Lecture Notes in Computer Science 11787

More information about this series at http://www.springer.com/series/7408

Giancarlo Guizzardi · Frederik Gailly ·
Rita Suzana Pitangueira Maciel (Eds.)

Advances in Conceptual Modeling

ER 2019 Workshops FAIR, MREBA, EmpER, MoBiD,
OntoCom, and ER Doctoral Symposium Papers
Salvador, Brazil, November 4–7, 2019
Proceedings

 Springer

Editors
Giancarlo Guizzardi
Free University of Bozen-Bolzano
Bolzano, Italy

Frederik Gailly
Ghent University
Ghent, Belgium

Rita Suzana Pitangueira Maciel
Federal University of Southern Bahia
Salvador, Brazil

ISSN 0302-9743 ISSN 1611-3349 (electronic)
Lecture Notes in Computer Science
ISBN 978-3-030-34145-9 ISBN 978-3-030-34146-6 (eBook)
https://doi.org/10.1007/978-3-030-34146-6

LNCS Sublibrary: SL2 – Programming and Software Engineering

This Springer imprint is published by the registered company Springer Nature Switzerland AG
The registered company address is: Gewerbestrasse 11, 6330 Cham, Switzerland

Preface

This volume contains the proceedings of a number of satellite events held in conjunction with the 38th International Conference on Conceptual Modeling (ER 2019), which took place in the beautiful Salvador, Bahia, Brazil. In addition to the papers accepted for presentation and publication in five workshops, the volume also includes the contributions of participants to the ER doctoral symposium.

Given the long tradition and broad scope of ER as a key conference in the area of conceptual modeling, the workshops organized therein play an important role, such as being a forum for: very interactive debates about emerging ideas; broadening the scope of what conceptual modeling is about; bridging conceptual modeling and other complementary communities; and reflecting on the scope and nature of the area itself. In that respect, this volume contains papers that were accepted for publication and presentation in the following five workshops: Workshop on Conceptual Modeling, Ontologies and Metadata Management for FAIR Data (FAIR 2019), the 6th Workshop on Conceptual Modeling in Requirements Engineering and Business Analysis (MREBA 2019), the Second International Workshop on Empirical Methods in Conceptual Modeling (EmpER 2019), the 8th International Workshop on Modeling and Management of Big Data (MoBiD 2019), and the 7th International Workshop on Ontologies and Conceptual Modelling (OntoCom 2019). Besides these, the 12th edition of the International i* Workshop (iStar 2019) was also held in conjunction with ER 2019. However, the iStar 2019 papers have been collected and published in a different volume.

The FAIR data movement has been gaining a lot of attention in the past years, with awareness and endorsement ranging from research institutions and funding agencies to international organizations such as the G7 and G20. In this first edition, the workshop was organized by Luiz Olavo Bonino (GO FAIR International Support and Coordination Office and Leiden University Medical Centre, The Netherlands), Maria Luiza M. Campos (Federal University of Rio de Janeiro, Brazil), Robert Pergl (Czech Technical University in Prague, Czech Republic), and Luana Sales (Brazilian Institute of Information in Science and Technology, Brazil). In this edition, three full papers were accepted for publication and presentation. The program of the workshop was complemented by an invited talk entitled "Towards the Internet of FAIR Data and Services – Challenges for the Ontology-Driven Conceptual Modeling Community" delivered by Luiz Olavo Bonino. Finally, in order to foster discussions and interest among specialists, a discussion panel was organized with researchers from data-intensive domains and institutions.

The MREBA workshop aims to provide a forum for discussing the interplay between Requirements Engineering topics and Conceptual Modeling, and in particular how requirements modeling can be effectively used as part of business analysis and systems engineering. This year's edition of MREBA was organized by Jelena Zdravkovic (Stockholm University, Sweden), Renata Guizzardi (Federal University of

Espírito Santo, Brazil), and Vítor E. Silva Souza (Federal University of Espírito Santo, Brazil). The workshop accepted four articles as full papers for publication and presentation. The organizers also invited Matthias Jarke (RWTH Aachen University and Fraunhofer FIT Institute for Applied Information Technology, Germany) to deliver the keynote talk entitled "Inter-Organizational Data Sharing: From Goals to Policies to Code."

The second edition of EmpER aimed at bringing together researchers with an interest in the empirical investigation of conceptual modeling languages, frameworks and practices. This year's edition of EmpER was organized by João Araújo (New University of Lisbon, Portugal), Jennifer Horkoff (Chalmers University of Technology and the University of Gothenburg, Sweden), and Sotirios Liaskos (York University, Canada). The workshop accepted three articles as full papers for publication and presentation, all of which describe empirical studies already conducted. The workshop involved presentations of the papers followed by discussion and audience feedback to the authors.

MoBiD aims at being an international forum for exchanging ideas on the latest and best proposals for modeling and managing big data in a data-driven paradigm. The workshop is a forum for researchers and practitioners who are interested in the different facets related to the use of the conceptual modeling approaches for the development of next generation applications based on Big Data. This year's edition of MoBiD was organized by Alejandro Maté (University of Alicante, Spain), Miguel A. Teruel (Lucentia Lab, Spain), Il-Yeol Song (Drexel University, USA), and Juan Trujillo (University of Alicante, Spain). The workshop accepted 4 articles as full papers for publication and presentation. The organizers also invited Ana León Palacio (Polytechnic University of Valencia, Spain) to deliver the keynote talk entitled "From Big Data to Smart Data in the Context of Genomic Information Systems."

OntoCom was created in order to bridge the conceptual modeling and ontology communities. In this spirit, every year the venue in which the workshop is organized in alternates: on one year, it is organized as a key formal ontology conference; every second year it is organized as a conceptual modeling conference. For quite some time now, it has been organized traditionally as a satellite ER event. This year's edition was organized by Sergio de Cesare (University of Westminster, UK), Mark Lycett (Royal Holloway University of London, UK), Chris Partridge (University of Westminster, and BORO Solutions, UK) and Oscar Pastor (Polytechnic University of Valencia, Spain). The workshop accepted four articles as full papers for publication and presentations. The organizers of OntoCom also invited the authors of four other papers to participate in the workshop by giving short 10-minute presentations. These papers were invited as they covered the scope of the workshop and had the potential to generate interesting discussions.

Although not having its papers included in this volume, we can report that the International i* Workshop is a community-building event, focusing on goal modeling and, in particular, in works using the i* modeling framework. This year's edition was organized by João Pimentel (Federal University of Pernambuco, Brazil), Juan Pablo Carvallo (University of Azuay, Ecuador), and Lidia López (Polytechnic University of Catalunya, Spain). The workshop's program comprised the presentation of 16 full papers and the aforementioned keynote talk given by Matthias Jarke, as a joint synergetic activity shared with MREBA 2019.

Finally, the ER doctoral symposium offers PhD students the opportunity to present and discuss their research, as well as interact with other researchers and experts in the field of conceptual modeling, who can provide feedback on their research. Samira Si-Said Cherfi (Conservatoire National des Arts et Métiers, France) and Vanessa Braganholo (Fluminense Federal University, Brazil) were responsible for organizing this year's edition of this traditional ER satellite event. Hence, closing this volume, we have six contributions selected by the doctoral symposium chairs.

We would like to thank the workshop and doctoral symposium chairs for the organization of the aforementioned high-quality and inspiring events. These events significantly increased the value of ER 2019. We are also indebted to the numerous reviewers for their time and expertise ensuring the quality of the workshops. Additionally, we express our gratitude to the general chairs of the conference for their continuous support. Finally, we are immensely grateful to Tiago Prince Sales and Claudenir Morais Fonseca for their hard work in supporting the creation of these proceedings!

September 2019

Giancarlo Guizzardi
Frederik Gailly
Rita Suzana P. Maciel

ER 2019 Conference Organization

Conference General Co-chairs

Vaninha Vieira dos Santos   Federal University of Bahia, Brazil
José P. M. de Oliveira   Federal University of Rio Grande do Sul, Brazil

Program Committee Co-chairs

Alberto H. F. Laender   Federal University of Minas Gerais, Brazil
Barbara Pernici   Politecnico di Milano, Italy
Ee-Peng Lim   Singapore Management University, Singapore

Workshop Co-chairs

Giancarlo Guizzardi   Free University of Bozen-Bolzano, Italy
Frederik Gailly   Ghent University, Belgium
Rita Suzana P. Maciel   Federal University of Bahia, Brazil

Poster and Tools Demonstration Co-chairs

Renata S. S. Guizzardi   Federal University of Espírito Santo, Brazil
Daniela Barreiro Claro   Federal University of Bahia, Brazil

Tutorial Co-chairs

Mirella M. Moro   Federal University of Minas Gerais, Brazil
Jolita Ralyte   University of Geneva, Switzerland

Doctoral Symposium Co-chairs

Samira Si-Said Cherfi   Conservatoire National des Arts et Métiers, France
Vanessa Braganholo   Fluminense Federal University, Brazil

ER Forum Chair

Ignacio Panach Navarrete   Universitat de València, Spain

Industrial Chair

Ana Carolina Salgado   Federal University of Pernambuco, Brazil

Publicity Chair

José P. M. de Oliveira   Federal University of Rio Grande do Sul, Brazil

Local Arrangements Co-chairs

Daniela Claro   Federal University of Bahia, Brazil
Fabiola Greve   Federal University of Bahia, Brazil
Rita Suzana Maciel   Federal University of Bahia, Brazil

Treasurer

Stephen W. Liddle   BYU Marriott School of Business, USA

ER Liaison

Sudha Ram   University of Arizona, USA

Conference Webmaster

Gabriel Machado Lunardi   Federal University of Rio Grande do Sul, Brazil

ER 2019 Workshop Organization

Conceptual Modeling, Ontologies and Metadata Management for FAIR Data (FAIR) 2019 Co-chairs

Luiz Olavo Bonino	GO FAIR International Support and Coordination Office and Leiden University Medical Centre, The Netherlands
Maria Luiza M. Campos	Federal University of Rio de Janeiro, Brazil
Robert Pergl	Czech Technical University in Prague, Czech Republic
Luana Sales	Brazilian Institute of Information in Science and Technology, Brazil

Conceptual Modeling in Requirements Engineering and Business Analysis (MREBA) 2019 Co-chairs

Workshop Organizers

Renata S. S. Guizzardi	Federal University of Espírito Santo, Brazil
Jelena Zdravkovic	Stockholm University, Sweden
Vítor E. Silva Souza	Federal University of Espírito Santo, Brazil

Steering Committee

Jennifer Horkoff	Chalmers University and the University of Gothenburg, Sweden
Colette Rolland	Université Paris 1 Panthéon-Sorbonne, France
Eric Yu	University of Toronto, Canada

Empirical Methods in Conceptual Modeling (EmpER) 2019 Co-chairs

João Araujo	Universidade NOVA de Lisboa, Portugal
Jennifer Horkoff	Chalmers University and the University of Gothenburg, Sweden
Sotirios Liaskos	York University, Canada

Modeling and Management of Big Data (MoBiD) 2019 Co-chairs

Alejandro Mate	University of Alicante, Spain
Miguel A. Teruel	Lucentia Lab, Spain

Juan Trujillo   University of Alicante, Spain
Il-Yeol Song   Drexel University, USA

Ontologies and Conceptual Modelling (OntoCom) 2019 Co-chairs

Sergio de Cesare   University of Westminster, UK
Mark Lycett   Royal Holloway, University of London, UK
Chris Partridge   BORO Solutions Ltd, UK
Oscar Pastor   Universidad Politécnica de Valéncia, Spain

i* 2019 Co-chairs

Workshop Organizers

João Pimentel   Federal University of Pernambuco, Brazil
Juan Pablo Carvallo   Universidad del Azuay, Ecuador
Lidia López   Universitat Politècnica de Catalunya, Spain

Steering Committee

Eric Yu   University of Toronto, Canada
John Mylopoulos   University of Ottawa, Canada
Xavier Franch   Universitat Politècnica de Catalunya, Spain

ER 2019 Workshop Program Committee

FAIR 2019 Program Committee

Tobias Kuhn	Vrije Universiteit Amsterdam, The Netherlands
Michel Dumontier	Maastricht University, The Netherlands
João Paulo A. Almeida	Federal University of Espírito Santo, Brazil
Renata S. S. Guizzardi	Federal University of Espírito Santo, Brazil
Sérgio M. S. da Cruz	Federal Rural University of Rio de Janeiro, Brazil
Patricia Henning	FioCruz/Unirio, Brazil
Claudio José S. Ribeiro	Unirio, Brazil
João L. R. Moreira	Vrije Universiteit Amsterdam, The Netherlands
Tiago Prince Sales	Free University of Bozen-Bolzano, Italy
Mark Thompson	Leiden University Medical Center, The Netherlands
Fernanda Baião	PUC-Rio, Brazil
Claudenir M. Fonseca	Free University of Bozen-Bolzano, Italy
Emilio Sanfilippo	LE STUDIUM Loire Valley, France
Kelli de Faria Cordeiro	Center of Naval System Analysis of Brazilian Navy, Brazil

MREBA 2019 Program Committee

Andreas Opdahl	University of Bergen, Norway
Angelo Susi	Fondazione Bruno Kessler, Italy
Carla Silva	Federal University of Pernambuco, Brazil
Elda Paja	University of Trento, Italy
Eric-Oluf Svee	Stockholm University, Sweden
Fabiano Dalpiaz	Utrecht University, The Netherlands
Genaína Rodrigues	University of Brasilia, Brazil
Grischa Liebel	Chalmers University of Technology, Sweden
Iris Reinhartz-Berger	University of Haifa, Israel
João Pimentel	Federal Rural University of Pernambuco, Brazil
Jolita Ralyté	University of Geneva, Switzerland
Joshua C. Nwokeji	Gannon University, USA
Lawrence Chung	University of Texas at Dallas, USA
Lidia Lopez	Universitat Politècnica de Catalunya, Spain
Lin Liu	Tsinghua University, China
Lucineia Thom	Federal University of Rio Grande do Sul, Brazil
Marcela Ruiz	Zurich University of Applied Sciences, Switzerland
Motoshi Saeki	Tokyo Institute of Technology, Japan

Okhaide Akhigbe	University of Ottawa, Canada
Paul Johannesson	Stockholm University, Sweden
Sam Supakkul	Sabre Travel Network, USA
Samira Si-Said Cherfi	Conservatoire National des Arts et Métiers, France
Sotirios Liaskos	York University, Canada
Tong Li	Beijing University of Technology, China

EmpER 2019 Program Committee

Alicia Grubb	University of Toronto, Canada
Ana Moreira	Universidade NOVA de Lisboa, Portugal
Carla Silva	Federal University of Pernambuco, Brazil
Geert Poels	Ghent University, Belgium
Grischa Liebel	University of Gothenburg, Sweden
Iris Reinhartz-Berger	University of Haifa, Israel
Jan Recker	University of Cologne, Germany
Jeffrey Parsons	Memorial University, Canada
Katsiaryna Labunets	Delft University of Technology, The Netherlands
Lin Liu	Tsinghua University, China
Marian Daun	University of Duisburg-Essen, Germany
Michel Chaudron	University of Gothenburg, Sweden
Miguel Goulão	Universidade NOVA de Lisboa, Portugal
Neil Ernst	University of Victoria, Canada
Nelly Condori-Frenandez	VU University Amsterdam, The Netherlands
Oscar Pastor	Universidad Politécnica de Valéncia, Spain
Robson Fidalgo	Federal University of Pernambuco, Brazil
Silvia Abrahão	Universitat Politècnica de València, Spain
Tong Li	Beijing University of Technology, China
Vincenzo Gervazsi	University of Pisa, Italy
Xavier Le Pallec	University Lille 1, France

MoBiD 2019 Program Committee

Dippy Aggarwal	Intel, USA
Okhaide Akhigbe	University of Ottawa, Canada
Jose F. Aldana Montes	University of Malaga, Spain
Raian Ali	Bournemouth University, UK
Faten Atigui	CNAM, France
Fatma Başak Aydemir	Boğaziçi University, Turkey
Fernanda Baião	PUC-Rio, Brazil
Judith Barrios Albornoz	University of Los Andes, Colombia
Ladjel Bellatreche	LIAS/ENSMA, France
Kawtar Benghazi	University of Granada, Spain
Sandro Bimonte	irstea, France
Carlos Blanco Bueno	Universidad de Cantabria, Spain
Shawn Bowers	Gonzaga University, USA

Cristina Cabanillas	Vienna University of Economics and Business, Austria
Cristina Cachero	Universidad de Alicante, Spain
Byron Choi	Hong Kong Baptist University, Hong Kong, China
Lawrence Chung	The University of Texas at Dallas, USA
Isabelle Comyn-Wattiau	ESSEC Business School, France
Nelly Condori-Fernández	Universidade da Coruña, Spain
Maya Daneva	University of Twente, The Netherlands
Marian Daun	University of Duisburg-Essen, Germany
Karen Davis	Miami University, USA
Valeria De Antonellis	University of Brescia, Italy
Elena de La Guía	University of Castilla-La Mancha, Spain
Jose L. Fernández Alemán	Universidad de Murcia, Spain
Xavier Franch	Universitat Politècnica de Catalunya, Spain
Sepideh Ghanavati	University of Maine, USA
Aditya Ghose	University of Wollongong, Australia
Giovanni Giachetti	Universidad Tecnológica de Chile INACAP, Chile
Matteo Golfarelli	University of Bologna, Italy
Cesar Gonzalez-Perez	Incipit-CSIC, Spain
Georg Grossmann	University of South Australia, Australia
Renata S. S. Guizzardi	Federal University of Espírito Santo, Brazil
Maria Hallo	Escuela Politécnica Nacional, Ecuador
Sven Hartmann	Clausthal University of Technology, Germany
Jennifer Horkoff	Chalmers and the University of Gothenburg, Sweden
Sergio Ilarri	University of Zaragoza, Spain
Arantza Illarramendi	Basque Country University, Spain
Peiquan Jin	University of Science and Technology of China, China
David Kensche	SAP, Germany
Tong Li	Beijing University of Technology, China
Yuchen Li	Singapore Management University, Singapore
Grischa Liebel	Reykjavik University, Iceland
Sebastian Link	The University of Auckland, New Zealand
Mengchi Liu	Carleton University, Canada
Lidia Lopez	Universitat Politècnica de Catalunya, Spain
Jiaheng Lu	University of Helsinki, Finland
Esperanza Marcos	Universidad Rey Juan Carlos, Spain
Raimundas Matulevicius	University of Tartu, Estonia
Judith Michael	RWTH Aachen University, Germany
Wilfred Ng	The Hong Kong University of Science and Technology, Hong Kong, China
Nan Niu	University of Cincinnati, USA
Joshua Nwokeji	Gannon University, USA
Antoni Olivé	Universitat Politècnica de Catalunya, Spain
Jeffrey Parsons	Memorial University of Newfoundland, Canada
Oscar Pastor	Universidad Politécnica de Valéncia, Spain
Zhiyong Peng	State Key Laboratory of Software Engineering, China
Jesus Peral	University of Alicante, Spain

Henderik Proper	Public Research Centre Henri Tudor, Luxembourg
Jolita Ralyté	University of Geneva, Switzerland
Iris Reinhartz-Berger	University of Haifa, Israel
Manuel Resinas	University of Seville, Spain
Carlos R. Rivero	Rochester Institute of Technology, USA
Stefano Rizzi	University of Bologna, Italy
Marcela Ruiz	Zurich University of Applied Sciences, Switzerland
Pablo Sanchez	University of Cantabria, Spain

OntoCom 2019 Program Committee

Sergio de Cesare	University of Westminster, UK
Frederik Gailly	Ghent University, Belgium
Giancarlo Guizzardi	Free University of Bozen-Bolzano, Italy
Mark Lycett	Royal Holloway, University of London, UK
Chris Partridge	BORO Solutions Ltd, UK
Oscar Pastor	Universidad Politécnica de Valéncia, Spain

i* 2019 Program Committee

Alejandro Maté	University of Alicante, Spain
Alexei Lapouchnian	University of Toronto, Canada
Angelo Susi	Fondazione Bruno Kessler, Italy
Anna Perini	Fondazione Bruno Kessler, Italy
Dolors Costal	Universitat Politècnica de Catalunya, Spain
Elda Paja	University of Trento, Italy
Enyo Gonçalves	Federal University of Ceará, Brazil
Fabiano Dalpiaz	Utrecht University, The Netherlands
Fatma Başak Aydemir	Boğaziçi University, Turkey
Fernanda Alencar	Federal University of Pernambuco, Brazil
Haralambos Mouratidis	University of Brighton, UK
Hugo Estrada	CENIDET, Mexico
Jaelson Castro	Federal University of Pernambuco, Brazil
Jelena Zdravkovic	Stockholm University, Sweden
Jennifer Horkoff	Chalmers and the University of Gothenburg, Sweden
João Araújo	Universidade NOVA de Lisboa, Portugal
Julio Leite	Pontifícia Universidade Católica - Rio, Brazil
Lin Liu	Tsinghua University, China
Luiz Cysneiros	York University, Canada
Malak Baslyman	University of Ottawa, Canada
Marcela Ruiz	Zurich University of Applied Sciences, Switzerland
Michalis Pavlidis	University of East London and University of Brighton, UK
Miguel Goulão	Universidade NOVA de Lisboa, Portugal

ER 2019 Doctoral Symposium Program Committee

Byron Choi	Hong Kong Baptist University, Hong Kong, China
Claudia P. Ayala	Universitat Politècnica de Catalunya, Spain
Giancarlo Guizzardi	Free University of Bozen-Bolzano, Italy
Marcos V. N. Bedo	Fluminense Federal University, Brazil
Mirella M. Moro	Federal University of Minas Gerais, Brazil
Oscar Pastor	Universidad Politécnica de Valéncia, Spain
Sergio De Cesare	University of Westminster, UK

Contents

Conceptual Modeling, Ontologies and Metadata Management for FAIR Data (FAIR) 2019

Preface

Luiz Olavo Bonino[1], Maria Luiza M. Campos[2], Robert Pergl[3],
and Luana Sales[4]

[1] Leiden University Medical Centre, The Netherlands
`luiz.bonino@go-fair.org`
[2] Federal University of Rio de Janeiro, Brazil
`jenho@chalmers.se`
[3] Czech Technical University in Prague, Czech Republic
`perglr@fit.cvut.cz`
[4] Brazilian Institute of Information in Science and Technology, Brazil
`luanasales@ibict.br`

The FAIR data movement has been gaining a lot of attention in the last years, with awareness and endorsement ranging from research institutions and funding agencies to international organisations such as G7 and G20. The FAIR principles define a set of expected behaviours in order to improve digital resources findability, accessibility, interoperability and reusability with the focus on machine actionability. In order to fulfil this goal, the FAIR principles require that more information is provided to the computational agents in clear and unambiguous form, which can be provided by ontology-driven conceptual model approaches. The objective of the 1st Workshop on Conceptual modelling, Ontologies and Metadata Management for FAIR Data is to create an international forum for discussing ideas and approaches on how to use conceptual models for effective realisation of the FAIR principles.

In this first edition, we had 6 submissions, and 3 were accepted as full papers to be presented and published. Although still a reduced number, we expect a growing interest in this area in the coming years and that was one of the motivations for planning the workshop co-occurring with the ER 2019 conference. Complementing the presentations, important parts of the technical program are an invited talk on the latest developments around FAIR and, to foster discussions and interest among specialists, a panel with researchers from data-intensive domains and institutions.

Acknowledgments. We would like to thank our Program Committee, composed by an international team of researchers, as well as the support from the ER Conference general chairs and staff.

Towards a Core Ontology for Scientific Research Activities

Patricia M. C. Campos[(⊠)], Cássio C. Reginato,
and João Paulo A. Almeida

Ontology & Conceptual Modeling Research Group (NEMO),
Federal University of Espírito Santo (UFES),
Av. Fernando Ferrari, 514, Goiabeiras, Vitória, ES 29075-910, Brazil
patricia.carnelli@aluno.ufes.br, cassio.reginato@inf.
ufes.br, jpalmeida@ieee.org

Abstract. The increasing volume and complexity of scientific research data associated with its semantic heterogeneity demands strategies to enable data integrated reuse. This is essential to improve global collaborations, in what has been called e-Science. A way to promote data integration is through the use of ontologies. Ontologies can play the role of a shared conceptualization, providing a common semantic background for data interpretation. In the case of scientific research, particularly empirical research, there are many concepts related to research activities that are general, despite any specific domain in which they may occur. Thus, they can be represented by means of a core ontology. In this paper, we propose the design of a core ontology to deal with research activities (e.g., sampling and measurement). As the concepts used are neutral with respect to different application domains, they can be reused to build ontologies for specific research domains, speeding up the development process. To illustrate this, we present an environmental research ontology developed based on this core ontology. The proposed core ontology is grounded in the Unified Foundational Ontology (UFO), which provides a solid basis for its key elements.

Keywords: Core ontology · Scientific research · Research activity · Unified Foundational Ontology

1 Introduction

In the last decades, scientific research has undergone major changes mainly due to the increasing volume and complexity of data produced and the need to share such data to improve global collaborations, in what has been called e-Science [1]. This new paradigm of scientific research aims to promote the development of science and technology through the use of methods that enable more powerful and synthetic data analyses from integrated data reuse. However, because of the variety of actors involved and the interdisciplinary nature of scientific research, scientific data are often available disconnected, using incompatible language and heterogeneous terminology. This brings up serious semantic interoperability concerns [2].

© Springer Nature Switzerland AG 2019
G. Guizzardi et al. (Eds.): ER 2019 Workshops, LNCS 11787, pp. 3–12, 2019.
https://doi.org/10.1007/978-3-030-34146-6_1

The FAIR Data initiative [3] presents a set of principles that must be regarded to address this problem. These principles cover aspects of how data should be semantically annotated with metadata in a way that it can be read, interpreted, and reused for humans and machines. One of the key principles establishes that metadata must meet domain-relevant community standards. This means that data produced must be annotated with metadata that, in turn, must reference domain-relevant community standards, such as ontologies. As presented in [4], ontologies can be used, among other possibilities, as global (or shared) conceptualization for data integration. In this sense, ontologies can promote data interoperability by providing a common semantic background for data interpretation, reducing conceptual ambiguities and inconsistencies, and supporting meaning negotiation.

In the case of scientific research [5], particularly empirical research, where evidence is gathered through experimentation or observation, there are many concepts related to research activities that are general, despite any specific domain in which they may occur. Thus, they can be represented by means of a core ontology. Core ontologies provide a precise definition of structural knowledge in a specific field that spans across different application domains in this field [6]. They can be reused and extended to incorporate particularities of the domains of interest, that is, for the construction of domain ontologies. So, in addition to providing a shared conceptualization, they enable the speeding up of the domain ontology development process.

In this paper, we propose the design of a core ontology to deal with the different types of research activities performed in empirical research, encompassing (physical) sampling, sample preparation and measurement. As the concepts used are neutral in relation to the various domains, they can be reused by a given domain. To illustrate this, we present an environmental research ontology developed on the basis of this core ontology. It is worth mentioning that the explicit modeling of research activities shows that provenance information (e.g., participation of actors, participation of devices, methods used, etc.), usually present in *metadata*, are actually properties of real-world events. The proposed core ontology is grounded in the Unified Foundational Ontology (UFO) [7, 8], from which basic notions of object, relation, property, event, and others are adopted.

This paper is structured as follows. Section 2 presents the background of the paper, which includes UFO concepts relevant to ground the core ontology development. Section 3 presents the *Core Ontology for Scientific Research Activities*. Section 4 illustrates the use of the core ontology to build a domain ontology for environmental research. Section 5 discusses related work, and Sect. 6 presents our final considerations.

2 Background

In developing a core ontology, it is desirable to use a solid modeling base given by a foundational ontology. Concepts and relationships defined in a core ontology should be aligned to the basic categories of a foundational ontology [6]. For the field of scientific research, we need the general concept of events to represent research activities. Also, the basic concept of object is necessary to deal with devices, procedures and physical samples. The concept of agent is necessary to represent people and organizations involved in research activities. In addition, to approach measurements, we need to speak of properties (qualities) and their quantification.

As the Unified Foundational Ontology (UFO) [7, 8] provides these basic concepts, we have used UFO to ground the construction of the *Core Ontology for Scientific Research Activities*. UFO has been developed based on theories from Formal Ontology, Philosophical Logics, Philosophy of Language, Linguistics and Cognitive Psychology. UFO consists of three main modules: UFO-A, an ontology of endurants (objects); UFO-B, an ontology of perdurants (events); and UFO-C, an ontology of social entities built up on UFO-A and UFO-B.

Figure 1 shows a fragment of UFO containing concepts from UFO-A, UFO-B and UFO-C. The root concept is *Entity*, which is specialized into *Universal* and *Individual*. Universals are patterns of features that can be realized in a number of different individuals [7]. Individuals can be *concrete* (e.g., a particular person, an explosion) or *abstract* (e.g., sets, numbers, and propositions). *Concrete Individuals* are divided into *Endurants* and *Events*. Endurants are individuals that are wholly present whenever they are present (e.g., a house, a person, an amount of sand, etc.). Events are individuals that may have temporal parts. They happen in time in the sense that they extend in time and accumulate temporal parts (e.g., a soccer match). Whenever an event is present, it is not the case that all its temporal parts are present [8].

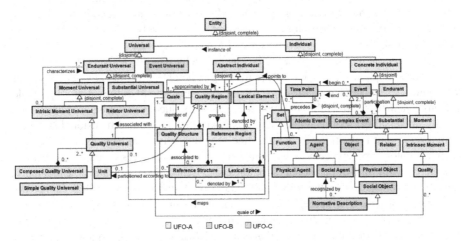

Fig. 1. A fragment of UFO-A, UFO-B and UFO-C.

The category of endurants can be further specialized into *Substantial* and *Moment*. Substantials are existentially-independent individuals (e.g., a house, a person). Moments are individuals that can only exist in other individuals, and, thus, they are existentially-dependent on their bearers (e.g., a color, an electric charge, a social commitment). *Intrinsic Moments* are moments that are dependent on one single individual (e.g., a color, a temperature). *Relators*, in turn, are moments that existentially depend on a plurality of individuals (e.g., an employment, a business process) [8].

Concerning the substantial hierarchy, a basic distinction is between agentive and non-agentive individuals, termed *Agents* and *Objects*, respectively. Agents can be divided into *Physical Agents* (e.g., a person) and *Social Agents* (e.g., an organization, a society). Objects can also be further categorized in *Physical Objects* and *Social Objects*. Physical objects include a book, a car, among others; social objects include money, language, etc. A *Normative Description* is a type of social object that defines one or more rules/norms recognized by at least one social agent. Examples of normative descriptions include contracts in general, but also sets of directives on how to perform actions within an organization [8].

Events can be atomic or complex. *Atomic Events* have no proper parts. *Complex Events* are aggregations of at least two disjoint events. Events are ontologically dependent entities in the sense that they depend on substantial participation to exist. Take for instance the event of measuring the height of a person. In this event, we have the participation of the measured person, the person that performs the measurement and the instrument used to measure the height. This event is composed of the individual participation of each of these entities and depends on them to exist. Besides that, each event is associated with two *Time Points*: a begin and an end time point. Time points are abstract individuals strictly ordered by a precedes relation [8].

Universals can be classified in *Endurant Universals* and *Event Universals*. Endurant universals are patterns of features of endurants. Event universals instead are patterns of features of events. *Substantial Universal* and *Moment Universal* are endurant universals whose instances are substantials and moments, respectively. Moment Universal is divided into *Intrinsic Moment Universal* and *Relator Universal* [7].

Regarding the intrinsic moment universal hierarchy, *Quality Universals* refer to the properties that characterize universals (e.g., weight, height). They are always associated with values spaces or *Quality Structures* that can be understood as the set of all possible regions (*Quality Regions*) that delimits the space of values that can be associated to a quality universal [7]. For example, height is associated with one-dimensional structure with a zero point isomorphic to the half-line of nonnegative numbers. Other properties such as color are represented by multidimensional structures. Quality universals associated with one-dimensional structures are called *Simple Quality Universals*. Quality universals associated with multidimensional structures are called *Composed Quality Universals*. The perception or conception of an intrinsic moment can be represented as a point in a quality structure. This point is named *Quale*. Quality regions and qualia are abstract entities. *Function* is a specialization of set that maps instances of a quality universal to points in a quality structure [9].

In order to allow quale communication, it is necessary to use *Lexical Elements* (e.g., 1.86 can be the lexical element used to communicate the height of a person) associated to *Reference Regions* and *Reference Structures*. A reference region is an abstract entity based on a quality region that acts as a bridge between that region and the lexical elements used to communicate the quale. A reference structure is associated to a quality structure and is a set of reference regions grounded in quality regions of that quality structure. When the 'value' of a particular quality is being referred by lexical elements (e.g., 1.86), what is actually being referred is a quality region that most approximates the quale. Reference structures associated to quality structures related to measurement act like scales grounded by quality structures. They can be partitioned in spaces with the same magnitude according to a *Unit* [9].

3 The Core Ontology for Scientific Research Activities

In this section, we present the *Core Ontology for Scientific Research Activities*, which deals with the different types of research activities performed in scientific research. We have identified that some characteristics are common to all types of research activities, such as temporal and spatial properties, actors involved in their execution, responsible actors, among others. They are related to provenance information and are generally addressed by the metadata domain, but the modeling of research activity shows that they are properties of events.

We have created a subontology to represent these properties: the *Research Activity Ontology*. This subontology must be specialized to handle the intrinsic characteristics of each type of research activity. We have specialized it in the following subontologies: *Sampling Ontology*, *Preparation Ontology* and *Measurement Ontology*. However, new specializations can be made to deal with other types of research activities, such as observations (e.g., an observation of the taxon of a beetle), assays, etc. Fig. 2 shows the *Core Ontology for Scientific Research Activities* and the UFO concepts used to ground it. Next, we explain each of these subontologies.

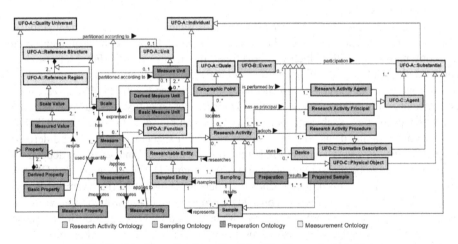

Fig. 2. The Core Ontology for Scientific Research Activities.

The *Research Activity Ontology* comprises concepts that are common to the different types of research activities. *Research Activity* is a UFO-B event used to generalize these types. Research activities are characterized by temporal and spatial properties, as well as the researched entity. Regarding temporal properties, research activities inherit begin and end time points from UFO-B. In relation to spatial properties, *Geographic Point* is a UFO-A quale that represents the coordinates corresponding to the spatial location of a research activity. *Researchable Entity* is a specialization of UFO-A individual because it can be a substantial (e.g., a river, a city) or an event (such as a process). A research activity is also characterized by the procedure adopted and the device employed. *Research Activity Procedure* is a UFO-C normative description that defines the rules to be followed for the execution of a research activity. *Device* is a specialization of UFO-C physical object. Examples of devices are: collectors, sensors, etc. In order to capture provenance, the *Agents* involved in the execution and the agent responsible for a research activity (the so-called *Principal*) are identified. They are specializations of UFO-C agent and can be physical (such as researches) or social agents (governmental agencies, research institutions, laboratories, etc.).

The *Sampling Ontology* deals with concepts related to the sampling activity. Sampling is the collection of samples for in situ and/or laboratory analysis. *Sampling* is a specialization of research activity, inheriting concepts related to research activity. *Sampled Entity* is a specialization of researchable entity and represents the target research entity. *Sample* represents a portion of a sampled entity that must be analyzed with the ultimate goal of characterizing the sampled entity. Sample is a specialization of UFO-A substantial. For instance, in the case of a water quality research of a river, a sample of water or sediment can be collected to verify the river water quality.

The *Preparation Ontology* address concepts related to the sample preparation activity. It refers to the ways in which a sample is treated before being analyzed. *Preparation* is a specialization of research activity. *Prepared Sample* represents a sample that has been prepared for analysis. Not all samples need to be prepared before they are analyzed.

The *Measurement Ontology* provides concepts related to the measurement activity. Most of the concepts presented here were extracted from the measurement core ontology presented in [9], which was developed in alignment with UFO. Measurement can be defined as a set of actions aiming to characterize an entity by attributing values to its properties. *Measurement* is a specialization of research activity. *Measured Entity* is a specialization of researchable entity. It represents an entity that has one or more measured properties, such as a person, a water sample, etc. *Property* is a UFO-A quality universal that deals with qualities of entities. It specializes in basic and derived property. *Basic Property* is a UFO-A simple quality universal that does not depend on other properties to be measured (e.g., weight and height). *Derived Property* is a UFO-A composed quality universal that depends on others to be measured (for example, Body-Mass Index). *Measured Property* represents a property that is measured. *Measures* are used for quantifying measured properties. Measure is a UFO-A function in the sense that it maps an instance of measured property to a measured value. Measures have *Scales* composed by all possible values (*Scale Value*) to be associated to a measured property. Scale is a specialization of UFO-A reference structure and scale value is a specialization of UFO-A reference region. Measures can be expressed in *Units* (e.g., meter, kilogram). A measure unit in which a measure is expressed partitions its scale.

4 Using the Core Ontology for Building an Environmental Research Ontology

In this section, we present how the proposed core ontology can be used as the basis for the development of a domain ontology. In this case, an environmental research ontology focused on water quality. This domain deals with the water quality assessment at monitoring points along rivers, lakes, sea, etc. This assessment is performed by analyzing measurements of physical, chemical and biological properties of water and sediment samples and ecotoxicological assays. We have used two other core ontologies to build this ontology: *Spatial Location Ontology* and *Material Entity Ontology*. The domain ontology, called *Environmental Research Ontology*, is divided into *Water Quality Ontology* and *Environmental Monitoring Ontology* (see Fig. 3).

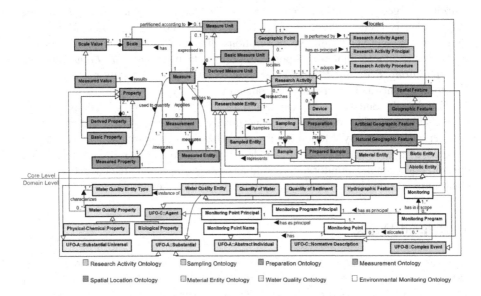

Fig. 3. The Environmental Research Ontology.

At the core level, the *Material Entity Ontology* comprises concepts for dealing with the existing types of material entities. The main concept is *Material Entity*, a UFO-A substantial that specializes into *Abiotic Entity* (non-living parts of an environment) and *Biotic Entity* (living parts of an environment).

The *Spatial Location Ontology* provides concepts related to spatial features (anything with spatial extent, such as a country, a river, etc.). *Spatial Feature* is a UFO-A substantial. It is specialized into *Geographic Feature*. Geographic features can be naturally-created (e.g., a river, a mountain) or artificially-created spatial features (e.g., a city, a water treatment plant). Spatial features are located in geographic points.

These other core ontologies are connected to the proposed core ontology by the researchable entity that is specialized in spatial feature and material entity. Also, sample is a specialization of material entity.

At the domain level, the *Water Quality Ontology* comprises concepts about water quality entities and properties. A *Water Quality Entity*, a UFO-A substantial, can be a *Hydrographic Feature*, a *Quantity of Water*, a *Quantity of Sediment*, among others. Hydrographic feature is a specialization of natural geographic feature and represents rivers, lakes, hydrographic basins, seas, etc. *Water Quality Property*, a UFO-A quality universal, refers to properties that are used to characterize water quality entities, encompassing both *Physical-Chemical* (e.g., temperature, dichloroethene concentration) and *Biological Properties* (e.g., concentration of coliforms, algae).

Finally, *the Environmental Monitoring Ontology* defines concepts related to environmental monitoring, monitoring points and monitoring programs. *Monitoring* consists of a set of research activities, performed periodically, for environmental quality control. Monitoring is a UFO-B complex event because it is composed of other research activities, such as sampling and measurement. *Monitoring Point* is a specialization of geographic point used to represent named geographic points. *Monitoring Point Name* is used to describe the location of the monitoring point. *Monitoring Programs* are UFO-C normative descriptions that have in their scope monitoring activities and allocate monitoring points to perform them. *Monitoring Point Principal* and *Monitoring Program Principal* are used to represent the agents responsible for monitoring points and monitoring programs, respectively.

The domain ontologies are connected to the proposed core ontology through researchable entity that specializes in water quality entity and property that specializes in water quality property. Monitoring is a specialization of research activity. It was not modeled as a core activity because it depends on particularities of the application domain. For example, monitoring program and monitoring point are concepts from the environmental domain, but not in every other scientific research domains.

5   Related Work

There are some models [10–14] related to scientific research based on the Observations and Measurements conceptual model from ISO 19156 [15]. This model defines an observation as an activity, the result of which is an estimate of the value of a property of the feature of interest, obtained using a specified procedure. Specializations of the observation have been classified by the result-type. For example, a measurement is an observation whose result is a scaled quantity, and a truth observation is an observation whose result is a Boolean value. As well as in [15], some ontologies [10, 11] do not represent the sampling activity; they represent only the sampling features. A sampling feature is used to support the observation process and may or may not have a persistent physical expression. Physical samples are modeled as the sampling feature specimen. In [10, 15], sample preparation is implemented using an association class with specimen. As sampling is not modeled as an activity, sampling properties need to be assigned to other entities. Specimen has properties related to sampling time, sampling location, etc. Observation has phenomenon time and result time to differentiate the moment of the sampling from the time of the ex-situ measurement of a sample, respectively. Thus, events and objects concepts are mixed. This shows the importance of developing core and domain ontologies based on a foundational ontology, characteristic not presented by these models.

The Semantic Sensor Network (SSN) ontology [12] describes sensors and their observations, the involved procedures, the studied features of interest, the samples used to do so, and the observed properties, as well as actuators. In SSN, the sampling activity is modeled. Sampling is used to represent both sampling and preparation activities. Location is not addressed. It is suggested that other models must be used to deal with location. Agents and devices involved in observations are treated by the same sensor entity. The Extensible Observation Ontology (OBOE) [13] is a formal ontology for capturing the semantics of scientific observation and measurement. OBOE does not handle other research activities. The Observation Data Model (ODM) [14] is an information model and supporting software ecosystem for feature-based earth observations, designed to facilitate interoperability across scientific disciplines and domain cyberinfrastructures. It models observation results, sample properties, monitoring locations, but does not model the research activities themselves, which we have shown key to capturing provenance information.

6   Conclusions

Improving scientific research based on data reuse requires adequate support for data semantics. We have addressed this challenge developing the *Core Ontology for Scientific Research Activities*. From this core ontology, we can develop domain ontologies that form the basis of mechanisms for finding, publishing and querying heterogeneous scientific research data. It promotes the application of FAIR principles in the scientific research field. As an example, we have developed a domain ontology for the environmental research. It was also possible to verify how the reuse of the core ontology facilitates the domain ontology development process.

The use of UFO as a foundational ontology supports the correct classification of the different concepts and relations about research activities, leveraging key notions that are domain independent. Activities are modeling as events, actors as agents, devices as objects, their participations in events revealed, and so on. The use of foundational ontology is a key feature of the proposed core ontology when contrasted with related work. By not adhering to a foundational ontology, some misconceptions arise, e.g., with event properties assigned to objects.

Besides that, the explicit modeling of research activity reveals that provenance information, usually present in the metadata domain, are actually properties of events, including the participation of agents and non-agentive objects in those events. In the case of scientific research, the modeling of these concepts is fundamental to support the integrated data reuse. Otherwise, there is a risk that such data will be misused. For example, data produced by incompatible methods can be compared, leading to inconsistent analysis; incorrect providers can be assigned to data since original data can be reprocessed by different agents; and so on.

As future work, other types of research activities should be modeled to broaden the scope of the core ontology. In addition, other aspects of scientific research, as well as research activities, can be incorporated. Some examples are types of scientific research, scientific research purpose, scientific research planning, etc.

Acknowledgements. This work is partly supported by CNPq (407235/2017-5 and 312123/2017-5), CAPES (23038.028816/2016-41) and FAPES (69382549).

References

1. Hey, T., Trefethen, A.: The data deluge: an e-Science perspective. In: Berman, F., Fox, G.C., Hey, T. (eds.) Grid Computing - Making the Global Infrastructure a Reality, pp. 809–824. Wiley, Chichester (2003)
2. Lenzerini, M.: Data integration: a theoretical perspective. In: Proceedings of the 21st ACM SIGMOD-SIGACT-SIGART Symposium on Principles of Database Systems, PODS 2002, pp. 233–246. ACM, New York (2002)
3. Wilkinson, M.D., et al.: Comment: the FAIR Guiding Principles for scientific data management and stewardship. Sci. Data **3**(1), 9 (2016)
4. Cruz, I.F., Xiao, H.: The role of ontologies in data integration. J. Eng. Intell. Syst. **13**(4), 245–252 (2005)
5. Çaparlar, C.Ö., Dönmez, A.: What is scientific research and how can it be done? Turk. J. Anaesthesiol. Reanim. **44**(4), 212–218 (2016)
6. Scherp, A., Saathoff, C., Franz, T., Staab, S.: Designing core ontologies. Appl. Ontol. **6**(3), 177–221 (2011)
7. Guizzardi, G.: Ontological foundations for structural conceptual models. CTIT Ph.D. thesis Ser (2005)
8. Guizzardi, G., Falbo, R., Guizzardi, R.S.S.: Grounding software domain ontologies in the Unified Foundational Ontology (UFO): the case of the ODE software process ontology. In: CIbSE, pp. 127–140 (2008)
9. Barcellos, M., Falbo, R., Frauches, V.: Towards a measurement ontology pattern language. In: Proceedings of 1st Joint Workshop ONTO.COM/ODISE on Ontologies in Conceptual Modeling and Information Systems Eng. of CEUR Workshop Proceedings, vol. 1301 (2014)
10. Cox, S.J.D.: An explicit OWL representation of ISO/OGC observations and measurements. In: Proceedings of the 6th International Conference on Semantic Sensor Networks, vol. 1063, pp. 1–18 (2013)
11. Cox, S.J.D.: Ontology for observations and sampling features, with alignments to existing models. Semant. Web **8**(3), 453–470 (2016)
12. Haller, A., et al.: The modular SSN ontology: a joint W3C and OGC standard specifying the semantics of sensors, observations, sampling, and actuation. Semant. Web **10**(1), 9–32 (2018)
13. Madin, J., Bowers, S., Schildhauer, M., Krivov, S., Pennington, D., Villa, F.: An ontology for describing and synthesizing ecological observation data. Ecol. Inform. **2**(3), 279–296 (2007)
14. Horsburgh, J.S., Tarboton, D.G., Piasecki, M., et al.: An integrated system for publishing environmental observations data. Environ. Model Softw. **24**(8), 879–888 (2009)
15. ISO 19156:2011: Geographic information - Observations and measurements. International Standard (2011)

Aligning DMBOK and Open Government with the FAIR Data Principles

Glaucia Botelho de Figueiredo[1][✉], João Luiz Rebelo Moreira[2][✉],
Kelli de Faria Cordeiro[3][✉], and Maria Luiza Machado Campos[1][✉]

[1] Federal University of Rio de Janeiro (UFRJ), Rio de Janeiro,
RJ 21941-916, Brazil
glaucia.botelho@ufrj.br, mluiza@ppgi.ufrj.br
[2] Vrije Universiteit Amsterdam, De Boelelaan 1081, 1081 HV Amsterdam,
The Netherlands
j.luizrebelomoreira@utwente.nl
[3] Center of Naval System Analysis of Brazilian Navy, Rio de Janeiro,
RJ 20091-000, Brazil
kelli@marinha.mil.br

Abstract. In enterprise organizations, the value of data has been considered on strategic level for a long time. As valuable assets, data need to be managed from source to disposal, considering their whole life cycle. To guide the data managing needs of enterprise organizations, the non-profit organization DAMA promotes the development and practice of data management as key enterprise assets. In 2017, DAMA has published the second edition of the DAMA International Guide to Data Management Body of Knowledge (DAMA DMBOK®). While the DAMA DMBOK focuses on corporate data, the FAIR data principles target research data management involving researchers and publishers in Academia. Data management is also a core issue in the Government sector, which has a great relevance in the open government initiatives, supporting the civil society to follow the actions of government bodies. This article makes a systematic analysis of these three data natures – research data, corporate data and government data – and the respective sets of principles that act as a basis for their management. These principles are correlated to identify similarities and possible complementarities focusing on the improvement of research data management, represented by the FAIR initiative, proposing an initial framework to support it.

Keywords: Research data · Corporate data · Government data · FAIR · FAIR principles · DMBOK · Open government data · Data management

1 Introduction

It is time for a paradigm shift in the conduct of scientific research data management. New practices, rules and policies are being reconfigured, as researchers, research institutes and funding agencies recognize research data as a valuable asset. In this regard, nowadays in Academia, data management is related with the FAIR Initiative.

© Springer Nature Switzerland AG 2019
G. Guizzardi et al. (Eds.): ER 2019 Workshops, LNCS 11787, pp. 13–22, 2019.
https://doi.org/10.1007/978-3-030-34146-6_2

FAIR is an acronym for Findable, Accessible, Interoperable and Reusable, i.e., principles designed with data-driven and machine-assisted open science in mind, aiming to serve as a guide for data management to researchers and publishers in Academia. GO-FAIR is an initiative that offers support and coordination to individuals, institutions and organizations committed to making research data FAIR, following the recommendations of the High Level Expert Group of the European Open Science Cloud (EOSC) [1].

In enterprise organizations, the value of data has been considered on strategic level for a long time. As valuable assets, data do need to be managed, taking into account their whole life cycle, from source to disposal [2]. To guide the data managing needs of enterprise organizations, a body of knowledge was organized by DAMA International. DAMA International is a non-profit organization whose primary purpose is to promote the development and practice of managing data as key enterprise assets. DAMA has been working for thirty years and, in 2017, it has published the second edition from DAMA International Guide to Data Management Body of Knowledge (DAMA DMBOK®) [3].

In the Government sector, new issues related to data management have arisen lately. There are initiatives on open government data to support civil society to check actions of government bodies and ensure that public institutions work for citizens, and not for themselves [4].

Considering these data management perspectives, this article makes a comparison between the data management strategy organized in DMBOK®, the FAIR initiative and the Open Government Data initiatives. Through a systematic analysis of their principles, we look for some common ground among them, discussing similarities, specific issues and possible complementarities between practices of data management in enterprises organizations, those employed in Academia and others management particularities needed by governments.

This article is structured as follows: in Sect. 2 characteristics of research data, corporate data and government data are discussed; Sect. 3 discusses data management principles employed in Academia, enterprises and government; in Sect. 4 the FADAM framework is proposed, as an early stage of an approach to FAIR Data Management generated from a mature data management strategy already used by enterprises; and, finally, Sect. 5 presents concluding remarks and topics for further investigation.

2 Essential Concepts

Regardless of the organization's nature, data are a valuable resource. For the purpose of this article, three types of organization's nature were identified: (i) research institutes, including universities and research centers; (ii) enterprises, representing private organizations, profit and non profit driven; and (iii) public sector, representing all public bodies, government and public administration. These organizations, naturally, produce and consume data. A number of aspects can characterize these data.

Research data are the data utilized or produced by a research, i.e., which are collected, observed or created to be used by a research [5]. Aligned to this definition, Arzberger et al. [6] define research data as the research input and highlight that they are a kind of raw material to the scientific processes. Expanding these concepts, Singh et al. [7] mention the value of research data in a concept called responsible research, which refers not only to use the research data to conclusions verification, but they also emphasize the data generated through research processes, that may be provided to other researchers for scrutiny. In Academia, both situations are possible: to assign property rights to researchers or to the institution itself [8].

In the literature, the terms scientific data and research data are used interchangeably [9]. In this article, the term research data refers to data used as input as well as resulting from research.

Corporate data are all data generated and maintained by the business processes of a company [2]. Otto et al. [10] remark that corporate data may help to develop efficient processes. As an organizational asset, corporate data belong to and are controlled by the enterprise [2]. Corporate data must be protected and safely stored, even if the data is available as part of some business-to-business service. Notwithstanding, some data might be open to satisfy existing compliance laws. Confidentiality is an important issue, not only referring to sensitive data, but also to internal and partners misuse, which can affect people's lives.

Enterprises might act as a research sponsor within a partnership with private or public research institute; or as a researcher itself, when they are looking for new technologies to develop new products and services. So, some research may require reuse of data from research data repositories; others may require the use of the enterprise data as research data (e.g. applying data mining in a data warehouse built by the company to generate new information); or another set of research may generate its own research data (e.g. an outcome of a market survey), as well as data created by enterprise funded research. Of course, some corporate can be, optionally, openly available to use.

Government data are any data created, collected and maintained by public bodies and by public administrations, indirectly "owned" by government (e.g., agencies) [4, 11]. In this article, all these data are considered as produced by the public sector business processes. So, they commune with the same needs of corporate data, since they are the outcome of business processes. The difference is that they are usually enforced by law as government responsibility to maintain data to support different functions and objectives. From an availability to use perspective, government data face a dichotomy between external (open) and internal use. On the one hand, Open Government Data (OGD) represent all data maintained by the public sector which could be made open, i.e., accessible to all, free of charge, without further restrictions. There are three main reasons to OGD: transparency, participatory governance and setting-up of new business and services that deliver social and commercial value. On the other hand, some data should be restricted for internal use, due to strategic and national defense issues [12].

Besides, government usually plays an important role in research, funding research institutes and universities, and developing research on its own organizations. Government may reuse research data as well as create new data. Furthermore, resulting data from public sector business processes can also be consumed by research, mainly those made open to public use.

As aforesaid, corporate data as well as government data may be utilized as input to research or as their output, becoming, in this way, research data. The boundaries between these types of data environment where data will be used are difficult to be established and, in this article as well as in reality, the use context may actually be a decisive factor to characterize data as governmental, research or corporate.

The increasing demands for open/shared data, and with distinct characteristics, prompted the need of keeping them under some level of control. Thus, the establishment of some guiding foundations can contribute to data preservation, keeping them organized, accessible and useful.

3   Data Management Principles

The three types of organizations depicted in Sect. 2 need to manage their data effectively. Managing involves knowing what data the organization produce and consume, and what might be accomplished with them. Thereafter, data stewardship is able to determine the most suitable manner to use data aiming to reach organization goals. To support data stewardship, some initiatives are committed to improve data management practices defining a set of principles to guide them [1, 2, 13]. These principles are aligned with data requirements of the context where they are used.

3.1   FAIR

Scientific progress requires cooperation and, therefore, data interoperability. Interoperability requires, firstly, discovering data utilized by prior researches or even produced by them. Due to the diverse nature of research, this is not an easy task and it does not depend on "who" (humans or machines) is searching for them.

In fact, it depends more on how these data had been classified before their storage. Considering the volume of research being produced around the world, some directives should be accomplished. From the challenge of optimal use of artifacts generated by scientific research, the FAIR Initiative has been proposed. As a first result, in 2016 fifteen foundational principles (named FAIR Data Principles) were published. These principles constitute a guide to make digital research artifacts Findable, Accessible, Interoperable and Reusable (FAIR) by both people and machines. They do not represent a standard or a specification [14], but these four perspectives are used to arrange the fifteen principles. Table 1 depicts the fifteen FAIR Data Principles.

Table 1. FAIR data principles [14]

Findable	Globally unique and persistent identifier
	Rich metadata
	Linking Metadata and data
	Register or index in a searchable resource
Accessible	Using a standardized communications protocol
	The protocol is open, free, and universally implementable
	The protocol must allow for an authentication and authorization
	Metadata are accessible, even when the data are no longer available
Interoperable	Usage a formal, accessible, shared, and broadly applicable language for knowledge representation
	Vocabularies must use globally unique and persistent identifiers
	Links between the datasets need to be described
Reusable	Metadata as detailed as possible
	Clear and accessible data usage license, defining legal interoperability
	Detailed provenance, including a description of the workflow that led to data
	Community standards or best practices for data archiving and sharing

3.2   DAMA DMBOK®

The DAMA DMBOK® body of knowledge is the result of the joint work of worldwide technical and business professionals, started in 1989. It is largely recognized nowadays as an essential resource for those organizations engaged in fostering data management, stewardship and governance [3].

According to DMBOK® [2], Data Management is the execution of policies, programs and practices to control the value of the data assets. DAMA DMBOK® defines twelve data management principles that balance business strategies and operational needs. Table 2 depicts DMBOK® Data Management Principles.

Table 2. DMBOK data management principles [2]

Effective data management requires leadership management
Data is an asset with unique properties
The value of data can and should be expressed in economic terms
Managing data means managing the quality of data
It takes Metadata to manage data
It takes planning to manage data
Data management requirements must drive Information Technology decisions
Data management is cross-functional
Data management requires an enterprise perspective
Data management must account for a range of perspectives
Different types of data have different lifecycle characteristics
Managing data includes managing the risks associated with data

3.3 Open Government

In December 2007, thirty open government advocates in the United States, such as Sunlight Foundation (https://sunlightfoundation.com/) and GovTrack.US (https://www.govtrack.us/), gathered to discuss why open government data is essential to democracy. The outcome of this meeting was a set of eight principles of open government (OG) data [13]. These principles are the basis to support how governments can make their data available in a way that enables a wide range of people to help making government functions more transparent, to monitor governmental actions and to create more opportunities for people to leverage government data to produce others business models[1] [13]. In 2011, a set of ten principles for improving public sector transparency was also identified in the United States and, a year later, another set of principles were published in the United Kingdom [11]. In this paper, the eight original principles are included, considering the number of participants who gathered together to agree. Table 3 presents the eight open government data principles.

Table 3. Open government principles [13]

Complete: All public data is made available. Public data is data that is not subject to valid privacy, security or privilege limitations.
Primary: Data is collected at the source, with the highest possible level of granularity, not in aggregate or modified forms.
Timely: Data is made available as quickly as necessary to preserve the value of the data.
Accessible: Data is available to the widest range of users for the widest range of purposes.
Machine processable: Data is reasonably structured to allow automated processing.
Non-discriminatory: Data is available to anyone, with no requirement of registration.
Non-proprietary: Data is available in a format over which no entity has exclusive control.
License-free: Data is not subject to any copyright, patent, trademark or trade secret regulation. Reasonable privacy, security and privilege restrictions may be allowed.

3.4 Similarities Among Principles

As previously mentioned, there are a set of data management principles focused on research institutions, other focused on enterprise organizations and another one focused on the public sector. These sets of principles were developed at different times, have not been cross-referenced or compared, as far as we know. We believe that a mutual reference would be beneficial for all parts.

To understand the principles, the characteristics of data must first be situated in a context. Context can help to explain why some principles were defined and also to understand how they are used and what they mean. The ordinary context for research data is represented by a controlled use environment, with a very low access concurrence rate. The archive mode and place, and retrieval mechanisms are key points, because research inputs and outcomes must be preserved to guarantee the continuity of

---

[1] David Orban interviews Larry Lessig at the conclusion of the workshop (https://youtu.be/AmlzW980i5A).

scientific progress. So, it is natural that most of the FAIR principles are related to quality metadata in order to benefit the findability, which is the root for accessibility, interoperability and reusability.

The corporate data context has an economic approach. High performance on data manipulation is usually important, even when there is high access concurrence rate, because companies deal with business processes which, usually, aiming at profiting. Thus, the data management principles profile defined in DMBOK is related to an enterprise perspective, aligned to business requirements. The context to government data focuses on data that should be made open, i.e., it considers the availability to use characteristic. Therefore, the open government data principles are outlined according to citizens' viewpoint, aiming at government actions transparency.

By considering the hybrid nature that data may have (Sect. 2), just one set of specific principles may not be enough to deal with the requirements of these data. In this sense, the management of these data may need principles defined in more than one context. So finding correspondences among different sets of principles can be helpful in adding new management guidelines. Thus, DMBOK principles were compared to OG principles and to FAIR principles in order to find a common ground. Table 4 shows the comparisons results and correlations found.

Table 4. DMBOK, open government and FAIR principles similarities.

DMBOK principle	Open government principle	FAIR principle
Data is an asset with unique properties	Primary machine processable	Unique and persistent data identifiers
		Vocabularies must use globally unique and persistent identifiers
The value of data can and should be expressed in economic terms	Timely	–
Managing data means managing the quality of data	Complete	Rich metadata
It takes Metadata to manage data	Machine processable	Rich metadata
	–	Linking metadata and data
	Non-proprietary Machine processable	Shared and broadly applicable language for knowledge representation
	–	Links described
		Metadata as detailed as possible
		Detailed provenance
–	Machine processable	Searchable resource
	Accessible	Authentication and authorization
		Protocol is open *and* free
	Non-proprietary Machine processable	Standardized communications protocol
	License-free	Defined legal interoperability
Different types of data have different life cycle characteristics	Accessible	Metadata are *always* accessible
		Standards for data archiving and sharing

Observing comparisons on Table 4 each of the fifteen FAIR principles is related to at least one DMBOK® or one OG principle. Also, although some of the fifteen principles are related to more than one OG principle, there are gaps between them.

Seven DMBOK® principles do not match with FAIR neither OG principles: "It takes planning to manage data"; "Data management requirements must drive Information Technology decisions"; "Data management is cross-functional"; "Data management requires an enterprise perspective"; "Data management must account for a range of perspectives"; "Managing data includes managing the risks associated with data"; and "Effective data management requires leadership management". "The value of data can and should be expressed in economic terms" is a DMBOK® principle related to only one OG principle; it does not have association to FAIR principles. In this case, this OG principle reveals a characteristic that add value and utility to data. In sum, eight DMBOK® principles are not related to FAIR principles. This does not mean, though, that these issues are not important to FAIR, even if they are not explicitly stated. FAIR has intentionally not included quality issues in its principles, by considering that the quality of a publication is taken by its ability of being properly found, reused and cited, i.e., as previously mentioned, to be considered FAIR, data need to be richly described [14].

The "Non-discriminatory" OG principle does not match with FAIR neither DMBOK principles. In fact, this principle is an opposition to Accessible FAIR principle, because FAIR allows authentication and authorization by a user account for a repository and an access can even be denied (role-based access control).

By similarities perspective on Table 4, the unique data identifier is a common ground among the three sets of principles, addressing machine processable requirements.

DMBOK principles emphasize the economic value of data which is considered a key asset used in enterprise decision-making processes. Therefore, it is important to have data timely available. This aspect is also aligned to OG initiatives: when data are timely available, they preserve their value to support data consumers' analyses. However, FAIR principles do not explicitly take them into account.

In OG initiatives, it is fundamental to have public data available, thus metadata should be as expressive as possible. Therefore, managing data requires managing the quality of metadata, which is essential to FAIR. It is important to highlight that specific data quality aspects are not explicit in the FAIR principles [14]; however, the metadata enrichment is addressed. Detailed metadata are essential to data management tasks and they give support to the tasks of linking data (for interoperability) and searching (for findability). Furthermore, using non-proprietary data formats eliminates restrictions over who uses the data, which also improves interoperability.

The aspects cited above should be considered in data life cycle. Metadata life cycle can last more than the data life cycle itself. This happens when data are no more relevant, but they still have historical contextual relevance, requiring metadata to remain accessible even when the data is no longer available.

From the FAIR perspective, these similarities motivated the discussion about how some aspects could be contemplated or at least have their non-inclusion option more clearly justified.

4   The FADAM Proposal

Considering research data management as an institutional issue, this article proposes the FADAM framework, which, in fact, is an early stage proposal to discuss a framework of data management to FAIR.

The FAIR principles do not cover all the features required for effective data management. Six from the eight DMBOK® principles, which have no association to FAIR, are the principles that treat data from the overall organization perspective, without data silos, regardless of data source or system whose maintain them. They consider a data policy involving senior management, i.e., beyond sector, system, project or local decisions (see Table 4). In this sense, add some features may give support FAIR principles to deal with all data management functions. The mapping from principles to features are described below:

- "It takes planning to manage data" → {"Management Planning"}
- "Managing data includes managing the risks associated with data" → {"Risk-based Data security"}
- "Effective data management requires leadership management" → {"Management Commitment"}
- {"Data management requires an enterprise perspective" | "Data management is cross-functional"} → {"Interoperability design | "Data Modeling"}
- "The value of data can and should be expressed in economic terms" → {"Data Timeliness Control"}

Considering the mapping described above, the FADAM proposal framework was built (see Fig. 1) to support FAIR data management.

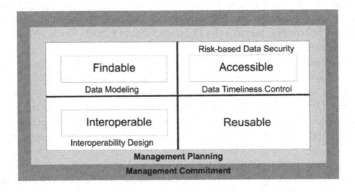

Fig. 1. FADAM proposal framework

"Data Modeling" gives support to Findability. "Risk-based Data Security" as well as "Data Timeliness Control" are add-ons features to Accessibility. "Interoperability Design" is a feature to improve Interoperability. "Management Planning" and "Management Commitment" underpin all FAIR principles to an effective data management.

5   Conclusions

The hybrid nature of data is characterized by the systematic analysis approaches of research, corporate and government data, as well as the context. In this paper we presented a comparison analysis that highlights the resemblance among data management principles employed on research, corporate and government data management approaches. These resemblances were key factors to the framework proposed here, coined as FADAM. In this first version, FADAM inherits data management features from DMBOK® that may also benefit government data management. Hence, these cross-references may mutually improve different data management approaches. Because of this, we intend to develop further research to improve FADAM by including data management frameworks, methods and tools, considering the context change along data life cycle.

References

1. GO FAIR. https://www.go-fair.org/. Accessed 09 July 2019
2. Henderson, D., Earley, S.: The DAMA Guide to the Data Management Body of Knowledge (DAMA-DMBOK2), 2nd edn. Technics Publications, New Jersey (2017)
3. Mission, Vision, Purpose and Goals | DAMA. https://dama.org/content/mission-vision-purpose-and-goals. Accessed 07 June 2019
4. Attard, J., Orlandi, F., Scerri, S., Auer, S.: A systematic review of open government data initiatives. Gov. Inf. Q. **32**(4), 399–418 (2015). https://doi.org/10.1016/j.giq.2015.07.006
5. Rice, R.: DISC-UK DataShare Project: Final Report (2009)
6. Arzberger, P., et al.: Promoting access to public research data for scientific, economic, and social development. Data Sci. J. **3**, 135–152 (2006). https://doi.org/10.2481/dsj.3.135
7. Singh, N.K., Monu, H., Dhingra, N.: Research data management policy and institutional framework. In: 5th International Symposium on Emerging Trends and Technologies in Libraries and Information Services (ETTLIS), pp. 111–115. IEEE, Noida (2018). https://doi.org/10.1109/ettlis.2018.8485259
8. Van den Eynden, V., Corti, L., Woollard, M., Bishop, L., Horton, L.: Managing and Sharing Data: Best Practice or Researchers, 3rd edn. UK Data Archive, Essex (2011)
9. Peng, G., et al.: A conceptual enterprise framework for managing scientific data stewardship. Data Sci. J. **17**, 15 (2018). https://doi.org/10.5334/dsj-2018-015
10. Otto, B., Wende, K., Schmidt, A., Osl, P.: Towards a framework for corporate data quality management. In: ACIS 2007 Proceedings, vol. 109 (2007). https://aisel.aisnet.org/acis2007/109
11. Ubaldi, B.: Open government data: towards empirical analysis of open government data initiatives. OECD Working Papers on Public Governance, No. 22. OECD Publishing (2013). https://doi.org/10.1787/5k46bj4f03s7-en
12. Geiger, C.P., von Lucke, J.: Open Government and (Linked) (Open) (Government) (Data). JeDEM EJournal EDemocracy Open Gov. **4**(2), 265–278 (2012). https://doi.org/10.29379/jedem.v4i2.143
13. The 8 Principles of Open Government Data (OpenGovData.org). https://opengovdata.org/. Accessed 23 July 2019
14. Wilkinson, M., et al.: The FAIR Guiding Principles for scientific data management and stewardship. Sci. Data **3** (2016). https://doi.org/10.1038/sdata.2016.18

Exploring Reproducibility and FAIR Principles in Data Science Using Ecological Niche Modeling as a Case Study

Maria Luiza Mondelli[1]([✉]), A. Townsend Peterson[2],
and Luiz M. R. Gadelha Jr.[1]([✉])

[1] National Laboratory for Scientific Computing, Petrópolis, RJ, Brazil
{mluiza,lgadelha}@lncc.br
[2] Biodiversity Institute, University of Kansas, Lawrence, KS, USA
town@ku.edu

Abstract. Reproducibility is a fundamental requirement of the scientific process since it enables outcomes to be replicated and verified. Computational scientific experiments can benefit from improved reproducibility for many reasons, including validation of results and reuse by other scientists. However, designing reproducible experiments remains a challenge and hence the need for developing methodologies and tools that can support this process. Here, we propose a conceptual model for reproducibility to specify its main attributes and properties, along with a framework that allows for computational experiments to be findable, accessible, interoperable, and reusable. We present a case study in ecological niche modeling to demonstrate and evaluate this framework.

Keywords: Reproducibility · FAIR principles · Data science · Ecological niche modeling

1 Introduction

Reproducibility is a fundamental aspect of science, and is related to the idea that a scientific process, or experiment, must be able to be reproduced, thus allowing its results to be validated or not [9]. If a scientific experiment can be reproduced, it can be reused or extended, leading to the validation of new findings and conclusions. However, ensuring that an experiment is reproducible is not a trivial task. It involves the need to record detailed documentation and specifications of the whole experimentation process and environment, and hence the need to plan these aspects and how they will be performed. If these aspects are not strategically thought out before performing the experiment, making it reproducible is time-consuming and unfeasible. Currently, this challenge has become increasingly important because many experiments are defined by a flow of computational steps. These steps typically perform data processing and prediction

© Springer Nature Switzerland AG 2019
G. Guizzardi et al. (Eds.): ER 2019 Workshops, LNCS 11787, pp. 23–33, 2019.
https://doi.org/10.1007/978-3-030-34146-6_3

activities using machine learning (ML) algorithms to extract knowledge and support decision-making, and are common in data science processes.

In 2016, a survey released by *Nature* [1] asked 1500 researchers from different disciplines about reproducibility in research. The study found that 52% of researchers believed that a crisis exists regarding reproducibility, but most said that they trusted the results of published papers. More than 70% of the researchers had tried but failed to replicate experiments of other scientists. At the same time, only 20% said that they had been contacted by another researcher who was trying to replicate their work. Other issues showed that few researchers follow some procedure to allow their experiments to be reproducible; for about 60% of participants, the most significant challenges include pressure to publish and selective reporting. In Ecology, the area of the case study of this work, interest in reproducibility is increasing thanks to the use of scripting languages and the need for more open sharing of data [2].

Given the importance that reproducibility plays in the scientific process and the relevance of developing methodologies and technologies to support it, we propose a conceptual model and a framework to formalize its main aspects. After introducing the challenge, we describe concepts and present a conceptual model for reproducibility. Next, we propose a framework in which computational experiments can be findable, accessible, interoperable, and reusable (FAIR) and describe a prototype implementation. We evaluate the framework using a case study in ecological niche modeling (ENM). Finally, we explore related work and derive conclusions.

2   A Conceptual Model for Reproducibility

The development of computational experiments that implement common data science steps has become an increasingly common practice in different scientific domains. This increase is thanks to the emergence of new technologies that have supported their execution, especially in cases in which experiments are complex, require high-performance computing, and involve manipulation of large volumes of data. Often, such experiments can be defined as a flow of activities, with execution managed by scientific workflow technologies [6]. However each such system has a specificity, which ends up requiring learning time, making it difficult to adopt. Many scientists use scripting languages, such as R and Python, to perform their experiments [12]. Both are well-established, open-source languages with broad user communities, and also offer great flexibility in the form of a large number of packages and libraries available, allowing customization of the steps that make up the experiment. Given researches' preference for these languages, recent efforts were applied to support the collection of provenance data [12].

Provenance comprises the production history of information or piece of data. By collecting provenance data from an experiment, it is possible to track all steps involved in producing a particular result. Scientists can benefit from provenance information to verify the sequence of computational steps performed to produce an output, to validate whether this sequence was executed correctly and used the appropriate parameters and inputs, and to compare different executions of the same experiment. Information about versions of libraries or packages, their dependencies, and aspects of the environment can also help in configuration of an environment more similar to the original when reproducing an experiment.

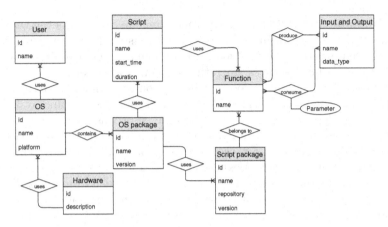

Fig. 1. Entity-Relationship diagram representing the aspects involved in the process of reproducibility of computational experiments.

In this work we propose a conceptual model that maps aspects that we consider essential for reproducibility, especially when experiments are modeled as workflows through scripting languages. This is because, with these aspects, it is possible to verify the executed steps and to retrieve information about application versions that may impact the results. The model is presented as an entity-relationship diagram, as shown in Fig. 1, with aspects we identified as essential mapped as entities. The main idea behind the model and the relationships between its entities is as follows: a *user* specifies and runs his/her experiment from an *operating system* (OS) using a specific *hardware*. This OS has some packages installed (*OS package*), and among them, we can consider the scripting language package that is used to specify the experiment, such as R or Python. The experiment is defined through a *script*, from an existing package in the OS, and can contain calls to user-defined functions or functions (*function*) that are part of a specific language package or module (*script package*). These specific language modules need to be installed in the OS. The functions comprise the executed activities of the experiment that consumed and produce *input* and *output*, respectively. Parameters can also be used as input to functions, and therefore constitute an attribute of the *consume* relation. This model will serve as a basis for the construction of a provenance database of the framework presented in Sect. 3.

The record of the aspects described through the entities of the proposed model can support the process of reproducibility on different levels, as addressed in [7]. We adapted the level definitions to cover the entities that we included in the model, as shown in Table 1 and described as follows:

Repeatable: executions of an experiment in the same computing environment, using the same code and data set, produce the same results or results consistent with the original finding. Thus, we must preserve all entities described in the proposed model.

Re-runnable: the results of an experiment remain consistent even with variations in the input data or in the parameter settings used. The implementation that concerns the script and function entities should not be modified, as well as the hardware, module packages, operating system, and its packages.

Portable: the experiment does not depend on the computing environment in which it was originally executed. Aspects such as versioning and availability of libraries and dependencies should be considered at this level. We must then preserve the input data, script, its functions, parameters, and module packages.

Extendable: an experiment can be reused for other purposes. This reuse includes integrating the original experiment into a new or existing experiment. For this aspect, one must have access to the script and its functions. We can preserve the operating system, its packages, and module packages.

Modifiable: changes can be made in the implementation of the original experiment for reuse purposes. As with the previous level, it is necessary to have access to the scripts and functions of the original experiment.

Table 1. Levels of reproducibility and the respective entities involved (adapted from [7]).

	Input	Script	Functions	Parameters	Script modules	OS	OS packages	Hardware
Repeatable	X	X	X	X	X	X	X	X
Re-runnable		X	X		X	X	X	X
Portable	X	X	X	X	X			
Extendable	X			X		X	X	X
Modifiable	X			X	X	X	X	X

By saying that we should preserve some entity, we mean that it should not be changed to ensure reproducibility at a certain level. We can observe that the level of repeatability for which we are aiming is the narrowest, and guarantees what we can call exact reproducibility. However, it is possible to combine aspects of more than one level depending on the desired degree of reproducibility.

3   A Framework for FAIR Computational Experiments

The FAIR principles [16] emerged from the efforts of a community including individuals from academia, industry, funding agencies, and scholarly publishers, to establish guidelines that allow for the findability, accessibility, interoperability, and reuse of scientific data or digital assets in general. Each of these four principles contains a set of requirements on how data, metadata, and infrastructure must be managed, allowing machines to retrieve them automatically, or at least with minimal human intervention. From a reproducibility point of view, the existence of such a guideline is beneficial. Although the principles do not suggest any specific technology to be used, they provide a means by which to solve aspects related to, for example, obtaining the input data for an experiment. However, as seen in the previous section, the reproducibility of an experiment is not limited to aspects related to its data. If we want to support the process of making an experiment reproducible, we can apply the FAIR principles to the experiment in its entirety. Therefore, each of the entities described in the conceptual model (Fig. 1) must have enough information to enable the user to reproduce the experiment at the desired level (Fig. 1).

Considering the scenario in which the user has implemented an experiment through a scripting language, we propose a framework (Fig. 2) to make this experiment reproducible. The main idea behind the framework is that, by following the proposed steps, the user will be able to share the experiment with enough information that meets, even minimally, the FAIR principles.

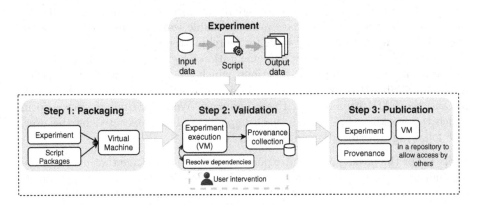

Fig. 2. Framework for FAIR computational experiments and its components.

Then, starting from an experiment that consumes input data, processes those data through the execution of a script like R or Python, and generates output data, the first step is to allow the encapsulation (or packaging) of that experiment. This packaging consists of importing the experiment and the packages or libraries used into a virtual machine (VM) using a standard operating system. It is important that the scripting language includes some dependency management system. With such a system, it is possible to identify which packages need to be included in the VM, avoiding installation of unused dependencies.

The second step is to access the VM created in the previous step and re-execute the experiment in this new environment. This step requires user interaction, which is responsible for validating the generated results. The user is responsible for resolving potential issues that may occur, such as installing the applications required to run the experiment and not previously installed in the VM. All modifications made to the VM, especially as regards installation of the new applications, must be recorded. One way to do this is to save the list of installed packages on the VM when it is created and check for modifications (i.e., if new applications have been installed) after the user has finished resolving possible dependencies. Then, the new applications and its version can be recorded in the provenance database. This record will allow to update the default VM specifications to include modifications. Thus, a user intending to reproduce the experiment will be able to rebuild the virtual environment in which it has been validated, without the need to install the required applications manually. During the experiment re-execution, it is also interesting to provide in the framework a way to collect provenance data and store, for example, into a database that can be subsequently queried for verification or validation purposes. Both R and Python have packages that can support this process.

Finally, the third step aims to gather the provenance database in the previous step, the experiment, and the VM specifications for publication. Publishing can be done in a repository that allows the sharing of research results. The choice of which repository is ideal for such sharing may vary depending on the application area of the experiment. However, initiatives and platforms such as FAIRsharing[1] and Repository Finder[2] have made available ways to support this process through recommendations and tools for searching repositories.

To exemplify the framework implementation for experiments defined with R, we encapsulated each step in R functions, which are available at GitHub[3], using a set of available R packages that meet the requirements to allow reproducibility and the FAIR principles of the experiment. We start from the scenario in which the workflow has already been implemented and executed by the user. The following describes the steps and tools used:

Step 1. For the packaging of the experiment, we use a package that manages the dependencies of the experiment called *packrat*. *Packrat* stores, in the experiment directory, the package installation files in the versions that were used in the script. Also, *packrat* has a bundle function, which compresses these packages and the script for later restoration. We then use *Vagrant*, a tool for building and managing VM environments, to create and start an Ubuntu VM containing the R installation for running the experiment. This step is achieved from the experiment directory, which is shared by default with the created VM, so that one can access the bundled experiment when connecting to the machine.

Step 2. In the validation step, we use *packrat* to unpack the experiment and install the packages. The installation of specific applications required by the experiment must be resolved by the user manually. We then provide a function

---

[1] https://fairsharing.org/.

[2] https://repositoryfinder.datacite.org/.

[3] https://github.com/mmondelli/reproduceR.

that re-executes the experiment using the *rdt* package, responsible for collecting the provenance. In this same function, we create a relational database (according to Fig. 1) to hold the provenance information collected.

Step 3. Finally, we put together the relational database containing the provenance, the bundled experiment generated by *packrat*, and the VM specification, which includes the installation of the new applications, and we compress these files for publication. We then use the *zen4R* package to publish on the Zenodo platform. Once this step is done, users can access the platform to add the necessary information and details about the publication.

4   Case Study in ENM and Evaluation

ENM is a technique that, based on data describing environmental factors, seeks to identify environmental requirements and predict the geographic distribution of a species. The environmental factors are generally abiotic, including aspects such as temperature and humidity, but can also be biotic, describing the interactions between species. Together they shape the environmental and geographic distributions of the species. The technique has been used widely in recent years, and has been applied in studies in conservation, ecology, and evolution.

The ENM process relies on the use of statistical and ML tools that allow analysis of environmental variables in relation to the geographic coordinates that represent the points of occurrence of a species. The end result is identification of a set of conditions associated with the occurrence of the species in question. Model-R [13] is a workflow, implemented in R, that automates some of the common steps for performing ENM. The following is an overview of each of these steps and the respective activities implemented by Model-R (Fig. 3):

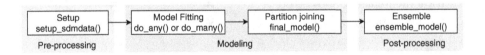

Fig. 3. Model-R workflow activities.

Pre-processing: comprises the data acquisition stage, including assembly of environmental layers and occurrence points, used as input to model algorithms. These data are usually obtained through known databases, such as GBIF, and require a cleaning step to eliminate uncertainties, duplications, and inconsistencies. In Model-R, *Setup* implements the data cleaning and partition procedures. It is worth mentioning that there is currently an effort by the biodiversity community to align data use and sharing practices with FAIR principles [5].

Modeling: consists of application of algorithms that generate the ecological niche models, based on the data obtained in the previous stage. In general, these algorithms use associations between the points of occurrence of the species and the environmental layers to predict the potential for occurrence of the species in other areas. This step is often achieved by using ML algorithms such as RandomForest and Maxent. This step is implemented in Model-R in two steps: (i) *Model Fitting*, which creates the ENM for a particular instance; and (ii) *Partition Joining*, which joins multiple models into a single result per species.

Post-processing: consists of the evaluation of the model generated in the previous step, to establish whether it is adequate and robust. Models can be evaluated using statistical methods, based on occurrence data not used in the preceding step. The *Ensemble* activity in Model-R joins the models for each algorithm into a final model, also known as a consensus model, which can then be analyzed and evaluated by the user.

To evaluate our framework, we used an example of the Model-R workflow for modeling the *Abarema langsdorffii* (Benth.) Barneby & J.W. Grimes plant species, available in its documentation[4], including the occurrence data. We executed the experiment on a machine locally, and followed the steps of the proposed framework for creating the VM. We highlight that, in the second step of the framework, we manually resolved one of the dependencies: the installation of the GDAL application in the VM. Next, we verified if it is possible to reproduce the experiment considering two different scenarios: (i) the user wants to reconstruct and reproduce the experiment locally, installing the packages used in the script, and not necessarily using the same versions; and (ii) the user wants to reproduce the experiment from a VM created by the framework.

Table 2. Results of the framework evaluation.

Config./Scenario	Machine 1	Machine 2	Machine 3
	Ubuntu 18.04 LTS R 3.6.0	CentOS Linux 7 R 3.4.4	Windows R 3.4.4
Local (no framework)	✘	✘	✘
VM (with framework)	✔	✔	✔

For this step, we used other machines with distinct hardware configurations. We took an intermediate file (sdmdata.txt), generated during the execution of the *Setup* step, as an example to verify if its content changed according to the machine used and the scenario in which the file was generated. This file contains clean data that are consumed by subsequent activity. The *Setup* activity has a random process and a seed is used as a parameter to ensure reproducibility. However, we were able to verify that only in the second scenario, with the use of the VM, the contents of the file remained the same when compared to the machine that originated the experiment (Table 2). The X symbol represents the executions that produced different results when compared to the machine that

---

[4] https://github.com/Model-R/modelr_pkg.

originated the experiment. The implementation of the framework and the execution of the experiment using the VM was robust enough to guarantee that the results were the same as the original, regardless of the machine used.

5   Related Work

A recent survey [9] raises the reasons why reproducibility of computational experiments is needed and the technical barriers and challenges that exist to achieve it. These barriers include issues ranging from managing and recording information from the execution environment to aspects related to the data that are consumed and generated by those experiments. Some efforts and initiatives have attempted to address these issues, especially as journals are increasingly encouraging submissions of reproducible computational research [14].

Among these efforts, we highlight *encapsulator* [15], a toolbox that relies on provenance data to produce an environment in which computational experiments can be reproduced. *ReproZip* [4] is a packaging tool that also uses provenance and focuses primarily on identifying the dependencies required to run an experiment. *WholeTale* [3] is a computational environment with features for data collection, identity management, data publication, and interfaces to analytical tools. These tools, as well as the framework proposed in this work, rely on VMs to allow reproduction of the experiment by others. However, we emphasize that in this work, we do not seek to implement a specific tool to guarantee reproducibility. Instead, we propose a framework that can benefit from existing tools to achieve different levels of reproducibility. We extend the proposal of *encapsulator* and *ReproZip* by indicating the need to publish the aspects related to the experiment so that it can be uniquely identified, accessed, and retrieved later. This work extends our previous work on provenance management [11]. The implementation of our framework provides provenance data, VM specifications, experiment script, and package versions used as a result. The user intending to run the experiment is not limited to using the VM, but can manually retrieve and reuse the experiment, or query the provenance database.

Addressing the FAIR principles, Madduri et al. [10] presented a set of tools to support the implementation of computational experiments and ensure the aspects related to the principles, using a case study in biomedicine. As in this paper, the need to apply FAIR principles in the experiment as a whole is discussed. However, in this work, we presented a more general and higher-level view of aspects of computational experiments that can be registered and the steps that can be followed to achieve reproducibility. In this way, the conceptual model and the framework can be more easily adapted to the specific needs of each experiment. Goble et al. [8] emphasizes the ability of computational workflows to process data and generate provenance information, which can therefore support the FAIR principles. They argued that the principles need to be extended to address the processual nature of workflows. This could lead further developments in our framework, since we are dealing with experiments that are, in essence, computational workflows.

6   Conclusions

In this paper, we discussed aspects of the reproducibility of computational experiments and the importance of allowing the application of FAIR principles to the experiment in its entirety. We indicate, through a conceptual model, the essential aspects of the experiments that must be recorded and how they relate to different levels of reproducibility. Also, we propose a generic framework for FAIR computational experiments and demonstrate its implementation through an ENM case study. As future work, we intend to evaluate and quantify which of the FAIR metrics are met with the implementation of the proposed framework. Future work may also include a mapping between the metrics and the different levels of reproducibility, and evaluation of what level of reproducibility is achieved according to the metrics obtained. We also intend to study the uncertainty quantification of the different results generated by the ML algorithms of the ENM experiment.

Acknowledgments. This work was supported by CNPq, CAPES, and FAPERJ. We thank Marinez Ferreira, Andrea Sánchez-Tapia and Sara Mortara, from the Botanic Garden of Rio de Janeiro, for their contributions.

References

1. Baker, M.: 1,500 scientists lift the lid on reproducibility. Nature **533**(7604), 452–454 (2016)
2. Borregaard, M.K., Hart, E.M.: Towards a more reproducible ecology. Ecography **39**(4), 349–353 (2016)
3. Brinckman, A., et al.: Computing environments for reproducibility: capturing the "whole tale". Future Gener. Comput. Syst. **94**, 854–867 (2019)
4. Chirigati, F., Rampin, R., Shasha, D., Freire, J.: ReproZip: computational reproducibility with ease. In: Proceedings of the 2016 International Conference on Management of Data, pp. 2085–2088. ACM (2016)
5. De Prins, J.: Global open biodiversity data: future vision of fair biodiversity data access, management, use and stewardship. Biodivers. Inf. Sci. Stand. **3**, e37190 (2019)
6. Deelman, E., et al.: Workflows and e-Science: an overview of workflow system features and capabilities. Future Gener. Comput. Syst. **25**(5), 528–540 (2009)
7. Freire, J., Chirigati, F.: Provenance and the different flavors of computational reproducibility. Bull. Tech. Comm. Data Eng. **41**(1), 15–26 (2018)
8. Goble, C., Cohen-Boulakia, S., et al.: Fair computational workflows (2019). https://doi.org/10.5281/zenodo.3268653
9. Ivie, P., Thain, D.: Reproducibility in scientific computing. ACM Comput. Surv. (CSUR) **51**(3), 63 (2018)
10. Madduri, R., Chard, K., D'Arcy, M., et al.: Reproducible big data science: a case study in continuous fairness. PloS one **14**(4), e0213013 (2019)
11. Mondelli, M.L., et al.: BioWorkbench: a high-performance framework for managing and analyzing bioinformatics experiments. PeerJ **6**, e5551 (2018)
12. Pimentel, J.F., Murta, L., Braganholo, V., Freire, J.: noWorkflow: a tool for collecting, analyzing, and managing provenance from python scripts. Proc. VLDB Endow. **10**, 1841–1844 (2017)

13. Sánchez-Tapia, A., et al.: Model-R: a framework for scalable and reproducible ecological niche modeling. In: Mocskos, E., Nesmachnow, S. (eds.) CARLA 2017. CCIS, vol. 796, pp. 218–232. Springer, Cham (2018). https://doi.org/10.1007/978-3-319-73353-1_15
14. Stodden, V., et al.: Toward reproducible computational research: an empirical analysis of data and code policy adoption by journals. PLoS One **8**(6), e67111 (2013)
15. Thomas, P., et al.: Sharing and preserving computational analyses for posterity with encapsulator. Comput. Sci. Eng. **20**(4), 111 (2018)
16. Wilkinson, M.D., Dumontier, M., Aalbersberg, I.J., et al.: The fair guiding principles for scientific data management and stewardship. Sci. Data **3**, 160018 (2016)

Conceptual Modeling in Requirements Engineering and Business Analysis (MREBA) 2019

Preface

Renata Guizzardi[1], Vitor E. Silva Souza[1], and Jelena Zdravkovic[2]

[1] Ontology and Conceptual Modeling Research Group (NEMO),
Department of Computer Science, Federal University of Espírito Santo, Brazil
{rguizzardi, vitorsouza}@inf.ufes.br
[2] Department of Computer and Systems Sciences, Stockholm University,
Postbox 7003, 164 07, Kista, Sweden
jelenaz@dsv.su.se

The MREBA workshop aims to provide a forum for discussing the interplay between Requirements Engineering and Business Analysis topics and Conceptual Modeling. These disciplines are nowadays common practices within organizations, and often applied in tandem. Moreover, the use of their methods and languages are an essential practice, for analysis, reasoning, development and evolution of Information Systems.

The 6th edition of MREBA received six submissions; each of them went through a thorough review process with at least three reviews from the program committee. This process ended up with 4 accepted full papers. The acceptance rate has been calculated considering all workshops together, thus complying with Springer standards. This explains our high acceptance number, which we owe to the authors of the submitted papers for the great quality of their work. We deeply thank them, as well as the reviewers for their valuable contributions.

The workshop started with a keynote Prof. Matthias Jarke from RWTH Aachen University & Fraunhofer FIT, joint with the i* workshop. The keynote was followed by the presentation of the four accepted full-papers and a discussion forum.

Acknowledgments. We must also thank the ER 2019 workshop chairs, and the remaining of the organizing committee for their trust and support. We have appreciated it!.

Realizing Traceability from the Business Model to Enterprise Architecture

W. Engelsman[1(✉)], R. J. Wieringa[2(✉)], M. van Sinderen[3(✉)], J. Gordijn[4(✉)], and T. Haaker[1(✉)]

[1] Saxion University of Applied Sciences, Enschede, The Netherlands
{w.engelsman,t.i.haaker}@saxion.nl
[2] The Value Engineers, Soest, The Netherlands
roel@thevalueengineers.nl
[3] University of Twente, Enschede, The Netherlands
m.j.vansinderen@utwente.nl
[4] The Value Engineers & Vrije Universiteit Amsterdam,
Amsterdam, The Netherlands
jaap@thevalueengineers.nl

Abstract. An enterprise architecture (EA) is a high-level representation of the enterprise, used for managing the relation between business and IT. In order to improve reasoning about the contribution of IT to the business, all elements of an EA should be traceable to the business model and vice versa. However, in practice this is not the case. Realizing this traceability would be useful because it would allow practitioners to reason about the contribution of IT to the Business Model of the organization. In addition to reasoning about cost structures and goal contributions of IT to the business, as is customary in EA, practitioners would also be able to reason about the contribution of IT to the value offerings of a business.

In this exploratory paper we investigate traceability between the EA, Business Model and Business Goals of an enterprise. We use ArchiMate as the EA language and e^3-*value* as the business modeling language, provide and motivate a hypothesis about how to realize traceability, and illustrate this with a real-world example. Our paper ends with a traceability hypothesis that will be further tested in future case studies.

1 Introduction

An enterprise architecture (EA) is a high-level representation of the enterprise, including business, IT and technology aspects. Large organizations maintain an EA in order to coordinate and steer IT projects and manage IT costs.

In our previous research we have clarified the relation between the business goals of the organization and its EA [6–8]. However, traceability to business goals captures only part of the motivation for an EA. High-level strategic goals are elaborated in a business model and the business model in turn motivates design choices in the EA [2]. In other words, an EA should not only be used to manage

© Springer Nature Switzerland AG 2019
G. Guizzardi et al. (Eds.): ER 2019 Workshops, LNCS 11787, pp. 37–46, 2019.
https://doi.org/10.1007/978-3-030-34146-6_4

IT costs but also to manage the contribution of IT to the value offerings of an enterprise. In this paper we extend our work on traceability with a hypothesis about traceability to business models. One could say that in this traceability relationship, the business model provides us with puzzle pieces and the EA will put these pieces together [17].

As the enterprise architecture modeling language we choose ArchiMate [19], both because it is well-known, the defacto standard for EA modelling and because we have been involved in its development [6].

We take an ecosystem approach to business models, which means that we see a company as part of a network of companies that coordinate to produce a value proposition. We use e^3-*value* as the ecosystem business modeling language [12]. e^3-*value* can be used to model the value exchanges in an ecosystem needed to jointly produce a value offering to a customer, and to analyze the long-term commercial viability of this. The current paper focusses on the implications of an ecosystem business model for the internal EA of an enterprise.

In this paper we show how the EA of one of the enterprises in an ecosystem, specified in ArchiMate, can be aligned with an ecosystem business model, specified in e^3-*value* . We expect that realizing this traceability provides us with the following advantages:

- Tracing not just to the business goals, but actually to quantifiable elements from the business model allows for better reasoning, especially in value networks where goals of different stakeholders need to be brought together to create a shared perception of the ecosystem, and to analyze the commercial viability of the ecosystem.
- To assess which projects that implement the architecture have the most business value in terms of contribution to the enterprise business goals and the ecosystem business model.

In Sect. 2 we analyze related work and, based on this, introduce a hypothesis about traceability links between ArchiMate and e^3-*value* models. In Sect. 3 we test this initial hypothesis on a real-world example and, based on this application, refine our initial traceability hypothesis in the form of a metamodel. In Sect. 4 we discuss the validity of our research method and outline some future research.

2   Value Modelling, Goal Modelling and Enterprise Architecture Modelling

There is some existing work done trying to link business models, goal modelling and EA. De Kinderen, Gaaloul and Proper propose to link ArchiMate to e^3-*value* using an intermedairy language. They do not propose a direct mapping [5]. Janssen and Gordijn directly map ArchiMate to e^3-*value* , but they use a different approach, which according to us, is incorrect. They link value activities to business processes instead of business services. Also, they determine much less instances of possible mappings. But they do agree that the business layer of ArchiMate should be mapped to e^3-*value* directly [20] Gordijn et al. [11] propose a method to combine i* with e³-*value* , with no focus realizing on traceabililty. Andersson et al. [3] describe the alignment of business models and goals. They have developed templates that align goal statements with value propositions. Meertens et al. [15] propose similar work, but instead of using e³-*value* they provide a mapping from the Business Model Canvas to ArchiMate. Pessoa et al. [16] developed a method for requirements elicitation for business models using an early version of the motivation extension of ArchiMate. Gordijn et al. [10] propose a method for requirements engineering for e-services. Aleda et al. [1] propose adaptations of ArchiMate to incorporate value modelling, but does not try to create traceability between different languages and the concepts introduced are less detailed than those using e³-*value* . In general, the major difference of our work with related work is our focus on traceability through meta-models.

Our earlier proposal to extend ArchiMate with a goal modelling language called ARMOR [6–8] is now part of Archimate 3.0 [19]. In follow-up empirical studies we observed that most of the concepts of ARMOR were conceptually too complex for practical use, and we proposed a simpler version of the language that is usable in practice, called ARMOR-light [7]. In ARMOR-light we only use the notions of stakeholder and goals. When a goal is realized by an element from ArchiMate then it is considered a requirement, similar to KAOS [4]. In this paper we will use ArchiMate 3.0 as if it only contains the constructs of ARMOR-light.

ArchiMate models have a business layer, an application layer, and a technology layer, that have traceability links among them. To realize traceability to e³-*value* models, we need to link the business layer of an ArchiMate model to e³-*value* models. Within the business layer, the Business Service is used to expose behavior and value of the organization to the environment. This is where we expect to find the link between ArchiMate and e³-*value* .

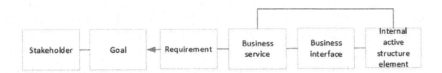

Fig. 1. Metamodel of ARMOR-Light with part of the metamodel of ArchiMate [7]. The lines represent many to many relations, the arrow represents a subset.

Figure 1 shows part of a meta-model of ARMOR-light and ArchiMate. For clarity reasons we have omitted the application and technology layers and a large part of the business layer. Requirements are the subset of goals allocated to a business service. Goals not allocated to an EA element are ends that a stakeholder wishes to achieve. In ArchiMate an internal active structure element is an abstraction of any actor or specialization thereof; e.g. roles, actors, collaborations, etc. A business service is the externally visible behavior of an internal active structure element. It exposes its behavior over a business interface of the internal active structure element, e.g. the sales channel.

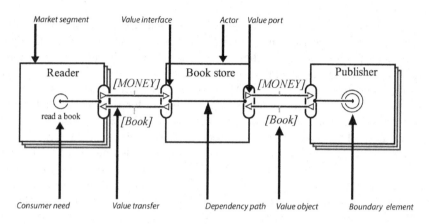

Fig. 2. Educational e³-*value* model

In Fig. 2 an educational e³-*value* model is presented, annotated with the name of the modeling constructs, which we discuss below. In e³-*value*, an actor is some entity capable of performing value activities, e.g. a business, department or partner. In the example, the book store is an actor. A special case of an actor is the market segment (e.g. the reader or the publisher). A market segment models that many actors of the same kind. In e³-*value* this means that all actors in a market segment assign economic value precisely in the same way. A value activity (not shown in the example) is a task performed by an actor which can lead to a positive net cash flow. The value activity differs from activities in process models in e.g. the BPMN. Value activities should be profitable while in BPMN it is perfectly allowed to include activities that only cost money. A value interface represents what the actors offers and requests to/from its environment in terms of value objects. Value objects are things that are perceived by at least one actor as of economic value. A value interface consists of at least one ingoing and one outgoing port, through which the actor requests or offers value objects from or to its environment. The value interface models (1) the notion of economic reciprocity and (2) bundling. Economic reciprocity is the idea that someone only offers something of value, of something else of higher economic value is obtained in return. In the example, the book is exchanged for money, hence the transfers are economically reciprocal. Bundling is the case where it is only possible to offer or obtain value objects in combination. Value ports between actors are connected by means of value transfers, which represent the willingness of actors to exchange things. Internally in an actor, there is the dependency path, which shows how value objects exchanged via a value interface require or assume exchanges via other value interfaces of that same actor. For example, the sale of a book by the book store requires that this store obtains the book from a publisher. The boundary element of a dependency path indicates the boundary of our modeling interest. Any further transactions that take place in the real world to satisfy the consumer need are not included in our model.

Figure 3 shows the meta-model for actors (left) and dependency paths (right) in e^3-*value* [9].

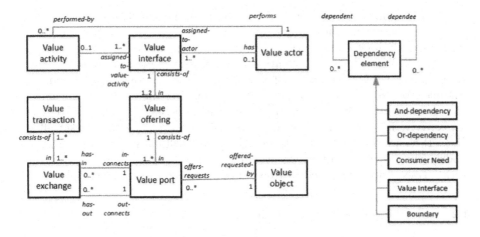

Fig. 3. Metamodel of actors and dependency paths in e^3-*value* [12]

Based on these two metamodels, we formulate our initial hypothesis about traceability between ArchiMate and e^3-*value* concepts in Table 1.

Table 1. Our initial hypothesis about correspondences between concepts in ArchiMate and in e^3-*value*.

ArchiMate	e^3-*value*	Argument
Stakeholder	Actor	An e^3-*value* actor is always an ArchiMate stakeholder, by definition. The other way around is not guaranteed
Goal	Customer need	Customer needs are customer goals. Goal models identify and refine customer needs
Business actor	Actor	Both are essentially the same thing. An actor in e^3-*value* performs activities that produce value. in ArchiMate actors perform behaviour as well
Business service	Value activity	Both concepts denote externally visible behavior performed by an actor and made available through an interface
Business interface	Value interface	Both are the interfaces in which the behavior is accessed

3   Application: Cirque du Soleil

3.1   The Example

Cirque du Soleil, based in Montreal, is known internationally for its innovative form of circus production. Cirque was one of the first to reinvent the circus production, without animal usage, but with a focus on artistic human performances [14]. We collected information about this example from public sources on the internet [13,21] supplemented with some assumptions to round out the example. We will show how Cirque du Soleil offers live shows and virtual shows, offered in an attractive location and through a Virtual Reality (VR) device, respectively. Tickets for the live shows are sold by an independent ticket office. The VR shows are distributed by Samsung. We will construct three different models, since there is no tool yet available to create a single model (see future work). Traceability links are described in the text explaining the models.

3.2   Goal Model, Business Model and EA Model

We start by constructing a goal model in ArchiMate (Fig. 4). For illustration purposes we have restricted ourselves to one goal per relevant actor. A goal model like this is often constructed in the strategic phase of EA development, similar to TOGAF's preliminary and vision phases [18].

Figure 5 contains the e³-*value* model that illustrates the value adding activities. Value activities are represented by rounded rectangles inside an actor. In our example Samsung enters into a collaboration with Cirque Du Soleil to distribute the VR media of the circus performance to customers. An external ticket office is used to offer a ticketing service. For example, Cirque du Soleil wants to perform a show and Samsung wants to distribute performances.

Customers are represented by two separate actors, Visitor and Digital Customer. Visitors have a need to enjoy a live artistic show, and satisfy this need by paying Cirque du Soleil for performing their value activity. Cirque du Soleil hires a ticket office to sell tickets. The inter-actor transactions and the intra-actor dashed lines form a dependency path in e³-*value* models, connecting a consumer need with all transactions in the ecosystem needed to satisfy the need. The customer need to enjoy a show from home is satisfied by a similar dependency path.

Figure 6 shows an ArchiMate model of the EA for Cirque du Soleil. We have identified two different main Business Services: the Circus Performance Service and the Digital Distribution Service. These two business services correspond to the value activities of the e³-*value* model from the actors Samsung and Cirque du Soleil. The ArchiMate model also contains four business actors, where Samsung and Cirque du Soleil collaborate together to deliver the digital distribution service. To model the different roles of the customers we have chosen to model the digital customer and the visitor as seperate roles.

The same can be seen with the ticket office, they collaborate (the business collaboration) to provide the ticketing service. Since ArchiMate allows for more detail in the modelling of the business services, design decisions like the composition of the ticketing service in the circus performance service are represented here.

It is also possible that these translate to supporting internal business services like the recording service. Before you can distribute a show you do need some sort of recording service. This is not necessarily a value adding activity and therefore not visible in the e³-*value* model.

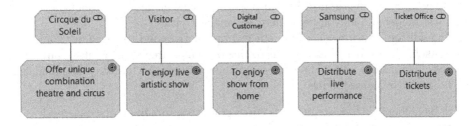

Fig. 4. Partial cirque du Soleil goal model

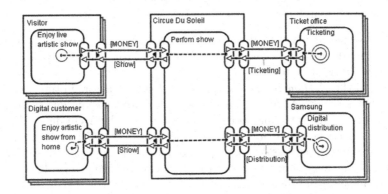

Fig. 5. e³-*value* model of Cirque du Soleil

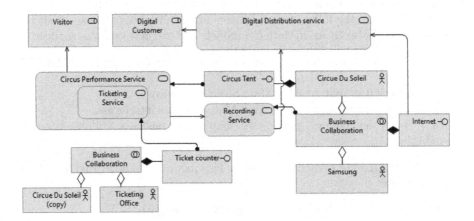

Fig. 6. ArchiMate model of the business layer of Cirque du Soleil

3.3 Observations

Linking ArchiMate goal models to e^3-value models. First, we see that in our example, goals in the goal model correspond to value activities of business actors in e^3-*value* . We believe this to be a general rule for strategic goals. There are goals at every level of the organization, but only strategic goals will be relevant for a business model and may appear there as value activities.

In addition, consumer needs in our example correspond to consumer goals in the stakeholder model. This leads us to the following three refinements of our initial two hypotheses about the correspondence between ArchiMate goals models and e^3-*value* business models:

- Stakeholders with strategic goals correspond to actors in an e^3-*value* model.
- Value activities in an e^3-*value* model correspond to lower level goals in a strategic goal model.
- Consumer needs in an e^3-*value* model correspond to lower-level consumer goals in a strategic goal model.

Linking e^3-value models to ArchiMate EA models. In our example all the value activities that do not have a consumer need attached to them correspond to business services in ArchiMate.

Actors in the e^3-*value* model correspond to business actors in the ArchiMate model. This may not be true in general as ArchiMate also contains the concept of a role. An e^3-*value* actor may correspond to a role in the ArchiMate EA rather than to a business actor. Future research should provide clarity about this.

The value interfaces in e^3-*value* map onto the business interface in ArchiMate. For example, the four value interfaces from Samsung to Cirque du Soleil translate to a single business interface in ArchiMate.

Finally, an e^3-*value* dependency path connects transactions among different actors. This may be mapped to business collaborations in an ArchiMate model. Whether this is true in general must be shown by future case studies.

This leads us to the following refinements of our initial hypotheses about the correspondence between ArchiMate EA models and e^3-*value* business models:

- e^3-*value* actors map to business actors and possibly roles in an ArchiMate EA models.
- e^3-*value* activities map to ArchiMate business services.
- e^3-*value* value interfaces map to ArchiMate business interfaces
- An e^3-*value* dependency path may map to a business collaboration in ArchiMate.

Figure 7 summarizes our traceability rules. This meta-model is divided into three different layers:

- The strategic layer where we find stakeholders and goals,
- The value layer, where we see the value adding activities and
- the technical layer where we find the designs of the organization in an EA.

Integrating e³-*value* into ArchiMate therefore happens between the Motivation layer and the Business Layer. This results in traceability from stakeholder to actor and ArchiMate equivalents. Conversely, from a business service we can trace to value activities and then to the value offerings, and directly and indirectly to goals.

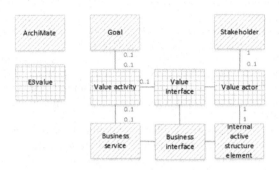

Fig. 7. Combined traceability model. All relationships are many-many unless otherwise stated.

4   Discussion and Future Work

This work is in its early stages and our current hypothesis is based on an analysis of metamodels plus an application to a single example. We cannot claim generalizability based on this.

To test generalizability, we will restrict our research to e³-*value* and ArchiMate. Generalizability to other languages therefore remains an open issue. However, we will investigate generalizability to other cases analyzed in e³-*value* and ArchiMate as a next step.

Within this scope, we need to refine the hypothesis by doing more complex real-world case studies. What is the exact meaning of the relations in our proposed integrated metamodel? What is the relation between value activity and goal? Could it be a realization or specialization? This could also be said for cross-abstraction level of traceability. How do concepts like value and goals relate?

We will test usability of our hypothesis in experiments like we did with ARMOR [6–8]. Utility in practice will be investigated by means of opinion research, e.g. a focus group of practitioners. A final step is to create a tool-supported method for designing an EA based on a business model, and for extracting a business model from a given EA.

References

1. Aldea, A., Iacob, M.E., van Hillegersberg, J., Quartel, D., Franken, H.: Modelling value with ArchiMate. In: Persson, A., Stirna, J. (eds.) CAiSE 2015. LNBIP, vol. 215, pp. 375–388. Springer, Cham (2015). https://doi.org/10.1007/978-3-319-19243-7_35

2. Alt, R., Zimmermann, H.-D.: Preface: introduction to special section-business models. Electron. Markets **11**(1), 3–9 (2001)
3. Andersson, B., Bergholtz, M., Edirisuriya, A., Ilayperuma, T., Jayaweera, P., Johannesson, P., Zdravkovic, J.: Enterprise sustainability through the alignment of goal models and business models. In: Proceedings of 3rd International Workshop on Business/IT-Alignment and Interoperability (BUSITAL 2008) CEUR Workshop Proceedings (2008)
4. Dardenne, A., van Lamsweerde, A., Fickas, S.: Goal-directed requirements acquisition. Sci. Comput. Program. **20**(1–2), 3–50 (1993)
5. de Kinderen, S., Gaaloul, K., Proper, H.A.: Bridging value modelling to archimate via transaction modelling. Softw. & Syst. Model. **13**(3), 1043–1057 (2014)
6. Engelsman, W., Quartel, D.A.C., Jonkers, H., van Sinderen, M.J.: Extending enterprise architecture modelling with business goals and requirements. Enterprise Inf. Syst. **5**(1), 9–36 (2011)
7. Engelsman, W., Wieringa, R.: Understandability of goal-oriented requirements engineering concepts for enterprise architects. In: Jarke, M., Mylopoulos, J., Quix, C., Rolland, C., Manolopoulos, Y., Mouratidis, H., Horkoff, J. (eds.) CAiSE 2014. LNCS, vol. 8484, pp. 105–119. Springer, Cham (2014). https://doi.org/10.1007/978-3-319-07881-6_8
8. Engelsman, W., Wieringa, R.: Goal-oriented requirements engineering and enterprise architecture: two case studies and some lessons learned. In: Regnell, B., Damian, D. (eds.) REFSQ 2012. LNCS, vol. 7195, pp. 306–320. Springer, Heidelberg (2012). https://doi.org/10.1007/978-3-642-28714-5_27
9. Gordijn, J.: E-business value modelling using the E3-value ontology. In: Value creation from e-business models, pp. 98–127. Elsevier (2004)
10. Gordijn, J., Eck, P.V., Wieringa, R.: Requirements engineering techniques for E-services. In: Service-Oriented Computing: Cooperative Information Systems Series, pp. 331–352 (2009)
11. Gordijn, J., Eric, Y., Van Der Raadt, B.: E-service design using i* and e/sup 3/value modeling. IEEE Softw. **23**(3), 26–33 (2006)
12. Gordijn, J., Akkermans, J.M.: Value webs: understanding E-business innovation. The Value Engineer (2018). http://www.thevalueengineers.nl
13. Kim, W.C., Mauborgne, R.A.: Blue Ocean Strategy. Expanded edition: how to create uncontested market space and make the competition irrelevant. Harvard Business Review Press, Brighton (2014)
14. Leslie, D., Rantisi, N.M.: Creativity and place in the evolution of a cultural industry: the case of cirque du soleil. Urban Stud. **48**(9), 1771–1787 (2011)
15. Meertens, L.O., Iacob, M.-E., Nieuwenhuis, L.J.M., van Sinderen, M.J., Jonkers, H., Quartel, D.: Mapping the business model canvas to archimate. In: Proceedings of the 27th Annual ACM Symposium on Applied Computing, pp. 1694–1701. ACM (2012)
16. Pessoa, R.M., van Sinderen, M., Quartel, D.A.C.: Towards requirements elicitation in service-oriented business networks using value and goal modelling. In: ICSOFT, vol. 2, pp. 392–399 (2009)
17. Teece, D.J.: Business models, business strategy and innovation. Long Range Plann. **43**(2–3), 172–194 (2010)
18. The Open Group. TOGAF Version 9. Van Haren Publishing, (2009)
19. The Open Group. ArchiMate 2.0 Specification. Van Haren Publishing (2012)
20. van Buuren, R., Gordijn, J., Janssen, W.: Business case modelling for E-services. In: BLED 2005 Proceedings, p. 8 (2005)
21. Computer Weekly. Case studies; the sytems behind the shows. Internet (2006)

Creation of Multiple Conceptual Models from User Stories – A Natural Language Processing Approach

Abhimanyu Gupta[1]([✉]), Geert Poels[1], and Palash Bera[2]

[1] Faculty of Economics and Business Administration, Ghent University,
Tweekerkenstraat 2, 9000 Ghent, Belgium
abhimanyu.gupta@ugent.be
[2] Saint Louis University, 1 N Grand Blvd, St. Louis, MO 63103, USA

Abstract. While Agile methodologies are used in software development, researchers have identified many issues related to requirements engineering in Agile approaches. Some of these issues relate to ambiguity in user stories, which is a widely-used requirements specification mechanism in Agile methodologies. This research proposes the use of conceptual models while developing user stories. We posit that the use of conceptual models helps reducing ambiguity in user stories. An important aspect of our research is the creation of an algorithm for automatic generation of such models while developing the user stories.

Keywords: User stories · Agile development · Conceptual models · Natural language processing · Behavior driven development

1 Introduction

In Agile software development, the software requirements documentation is mainly limited to the creation of user stories [1]. A user story is a simple description of a feature of the working software written from the user's perspective [2, 3].

Because of the substantial number of user stories that are developed in an Agile software development project, the development team may encounter difficulties in maintaining, tracing, and managing the user stories [4]. Even for moderately complex software, the number of user stories easily exceeds the human capacity of overview and understanding. To alleviate this problem, we suggest using a tool to automatically generate conceptual models while developing user stories and corresponding BDD acceptance criteria. Conceptual models are visual representations that are commonly used for understanding requirements and communicating with system stakeholders [5].

There has been limited research in developing conceptual models automatically from user stories. For example, Mesquita et al. [6] automatically extracted goal models (in i* language) from user stories. Robeer et al. [7] built a tool that automatically generates an ontological model of the domain (in OWL ontology) from user stories. And Lucassen et al. ([8]) developed the Visual Narrator tool to visually show concepts and relationships extracted from user stories. However, each of these tools have targeted only one type of conceptual model.

© Springer Nature Switzerland AG 2019
G. Guizzardi et al. (Eds.): ER 2019 Workshops, LNCS 11787, pp. 47–57, 2019.
https://doi.org/10.1007/978-3-030-34146-6_5

What is currently missing in the state-of-the-art is the automated generation of conceptual models that show both the functional (de) composition of the domain (i.e., the process view) and the domain concepts and relationships (i.e., the object view). Moreover, the tools have focused only on the standard structure of user stories (As a [user], I want [some goal] so that [some reason]), and not on extended versions as used in Behavior-Driven Development (BDD) [9].

2   Research Goal

In this paper, we extend the current research by extracting multiple conceptual models from user stories. Multiple conceptual models provide rich perspectives of the domain from multiple points of view (e.g., considering both a structural and dynamic perspective of a domain) [9]. Recker and Green [18] suggest using multiple conceptual models as no one model is a complete representation of a domain as no single available grammar is ontologically complete.

There is also growing evidence of using multiple conceptual models simultaneously. Surveys conducted on the use of conceptual models indicate that practitioners indeed use more than one conceptual model for different types of tasks [13–16]. For instance, Recker [17] found that process modelers use other models than process models when modeling business processes. Jabbari et al. [16] found that practitioners use multiple interrelated conceptual models since information systems are getting more complex and interrelated models can be used to represent different aspects of the system.

In Agile development, where there is less focus on documentation, it will be unrealistic to expect that users will develop and maintain (multiple) conceptual models in the process of creating the user stories. Therefore, we developed an algorithm that automatically creates multiple conceptual models when user stories are fed to it. In order to do so, we supplement the standard structure of user stories with acceptance criteria, as is common practice in BDD [9]. Acceptance criteria define the acceptable functionality of a user story [3]. They are usually formulated in terms of preconditions, triggering events, and postconditions. The conceptual models that are generated by our algorithm are: Domain Model [10], Process Model [11], Finite State Machine [12], and Use Case Model [12].

The objective of this paper is to demonstrate this algorithm. In future research, the effectiveness and usefulness of this algorithm will be validated by conducting a case study. The feedback obtained from the case study will inform us on the further development and fine-tuning of our solution.

3   Proposed Solution

We add acceptance criteria to user stories using BDD scenarios. BDD is a set of Agile practices from test driven development and domain driven design, that allow developing high-quality software faster [19]. BDD provides a common language based on simple structured English that facilitates communication between project team members and business stakeholders [9]. A BDD scenario consists of a feature title, an associated user story and the scenario proper which is defined by three keywords – Given, When, and Then [3]. Given describes the context of the user story, i.e., the preconditions for performing the action specified in the user story. When specifies the event that triggers this action, whereas Then describes the outcome of the user story, i.e., the postconditions of performing the action specified in the use story. Table 1 shows the BDD scenario template recommended by the Agile community [9] (an example is in Table 5).

Table 1. The BDD scenario template [9].

Feature: [title]
As a [role] I want [feature] so that [benefit]
Scenario: [title]
Given [context] And [some more context]
When [some event occurs] And [some other event]
Then [outcome] And [some other outcome]

To analyze the structure and content of BDD scenarios, we first developed an agent-based framework for user stories (Fig. 1). This framework will guide the algorithm that generates multiple conceptual models from a given set of user stories.

The agent-based framework considers the [role] as an Agent that wishes to use the system to perform an Action on an Object. Each User Story is a triad of Agent-Action-Object, where the action-object pair is captured by the [feature] segment of the user story. Figure 1 shows that agents, actions and objects may be part of many user stories, but of course no two user stories can share the same triad of Agent-Action-Object.

Figure 1 shows that objects have states. A State can be a pre- or postcondition for one or more actions and such object-state pairs are captured respectively in the [context] and [outcome] segments of the BDD scenario. We observed, when investigating real user stories, that pre- and postconditions might also refer to states of agents, in which case we can include those agents also amongst the objects (i.e., being an agent or object is a role played by entities in the context of user stories).

Finally, Fig. 1 shows that actions are triggered by events. An Event is captured in the [some event occurs] segment of the BDD scenario. An action is an event, but there might be other kinds of event like time events (e.g., 3.00 PM or every 30 min) and events occurring in the system's environment (e.g., detection of an earthquake). Still missing in our framework is the [benefit] segment of the user story. For the moment, information on the goal of or motivation for a user story is not used to generate conceptual models. We consider this as a topic for future research.

While model generation from user stories and use of models to help assuring the quality of user stories is not new (see, e.g., [17]), the novelty of our approach is in the generation of multiple models reflecting different views on the system. Hence, we develop interrelated models that complement each other in terms of representing different aspects of the envisioned system as captured through the user stories. Booch,

Rumbaugh, and Jacobson [20] provide a basic classification of conceptual models - behavioral and structural models. These two types reflect the dynamic and static nature of the systems respectively.

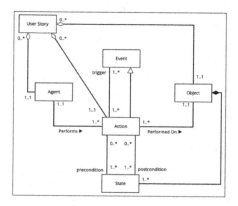

Fig. 1. Agent-based framework for user stories

From the user stories, we will develop all possible conceptual models, given the information in user stories and BDD acceptance criteria, which include both behavioral and structural models (Table 2). The domain model or concept map is used to show the interrelated domain concepts [21] and is considered as a structural model. Process models, Finite State Machine and Use Case models are treated as behavioral models.

Table 2. Types of conceptual models generated

Conceptual model	Type
Domain model	Structural
Process model	Behavioral
Finite state machine(s)	Behavioral
Use case model	Behavioral

4 Solution Design

We designed an algorithm that applies Natural Language Processing (NLP) to a given set of user stories to translate them into a canonical form that instantiates the concepts of the agent-based framework presented in Sect. 3. The canonical form is then the starting point for generating the four types of model shown in Table 2.

The algorithm starts by splitting (based on indicators like "As a", "I want", etc.) the user stories and their acceptance criteria into six segments – Role, Feature, Benefit, Context, Event and Outcome. After this step, the Parts of Speech (PoS) of all the words appearing in those six segments are identified. Then, the PoS fragments are used to identify the instances of the concepts of the agent-based framework. These instances are then entered for all user stories into a table which represents the canonical form of the user stories.

Next, a thorough reconciliation process takes place to ensure that all required instances are present in all user stories and their acceptance criteria. If instances are missing (e.g., no object is identified on which the action is performed), then heuristics are applied to approximate these missing components from the information obtained from previously processed user stories. After completing the canonical form with missing information, the Domain Model, Process Model, Finite State Machines (one for each object) and Use Case Model are generated (i.e., drawn by the tool that implements the algorithm).

Table 3 elaborates on the NLP rules that are used to translate user stories into their canonical form.

Table 3. Mapping between PoS and model components

Rule	Parts of Speech (If)	Component (then)	Rule	Parts of Speech (If)	Component (then)
	Segment: Role			**Segment: Context**	
A1	Singular Noun	Agent	C1	Singular Noun	Concept of Precondition
A2	Plural Noun	Agent	C2	Plural Noun	Concept of Precondition
A3	Singular Noun + space + Singular Noun	Agent	C3	Singular Noun + space + Singular Noun	Concept of Precondition
A4	Singular Noun + space + Plural Noun	Agent	C4	Singular Noun + space + Plural Noun	Concept of Precondition
A5	Plural Noun + space + Plural Noun	Agent	C5	Plural Noun + space + Plural Noun	Concept of Precondition
A6	Adverb	Agent	C6	Adverb	Concept of Precondition
	Segment: Feature		C7	Verb in Past Participle Form	State of Precondition
B1	Verb	Action	C8	Adjective	State of Precondition
B2	Verb + space + Preposition	Action		**Segment: Outcome**	
B3	Singular Noun	Object	D1	Singular Noun	Concept of Postcondition
B4	Plural Noun	Object	D2	Plural Noun	Concept of Postcondition
B5	Singular Noun + space + Singular Noun	Object	D3	Singular Noun + space + Singular Noun	Concept of Postcondition
B6	Singular Noun + space + Plural Noun	Object	D4	Singular Noun + space + Plural Noun	Concept of Postcondition
B7	Plural Noun + space + Plural Noun	Object	D5	Plural Noun + space + Plural Noun	Concept of Postcondition
B8	Adverb	Object	D6	Adverb	Concept of Postcondition
			D7	Verb in Past Participle Form	State of Postcondition
			D8	Adjective	State of Postcondition

Table 4a. Pseudo-code to create the Canonical Form

```
#Create table containing agent, action, object, precondition and postcondition
1:   user story: {As a..., I want to..., so that... (Given..., when..., then...)}
2:   for each (user story)
3:       segment1 ← "As a..."
4:       segment2 ← "I want to..."
5:       segment3 ← "so that..."
6:       segment4 ← "Given..."
7:       segment5 ← "when..."
8:       segment6 ← "then..."
9:       posSegment1 ← part-of-speech of segment1
10:      posSegment2 ← part-of-speech of segment2
11:      posSegment3 ← part-of-speech of segment3
12:      posSegment4 ← part-of-speech of segment4
13:      posSegment5 ← part-of-speech of segment5
14:      posSegment6 ← part-of-speech of segment6
15:      If ((posSegment1==NN) || (posSegment1==NNS) || (posSegment1==RB))
16:          agent ← add (token)
17:      If ((posSegment2==NN) || (posSegment2==NNS) || (posSegment2==RB))
18:          object ← add (token)
19:      If (posSegment2==VB)
20:          action ← add (token)
21:      If ((posSegment4==NN) || (posSegment4==NNS) || (posSegment4==RB))
22:          concept of precondition ← add (token)
23:      If ((posSegment4==JJ) || (posSegment4==VBN))
24:          state of precondition ← add (token)
25:      If ((posSegment6==NN) || (posSegment6==NNS) || (posSegment6==RB))
26:          concept of postcondition ← add (token)
27:      If ((posSegment6==JJ) || (posSegment6==VBN))
28:          state of postcondition ← add (token)
29:      table ← add (agent, action, object, precondition, postcondition)
```

Following are the steps involved in creating the conceptual models. The steps are formulated in pseudo-code in Tables 4a, 4b, and 4c. The procedure starts in line 2 (Table 4a) by splitting the user stories and their acceptance criteria in six segments – Role, Feature, Benefit, Context, Event and Outcome (lines 2–8). In lines 9–14, parts of speeches of all the words appearing in those six segments are identified. For example, in line 9, the parts of speech of segment 1 which is "As a ..." are identified. Then the identification of various components like agent (lines 15–16, using rules A1–A6), object (lines 17–18, using rules B3–B8), action (lines 19–20, using rules B1–B2), concept of precondition (lines 21–22, using rules C1–C6), state of precondition (lines 23–24, using rules C7–C8), concept of postcondition (lines 25–26, using rules D1–D6) and state of postcondition (lines 27–28, using rules D7–D8) are completed and all information is stored into a table representing the user stories in the canonical form (line 29).

The process of reconciliation is described in Table 4b. The instructions in lines 30–70 ensure that all components are present in all user stories and their acceptance criteria. If components are not present, then they are populated from appropriate components of the previous user story. For example, if an object is not present in a user story, the object from the previous user story is used. Similarly, if the concept of precondition is not available, the concept of precondition or object from the previous user story is used depending on whether the agent is also missing or not. Another example is if the concept of postcondition is missing in a user story, then the concept of postcondition is reused from the previous user story. We reckon that this reconciliation mechanism is only approximative and depends on the order in which the user stories and their acceptance criteria are processed by the algorithm, but leave improvements for future research. The table representing the user stories in canonical form is updated as output of this part of the algorithm (line 71) (Table 4c).

Table 4b. Pseudo-code to validate the Canonical Form

```
#Reconcile lists of agent, action, object, precondition and postcondition
30:   for each (row in table)
31:       if (count of object < count of agent)
32:           object ← previous object
33:       if (count of concept of precondition < count of object)
34:           if (count of concept of precondition < count of agent)
35:               concept of precondition ← previous concept of precondition
36:           else
37:               concept of precondition ← previous object
38:       if (count of concept of postcondition < count of concept of precondition)
39:           if (count of concept of postcondition < count of agent)
40:               concept of postcondition ← previous concept of postcondition
41:           else
42:               concept of postcondition ← previous concept of precondition
43:       if (count of agent < count of state of precondition)
44:           agent ← previous agent
45:       if (count of action == < count of state precondition)
46:           action ← previous action
47:       if (count of object < count of state of precondition)
48:           object ← previous object
49:       if (count of concept of precondition < count of state of precondition)
50:           concept of precondition ← previous concept of precondition
51:       if (count of concept of postcondition < count of state of precondition)
52:           concept of postcondition ← previous concept of postcondition
53:       if (count of state of postcondition < count of state of precondition)
54:           state of postcondition ← previous state of postcondition
55:       if (count of agent < count of concept of precondition)
56:           agent ← previous agent
57:       if (count of action == < count of concept precondition)
58:           action ← previous action
59:       if (count of object < count of concept of precondition)
60:           object ← previous object
61:       if (count of state of precondition < count of concept of precondition)
62:           state of precondition ← previous state of precondition
63:       if (count of concept of postcondition < count of concept of precondition)
64:           concept of postcondition ← previous concept of postcondition
65:       if (count of state of postcondition < count of concept of precondition)
66:           state of postcondition ← previous state of postcondition
67:   if table == valid
68:       continue
69:   Else
70:       exit
```

The generation of multiple conceptual models starting from the canonical representation of the user stories and their acceptance criteria is presented in Table 4c. The domain model is drawn in lines 72–79; the process model is drawn in lines 80–89; finite state machines are drawn in lines 90–96 and the use case diagram is drawn in lines 97–102.

Table 4c. Pseudo-code to draw various models

```
#Publish table containing agent, action, object, precondition and postcondition       #Draw Finite State Machine Diagram
71:    write(table)                                                                    90:    for each (precondition of table)
                                                                                       91:            unique state ← add (unique state from precondition from table)
#Draw Entity-Relationship (ER) Diagram                                                 92:    for each (postcondition of table)
72:    for each (agent of table)                                                       93:            unique state ← add (unique state from postcondition from table)
73:            unique agent ← add (unique agent from table)                            94:    draw circle ← unique state
74:    for each (object of table)                                                      95:    for each (action of table)
75:            unique object ← add (unique object from table)                          96:            draw arrow ← connect (state of precondition, state of postcondition)
76:    draw rectangle ← unique agent
77:    draw rectangle ← unique object                                                  #Draw Use Case Diagram
78:    for each (action of table)                                                      97:    for each (agent of table)
79:            draw line ← connect (unique agent, unique object)                       98:            unique agent ← add (unique agent from table)
                                                                                       99:    draw human ← unique agent
#Draw Business Process Model Notation (BPMN) Diagram                                    100:   draw ellipse ← action + object
80:    for each (agent of table)                                                       101:   for each (action of table)
81:            unique agent ← add (unique agent from table)                            102:           draw line ← connect (unique agent, action + object)
82:    for each (action of table)
83:            unique action ← add (unique action from table)
84:    draw swim lane ← unique agent
85:    draw rectangle ← unique action
86:    for each (precondition of table)
87:            for each (postcondition of table)
88:                    if (precondition == postcondition)
89:                            draw arrow ← connect (unique action, unique action)
```

5 Proof of Concept

We demonstrate how a sample set of user stories (Table 5) is translated into their canonical form and represented in the table that is generated by our algorithm. Next, we show how our algorithm derives the conceptual models for this sample set.

Table 5. Sample user stories

1.	As a customer, I want to create a service request so that I can have my problem solved. Given that the customer is active, when he submits a service request then the service request should be submitted
2.	As a support assistant, I want to accept so that I can start working on it. Given it is submitted, when the team starts working on it then it is open
3.	As a support assistant, I need to resolve so that the customer can close the ticket. Given a service request is open, when the team resolves it, then it is fixed
4.	As a customer, I need to approve the service request so that it can be closed. Given a service request is fixed, when I approve it, then the service request becomes closed
5.	As a customer, I need to reject the service request so that it can be reopened. Given a service request is fixed, when I reject it, then the service request is open
6.	As a customer, I want to cancel a service request so that the team can focus on other active requests. Given a service request is submitted or closed when customer cancels it then it will be canceled

Each of the above user stories is first decomposed into six segments using the following keywords: "As a", "I want to", "so that", "Given", "when" and "then". After that, the NLP rules from Table 3 are applied to identify the agent, action, object, precondition and postcondition of each user story. The result of applying the instructions in lines 1–71 of the algorithm is Table 6, which shows the sample of user stories in their canonical form.

Table 6. Canonical form of sample user stories

Agent	Action	Object	Agent/object	Precondition state	Agent/object	Postcondition state
customer	create	service request	customer	active	service request	submitted
support assistant	accept	service request	service request	submitted	service request	open
support assistant	resolve	service request	service request	open	service request	fixed
customer	approve	service request	service request	fixed	service request	closed
customer	reject	service request	service request	fixed	service request	open
customer	cancel	service request	service request	submitted	service request	canceled
customer	cancel	service request	service request	closed	service request	canceled

Rules A1 – A6 identify agents. A customer performs actions in user stories 1, 4, 5 and 6. Therefore customer is an entry in the agent column of Table 6 for rows 1, 4, 5 and 6. A support assistant performs actions in user stories 2 and 3. Therefore support assistant is an entry in the agent column for rows 2 and 3.

Following are the actions performed by the agents, which are identified by rules B1 and B2 in the six user stories: create (from user story 1), accept (from user story 2), resolve (from user story 3), approve (from user story 4), reject (from user story 5) and cancel (from user story 6). Therefore, these six actions are entered the action column of Table 6.

The following are the objects on which the actions are performed. These objects are identified by rules B3–B8. In this set of user stories, all the actions are performed on the same object, i.e., service request. Note that the object was missing in the Feature segment of user stories 2 and 3. If the user stories are processed in the given order, then the algorithm assumes that the actions of user stories 2 and 3 are performed on the object identified in user story 1.

Next, rules C1 – C8 and D1 – D8 identify pre- and postconditions as (conjunct) object-state pairs. In this example:

- The object customer (also an agent) has only one state: active
- The object service request has five states: submitted, open, fixed, closed and canceled.

The above object-state pairs are added to columns 4 and 5, respectively 6 and 7 of Table 6, depending on whether they are pre- or postconditions.

Based on the relationships among agents, actions, objects and states, as depicted in Fig. 2, the following models are created by our prototype tool, as output, that implements the designed algorithm (Fig. 3).

To create the domain model and use case model, the first three columns of Table 6 (i.e., agent, action and object) are combined and represented in the appropriate format. To create finite state machine(s), the fourth and fifth columns of Table 6 (i.e., agent/object and pre-condition state) are compared to the sixth and seventh columns of Table 6 (i.e., agent/object and post-condition state) to find if an action (i.e., second column) exists for which the agent/object of pre-condition and post-condition are same but the states are different. The transitions are then represented using arrows. Similarly,

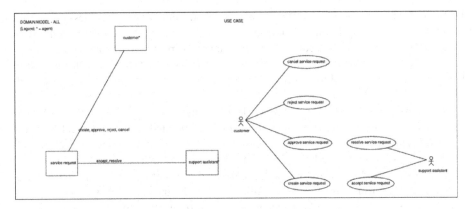

Fig. 2. Domain model and use case model from user stories

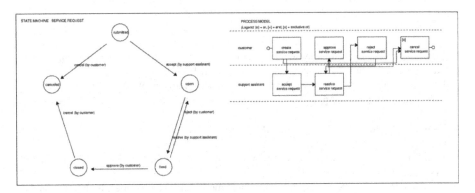

Fig. 3. Finite state machine model and process model from user stories

to create process model, the fourth and fifth columns of Table 6 (i.e., agent/object and pre-condition state) are compared to the sixth and seventh columns of Table 6 (i.e., agent/object and post-condition state) to find if a pre-condition (i.e., both agent/object and state) of a later user story matches with a post-condition (i.e., both agent/object and state) of a previous user story. The dependencies are then represented using arrows.

6   Conclusion

A key component of this research is to develop a tool that automatically creates conceptual models from a given set of user stories. We posit that conceptual models that offer different perspectives on the system to be developed, help in developing user stories.

Python text analytics (NLTK) [22] has been used to create a prototype of the envisioned tool that implements the algorithm presented in the paper. The tool takes user stories with acceptance criteria as input and produces four conceptual models (i.e.,

Domain Model, Process Model, Use Case Model and Finite State Machines) as output. Currently a case study in an organization is being performed to demonstrate the feasibility of our approach and evaluate the accuracy of the proposed algorithm of creating multiple conceptual models from user stories. A series of interviews with the stakeholders will be conducted to receive their feedback on the usefulness of the generated models.

In future research, we plan to further develop our solution. The Benefit and Event segments of the BDD scenarios have not been incorporated in the canonical form of user stories produced by the tool. Next, based on the initial results of the case-study and interviews, an empirical study is planned to assess the benefits and costs (in terms of effort of using models) of automatically generated conceptual models in developing and quality assuring user stories. This study will in particularly consider the benefits/costs of using multiple conceptual models (compared to using models for a single system perspective).

References

1. Inayat, I., et al.: Review: a systematic literature review on agile requirements engineering practices and challenges. Comput. Hum. Behav. **51**, 915–929 (2015)
2. Leffingwell, D.: Agile Software Development Series. Addision-Wesley, Boston (2011)
3. Cohn, M.: User Stories Applied: For Agile Software Development. Addison-Wesley, Boston (2004)
4. Ramesh, B., Lan, C., Baskerville, R.: Agile Requirements Engineering Practices and Challenges: An Empirical Study. Inf. Syst. J. **20**(5), 449–480 (2010)
5. Wand, Y., Weber, R.: Information systems and conceptual modeling: a research agenda. Inf. Syst. Res. **13**(4), 363–376 (2002)
6. Mesquita, R., et al.: US2StarTool: generation i* models from user stories. In: International i* Workshop (iStar) (2015)
7. Robeer, M., et al.: Automated extraction of conceptual models from user stories via NLP. In: RE Conference (2016)
8. Lucassen, G., Dalpiaz, F., van der Werf, J.M.E.M., Brinkkemper, S.: Visualizing user story requirements at multiple granularity levels via semantic relatedness. In: Comyn-Wattiau, I., Tanaka, K., Song, I.-Y., Yamamoto, S., Saeki, M. (eds.) ER 2016. LNCS, vol. 9974, pp. 463–478. Springer, Cham (2016). https://doi.org/10.1007/978-3-319-46397-1_35
9. Smart, J.F.: BDD in Action: Behavior-Driven Development for the Whole Software Lifecycle, vol. 3. Manning Publications Company, New York (2014)
10. Kinchin, I.M., Hay, D.: How a qualitative approach to concept map analysis can be used to aid learning by illustrating patterns of conceptual development. Educ. Res. **42**(1), 43–57 (2000)
11. White, S.: Business Process Modeling Notation (2004)
12. Booch, G., Rumbaugh, J., Jacobson, I.: The Unified Modeling Language User Guide, 2nd edn. Addison-Wesley, New Jersey (2005)
13. Davies, I., et al.: How do practitioners use conceptual modeling in practice? Data Knowl. Eng. **58**(3), 358–380 (2006)
14. Dobing, B., Parsons, J.: How UML is used. Commun. ACM **49**(5), 109–113 (2006)
15. Fettke, P.: How conceptual modeling is used. Commun. AIS **25**(1), 571–592 (2009)

16. Jabbari, S., Mohammad, A., Recker, J.: Combined use of conceptual models in practice: an exploratory study. J. Database Manage. **28**(2), 56–88 (2017)
17. Recker, J., et al.: How agile practices impact customer responsiveness and development success: a field study. Proj. Manage. J. **48**(2), 99–121 (2017)
18. Recker, J., Green, P.: How do individuals interpret multiple conceptual models? a theory of combined ontological completeness and overlap. J. Assoc. Inf. Syst. **20**(8), 1210–1241 (2019). forthcoming
19. Matula, J., Hunka, F.: Enterprise ontology-driven development. In: Pergl, R., Babkin, E., Lock, R., Malyzhenkov, P., Merunka, V. (eds.) EOMAS 2018. LNBIP, vol. 332, pp. 3–15. Springer, Cham (2018). https://doi.org/10.1007/978-3-030-00787-4_1
20. Booch, G.: Object Oriented Analysis and Design with Applications. Redwood City, Benjamin/Cummings (1994)
21. Markham, K., Mintzes, J., Jones, M.: The concept map as a research and evaluation tool: further evidence of validity. J. Res. Sci. Teach. **31**(1), 91–101 (1994)
22. Bird, S., Loper, E., Klein, E.: Natural Language Processing with Python. O'Reilly Media, Newton (2009)

Towards a Catalog of Goals
for Strategic Coopetition

Vik Pant[1(⊠)] and Eric Yu[1,2]

[1] Faculty of Information, University of Toronto, Toronto, Canada
vik.pant@mail.utoronto.ca, eric.yu@utoronto.ca
[2] Department of Computer Science, University of Toronto, Toronto, Canada

Abstract. Coopetition describes a phenomenon in which actors cooperate and compete simultaneously. Actors cooperate to grow collective benefits and compete to maximize individual shares. Coopetition is undergirded by concomitantly cooperative and competitive intent. This paper presents catalogs of cooperation and competition goals that are useful for designing business strategies. The content in these goal catalogs is based on an exploratory literature review of scholarly publications in the business and management domains. Hyperlinks are provided to online interactive versions of these goal catalogs as well as bibliographies listing their sources. These goal catalogs are instantiated in an empirical case of businesses in the market of data science professional development programs in Toronto. We adopted an action research methodology to study and intervene in this empirical setting concurrently. Strategies based on recommendations and suggestions from our study are being piloted by focal businesses in this empirical case.

Keywords: Coopetition · Win-Win · Strategy · Design · Analysis

1 Introduction

Strategic coopetition refers to a relationship in which actors cooperate and compete concomitantly [1]. It is a counter-intuitive phenomenon that is commonplace in economic, political, social, and civic contexts. The durability of a coopetitive relationship depends upon the existence of win-win outcomes for actors in that relationship. A win-win outcome exists when all actors in a relationship are better off as a result of being in that relationship. In [7–9], we propose a methodology that combines *i** modeling with Game Trees to generate win-win strategies. This methodology can be used for discriminating strategies (i.e., identifying whether a strategy is win-win) as well as generating new win-win strategies.

The generation of a win-win strategy entails systematic experimentation with new relational configurations. Our methodology [7–9] proposes five non-deterministic steps that can be applied iteratively to develop new or different configurations of a focal relationship. One of these steps involves the addition, change, or elimination of the goals of some actor in the relationship. Professionals, such as subject matter experts (SMEs) and domain specialists, can apply their knowledge to build and compare configurations of goal models representing a focal relationship. In this paper, we offer a

© Springer Nature Switzerland AG 2019
G. Guizzardi et al. (Eds.): ER 2019 Workshops, LNCS 11787, pp. 58–69, 2019.
https://doi.org/10.1007/978-3-030-34146-6_6

catalog of cooperative and competitive goals that can be used by professionals to aid their exploration of a win-win strategy. This catalog can augment the knowledge base of professionals thereby: (i) increasing the variety of relational configurations considered by them, as well as, (ii) reducing the duration needed to develop new relational configurations.

2   Goal Catalogs: Compilation and Content

We performed an exploratory literature review of competition goals and cooperation goals on Google Scholar (GS) to compile the goal catalogs of competition and cooperation respectively. Our decision to use GS was justified by Martín-Martín et al.'s [15] findings that "GS finds significantly more citations than the WoS Core Collection and Scopus across all subject areas" and "Spearman correlations between GS and WoS, and GS and Scopus citation counts are very strong across all subject categories".

Between February 2019 and May 2019, we searched GS for the phrases "goals of competition", "aims of competition", "objectives of competition" and "purpose of competition" as well as "goals of cooperation", "aims of cooperation", "objectives of cooperation" and "purpose of cooperation". In each search we added the terms "business" and "management" using AND operators to target only results pertaining to business and management contexts. We sorted the result sets for each search by relevance and read the most highly cited research papers and book chapters from each result set. We constructed separate conceptual hierarchies of competition and cooperation goals by progressively refining relatively higher-level goals into their lower-level goals based on the content of these research papers and book chapters. When sources disagreed about the relationships among any goals then we based our conclusions on textual majority.

Goals in these catalogs are connected via three main types of links which are: intentional Help contribution link, incidental Help contribution link, and incidental Hurt contribution link. A Help contribution link indicates goal refinement wherein a lower-level goal intentionally impacts the higher-level goal with which it is associated positively. An incidental Help/Hurt contribution link shows an unintentional positive/negative side-effect of a goal on any other goal in the catalog. The presence of positive and negative contribution links in these goal catalogs necessitates decision-makers to perform trade-off analysis among various configuration of goals. Decision-makers utilizing these catalogs, to inform their business strategies, will need to compare and contrast goals of interest taking into account their intended effects and incidental side-effects.

Figure 1 depicts a competition goal catalog and Fig. 2 presents a cooperation goal catalog derived from these sources. An online and interactive version of these goal catalogs can be accessed online at http://research.vikpant.com. Each goal in these interactive catalogs is hyperlinked to its source from the literature in an online bibliography. The full bibliographies from which each of these goals catalogs are compiled can also be accessed online at http://research.vikpant.com. Figures 1 and 2 display visual snippets of these goal catalogs when accessed using a web browser. Each goal catalog is comprised of one hundred and twenty goals distributed over six levels.

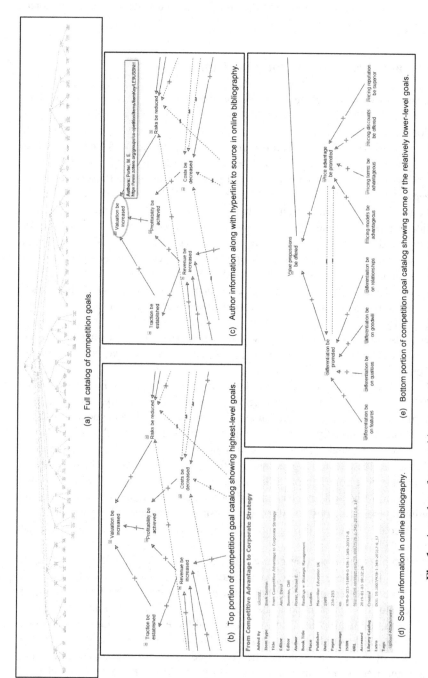

Fig. 1. A catalog of competition goals (Source of each goal can be identified and accessed via http://research.vikpant.com)

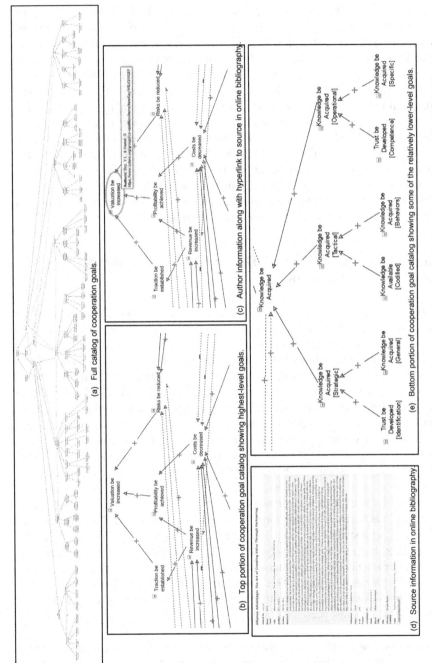

(a) Full catalog of cooperation goals.

(b) Top portion of cooperation goal catalog showing highest-level goals.

(c) Author information along with hyperlink to source in online bibliography.

(d) Source information in online bibliography.

(e) Bottom portion of cooperation goal catalog showing some of the relatively lower-level goals.

Fig. 2. A catalog of cooperation goals (Source of each goal can be identified and accessed via http://research. vikpant.com)

A professional can benefit from this goal catalog in two main ways which are goal search and impact evaluation. In the first case, a professional can start with a higher-level goal, such as "profitability be achieved" and explore relatively lower-level goals that can be used to achieve that higher-level goal, such as "revenue be increased" and "costs be decreased". This top-down approach can assist a professional in identifying potential lower-level options for satisfying their higher-level objectives. In the second case, a professional can start with a focal goal and trace its intentional and incidental contributions to other goals. This is useful for understanding the impact of a goal on other goals holistically. For example, in the competition goal catalog, the goal "channels be established" (i.e., marketing, sales, and distribution) makes an intentional help contribution to "revenue be increased" but makes an incidental hurt contribution to the "costs be decreased". Mutual exclusivity among goals at the same conceptual level can also be discerned in this way. For instance, in the competition goal catalog, "differentiation be promoted" (D) and "price advantage be promoted" (P) are at the same level relative to "value propositions be offered" (V). Both D and P make intentional help contributions to V but they make incidental hurt contributions to each other. This reflects Porter's [16] observations that a business that attempts to adopt both goals at the same time risks getting "stuck in the middle".

3   Empirical Case: Market of Data Science Professional Development Programs

The market for data science talent in Toronto is large and growing due to the surge in popularity of applied artificial intelligence in the industry. Many educational institutions offer professional development programs to learners that aspire to enter and succeed in this attractive job market. Learners can enroll in data science educational programs at privately-owned businesses such as private colleges (PC), training bootcamps (TB), and mentorship academies (MA). Similarly, graduates and alumni from these programs can be placed into jobs in the industry by corporate staffing scouts (CS), that hire staff for their organizations, as well as agency recruiters (AR), that hire employees for their client organizations. The empirical case presented in this section illustrates a facet of this market – a real-world business relationship between two startups (TB, MA), an established business (PC), and their customers (CL, AR, and CS) in Toronto.

One of the authors of this paper was known by the founders of a TB as well as a MA that offer data science professional development programs in Toronto. Each of these founders approached this co-author individually to request strategic advice for their respective businesses separately. Data for this empirical case were gathered through five separate sixty-minute interviews with the founders of each of startup (i.e., ten one-hour interviews in total). This co-author notified the founders of each startup that the authors would apply the methodology in [7–9] along with the cooperation and competition goal catalogs presented in this paper to get at a win-win strategy for TB and MA.

The models developed during this advisory engagement as well as the resulting analyses were communicated separately to the founders of each startup in verbal and diagrammatic form. The recommendations emerging from this advisory engagement were favorably received by the founders of each startup and these founders are referring to these suggestions in their decision-making processes. The research approach used in this paper represents an application of action research wherein a researcher instigates a change in the domain that is being investigated during the research [2]. The activities performed by the authors to advise and counsel the founders of TB and MA can be regarded as interventions [3], which are purposeful acts to bring about changes.

Figure 3 presents an *i** SR diagram portraying relationship between TB, MA, PC, CL, AR, and CS in the past (i.e., As-Is configuration). Figure 4 presents an *i** SR diagram portraying relationship between these organizations in the future (i.e., To-Be configuration). *i** is a modeling language that can be used to articulate and analyze the relationship between multiple actors in terms of their distributed intentionality [4]. It has been applied to represent and reason about a variety of business phenomena including coopetition [5–10] and pivoting [11–13]. In this empirical case, CL, AR, and CS source data science talent from TB, MA, and PC. TB and MA target different client segments (i.e., AR and CS respectively) but PC targets both client segments. PC is a mature business and thus it can address a larger market as well as offer a wider range of services than TB and MA can individually as startups.

In *i**, an *actor* is an intentional entity that seeks to satisfy its *goals* by performing *tasks* and applying *resources* while achieving quality criteria (referred to as *softgoals*). *Goals* are states of affairs in the world that an *actor* wishes to attain. In Figs. 2 and 3, *actors* include TB, MA, PC, CL, AR, and CS. Moreover, AR and CS are specializations of the CL actor wherein AR and CS extend the intentional model of CL differently. We follow the approach for specializing *i** actors that is presented in [14]. CL has a goal "Data Scientists be hired" which is a common objective for AR and CS. However, AR and CS adopt different means to achieve this end. CS sources "individually-mentored candidates" while AR sources "classroom-trained candidates" which are represented as *tasks*. A *task* is a specific way of fulfilling a *goal* via the application of know-how.

A *task* is connected to a *goal* using a *means-end* link that shows an OR relationship. A *goal* is regarded as satisfied if any *task* that is associated with it, using a *means-ends* link, is performed. In our empirical case, an AR can source "classroom-trained candidates" from a TB or a PC and a CS can source "individually-mentored candidates" from a MA or a PC. Such choices are typically depicted in *i** using means-ends links wherein separate means (i.e., *tasks*) would be used to represent each choice. However, we have chosen a to present this information differently in order to declutter our diagrams and simplify their visual layout. This deviation from standard *i** usage is described below.

A *task* can be decomposed into lower-level *tasks* using *task decomposition* links, wherein all the child elements of a *task* must be satisfied for the parent *task* to be completed (i.e., AND relationship). To achieve its highest-level task, AR requires lower-level tasks to be performed including "access broad pool of skillsets", "avail technical coaching post placement", "choose lowest cost option", and "search large

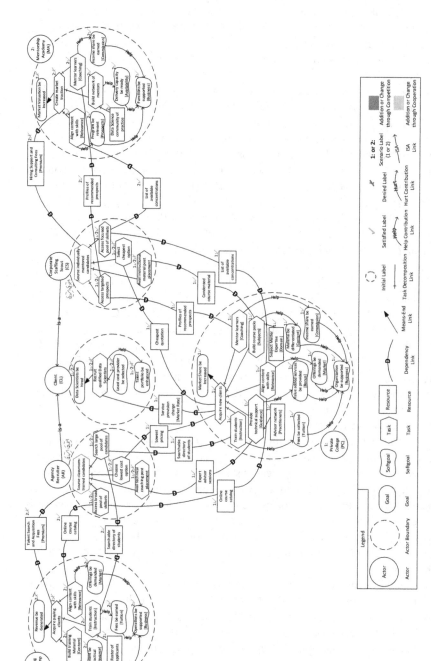

Fig. 3. *i** SR diagram portraying relationship between TB, MA, PC, CL, AR, and CS in the past (i.e., as-is configuration)

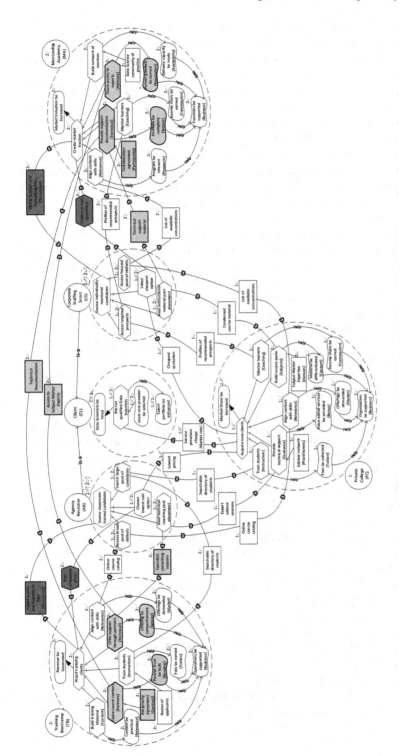

Fig. 4. *i** SR diagram portraying relationship between TB, MA, PC, CL, AR, and CS in the future (i.e., to-be configuration)

pool of candidates". Similarly, to achieve its highest-level task, CS also requires lower-level tasks to be performed including "access targeted prospects", "avail instructional material post placement", "select cheapest option", and "access focused pool of skillsets".

In *i**, an *actor* can rely on one or more *actors* to satisfy a *goal*, perform a *task*, obtain a *resource*, or achieve a quality criterion. Reliance among *actors* can be shown using *dependency* links wherein the flat side of the D points towards the *actor* that is depending and the curved side of the D points towards the *actor* that is depended upon. The subject of the *dependency* is inscribed on that *dependency* link. The satisfaction/denial of an inbound *dependency* can positively/negatively impact the achievement of the receiving model element. AR depends on TB for "online course catalog" and "searchable directory of students" while TB depends on AR for "talent search and acquisition fees" which is a premium service. AR depends on PC for "online course catalog", "searchable directory of students", "expert advisor sessions", and "lowest pricing" while PC depends on CL (of which AR is a specialization) for "service provision charge" which is based on the market rate. Similarly, CS depends on MA for "profiles of recommended prospects" and "list of available concentrations" while MA depends on CS for "hiring support and consulting fees" which is a premium service. CS depends on PC for "profiles of recommended prospects", "list of available concentrations", "condensed course materials", and "cheapest quotation" while PC depends on CL (of which CS is a specialization) for "service provision charge" which is based on the market rate.

In standard *i** usage, when a receiving model element has multiple inbound dependencies then it means that it depends on all of the dependencies simultaneously. However, Figs. 2 and 3, we show inbound dependencies to a model element from different actors (that are depended upon) as representing separate scenarios. This is necessary for avoiding proliferation of duplicate model elements corresponding with each scenario. For example, AR comprises a *task* "search large pool of candidates" that depends on both TB and PC for "searchable directory of students". Here, we do not wish to imply that AR depends on both TB and PC at the same time (i.e., standard *i** usage) but rather that either TB or PC can fulfil AR's requirement of a "searchable directory of students". This implies that TB and PC serve as substitutes from the perspective of AR. Similarly, MA and PC serve as substitutes from the perspective of CS.

We have labeled scenarios as 1 and 2 to express these modified visual semantics more clearly in Figs. 2 and 3. In scenario 1, AR and MA conduct business with PC while in scenario 2 AR conducts business with TB while CS conducts business with MA. In the as-is configuration, AR can only perform two of its four sub-tasks by relying on TB (scenario 2) but it can perform all four of the sub-tasks by relying on PC (scenario 1). TB can only support two of AR's sub-tasks because for one sub-task ("avail technical coaching post placement") it does not offer any support (i.e., there is no inbound dependency from TB to AR) and for the other sub-task ("choose lowest cost option") it does not offer a suitable proposition because its offering is premium rather than cut rate. Similarly, CS can only perform two of its four sub-tasks by relying on MA (scenario 2) but it can perform all four of the sub-tasks by relying on PC (scenario 1). MA can only support two of CS's sub-tasks because for one sub-task ("avail instructional material post placement") it cannot offer any support (i.e., there is no inbound dependency from MA to CS) and for the other sub-task ("select cheapest option") it does not offer an appropriate proposition as its offering is premium rather than economical.

This reasoning suggests that PC is preferred by both AR and CS in the as-is configuration as neither TB nor MA can address their respective needs individually. This means that TB will not be able to satisfy its top-level goal of "revenue be generated" since it depends on a task "acquire paying clients" which depends on "talent search and acquisition fees" from AR. Similarly, MA will not be able to satisfy its top-level goal of "market valuation be increased" since it depends on a task "create market traction" which depends on "hiring support and consulting fees" from CS. Recognition of this inability to succeed in their targeted market segments engendered a search for viable business strategies by the founders of TB and MA. This search comprised of two phases and their end result is depicted in the to-be configuration.

In the first phase, TB and MA needed a cooperative arrangement so each could help the other to fill their respective capability gap. This search was supported by our cooperation goal catalog. In the as-is configuration, TB was unable to offer "avail technical coaching post placement" by itself and MA was unable to offer "avail instructional material post placement" on its own. However, TB could support MA by providing access to its "technical documentation" ("technology be pooled" in the cooperation goal catalog) and MA could assist TB by providing "access to subject matter experts" ("talent be pooled" in the cooperation goal catalog). By doing this, TB would be able to support AR's sub-task of "avail technical coaching post placement" and MA would be able to support CS's sub-task of "avail instructional material post placement".

In the second phase, TB and MA needed to devise competitive positions whereby each could individually challenge PC in the AR and MA market segments respectively. This was supported by our competition goal catalog. TB and MA recognized that AR and CS were cost-conscious and exhibited high elasticity of demand (i.e., price was the primary factor in their decision-making). Therefore, TB adopted a competitive position of "beat competitor prices" ("pricing models be advantageous" in the competition goal catalog) and MA adopted a competition position of "undercut rival quotation" ("pricing discounts be offered" in the competition goal catalog). This allowed TB and MA to replace PC as the preferred service provider for AR and CS respectively in the to-be configuration. Based on this reasoning, the founders of TB and MA are currently piloting strategic positions in the market of data science professional development programs in Toronto.

4 Related Work

$i*$ has been used to represent and reason about business strategies. In [5, 6] we outlined the main characteristics of coopetition and identified requirements for modeling and analyzing them. In [7–9] we applied game-theoretic methods together with $i*$ to discriminate and generate win-win strategies. In [10] we combined $i*$ with a value modeling technique to express and evaluate complementarity and synergy in business relationships. In [11–13] we used i^* to depict and discern pivoting in startups as well as large enterprises. Overall, our work is associated with the body of literature that focuses on the application of i^* in empirical cases. Our work is also related to the body of literature associated with the application of action research in business scenarios [2, 3].

5   Conclusion and Future Work

In this paper we presented goal catalogs for designing competitive and cooperative strategies. Our future work pertains to two streams of research which are extending these goal catalogs and devising methods to overcome the challenges faced in this research. The first stream in our research is to introduce additional goals at all levels of the goal catalog. This will be done by continuing our exploration of the business and management literature focusing on competition and cooperation. It will also be done by socializing these goal catalogs in suitable research communities to encourage the participation and involvement of other scholars wishing to contribute to this research endeavor. The second stream in our research is to address limitations of i^* modeling that were encountered during this research. These include the inability to show conditionality and temporaility in i^* models. To overcome the first limitation, we adapted i^* slightly through the inclusion of scenario labels to demonstrate separate configurations associated with different conditions. To overcome the second limitation, we developed separate as-is and to-be i^* models to show different points in time. Our future work shall include addressing of these limitations.

References

1. Brandenburger, A.M., Nalebuff, B.J.: Co-Opetition. Doubleday, New York (1996)
2. Eden, C., Huxham, C.: Action research for management research. British J. Manage. **7**(1), 75–86 (1996)
3. Midgley, G.: Systemic intervention. In: Systemic Intervention, pp. 113–133. Springer, Boston (2000)
4. Yu, E.S.: Towards modelling and reasoning support for early-phase requirements engineering. In: Proceedings of the Third IEEE International. Symposium on Requirements Engineering (RE), pp. 226–235. IEEE (1997)
5. Pant, V., Yu, E.: Modeling simultaneous cooperation and competition among enterprises. Bus. Inf. Syst. Eng. **60**(1), 39–54 (2018)
6. Pant, V., Yu, E.: Coopetition with frenemies: towards modeling of simultaneous cooperation and competition among enterprises. In: Horkoff, J., Jeusfeld, M.A., Persson, A. (eds.) PoEM 2016. LNBIP, vol. 267, pp. 164–178. Springer, Cham (2016). https://doi.org/10.1007/978-3-319-48393-1_12
7. Pant, V., Yu, E.: Getting to win-win in industrial collaboration under coopetition: a strategic modeling approach. In: Zdravkovic, J., Grabis, J., Nurcan, S., Stirna, J. (eds.) BIR 2018. LNBIP, vol. 330, pp. 47–66. Springer, Cham (2018). https://doi.org/10.1007/978-3-319-99951-7_4

8. Pant, V., Yu, E.: Generating win-win strategies for software businesses under coopetition: a strategic modeling approach. In: Wnuk, K., Brinkkemper, S. (eds.) ICSOB 2018. LNBIP, vol. 336, pp. 90–107. Springer, Cham (2018). https://doi.org/10.1007/978-3-030-04840-2_7

9. Pant, V., Yu, E.: A modeling approach for getting to win-win in industrial collaboration under strategic coopetition. Complex Syst. Inform. Model. Q. **19**, 19–41 (2019)

10. Pant, V., Yu, E.: Modeling strategic complementarity and synergistic value creation in coopetitive relationships. In: Ojala, A., Holmström Olsson, H., Werder, K. (eds.) Software Business ICSOB 2017. Lecture Notes in Business Information Processing, vol. 304. Springer, Cham (2017). https://doi.org/10.1007/978-3-319-69191-6_6

11. Pant, V., Yu, E., Tai, A.: Towards reasoning about pivoting in startups and large enterprises with i*. In: Poels, G., Gailly, F., Serral Asensio, E., Snoeck, M. (eds.) The Practice of Enterprise Modeling PoEM 2017. Lecture Notes in Business Information Pro, vol. 305. Springer, Cham (2017). https://doi.org/10.1007/978-3-319-70241-4_14

12. Pant, V., Yu, E.: Conceptual modeling to support pivoting – an example from Twitter. In: Woo, C., Lu, J., Li, Z., Ling, T., Li, G., Lee, M. (eds.) Advances in Conceptual Modeling ER 2018. Lecture Notes in Computer Science, vol. 11158. Springer, Cham (2018). https://doi.org/10.1007/978-3-030-01391-2_31

13. Pant, V., Yu, E.: Conceptual modeling to support the "Larger Goal" pivot – an example from Netflix. In: Buchmann, R., Karagiannis, D., Kirikova, M. (eds.) The Practice of Enterprise Modeling PoEM 2018. Lecture Notes in Business Information Processing, vol. 335. Springer, Cham (2018). https://doi.org/10.1007/978-3-030-02302-7_26

14. López, L., Franch, X., Marco, J.: Specialization in i* strategic rationale diagrams. In: International Conference on Conceptual Modeling, pp. 267–281. Springer, Berlin (2012). https://doi.org/10.1007/978-3-642-34002-4

15. Martín-Martín, A., Orduna-Malea, E., Thelwall, M., López-Cózar, E.D.: Google scholar, web of science, and scopus: a systematic comparison of citations in 252 subject categories. J. Inform. **12**(4), 1160–1177 (2018)

16. Porter, M.E.: What is strategy? Harvard Bus. Rev. **74**(6), 61–78 (1996)

Early Identification of Potential Distributed Ledger Technology Business Cases Using e³value Models

Geert Poels[1](✉) , Fadime Kaya[2] , Michaël Verdonck[1] ,
and Jaap Gordijn[2]

[1] Faculty of Economics and Business Administration, Ghent University,
Tweekerkenstraat 2, 9000 Ghent, Belgium
{geert.poels,michael.verdonck}@ugent.be
[2] Department of Computer Science, Vrije Universiteit Amsterdam,
De Boelelaan 1081, 1081 HV Amsterdam, The Netherlands
{fadime,jaap}@thevalueengineers.nl

Abstract. Many Distributed Ledger Technology (DLT) projects end prematurely without reaping benefits. Previous research has indicated a lack of sustainable business cases for many Blockchain projects. A successful project has a disruptive impact on the business ecosystem. The paper investigates how e³value modeling can contribute to identifying the potential success of DLT implementation. Using insights from a first DLT case-study, an abstract e³value model fragment is defined that indicates potential success. As a test, the e³value model fragment is subsequently applied to a second case-study that is currently being implemented as a DLT-based platform. The paper concludes by reflecting on how an e³value model can provide evidence of meeting the requirements for building a sustainable DLT business case.

Keywords: Blockchain · e³value modeling · Business case requirements

1 Introduction

Distributed Ledger Technology (DLT) has emerged as a disruptive technology that could influence the mechanisms of enterprises and society in the years to come. DLT has been defined as a consensus of replicated, shared, and synchronized digital data geographically spread across multiple sites, countries, or institutions [1]. The inherent characteristics of DLT provide benefits such as transparency, robustness, auditability, and security, allowing certain industries to minimize their transaction costs as they become inherently safer, transparent and in some cases even faster [2, 3].

Despite its potential, a study by Deloitte showed that, as of October 2017, only 8 percent of more than 86,000 open-source DLT projects developed on GitHub were actively maintained with an average life span of only 1.2 years [4]. This entails that many resources are invested in DLT projects without reaping any benefits. This clearly indicates that there is a call for an early identification of potential success of a DLT project, in order to avoid wasting resources on projects which hold a weak business

G. Guizzardi et al. (Eds.): ER 2019 Workshops, LNCS 11787, pp. 70–80, 2019.
https://doi.org/10.1007/978-3-030-34146-6_7

case [5]. We believe that conceptual modeling can contribute in analyzing and designing a sustainable DLT business case. Particularly, conceptual modeling techniques that take a business ecosystem perspective could indicate in an early stage of analysis whether the introduction of DLT will be disruptive in terms of impacting the composition of the ecosystem (e.g., removal of the middleman that acts as a trusted third party) [6].

The e^3value approach [7] is an enterprise modelling technique that has been positioned as an early Requirements Engineering (RE) technique for systems supporting business ecosystems. In a study of 65 MSc student projects on digital innovation, all cases of digital innovation through DLT (9 out of 65) were analyzed using e^3value models [8]. The students were free to choose amongst different enterprise modeling techniques, but they all choose e^3value modeling. This clearly demonstrates that a business ecosystem perspective when analyzing DLT cases is required.

This observation leads to the research question that we address in this paper: *How can an e^3value model identify a potential business case for DLT?* The goal of our research is to investigate whether an e^3value model can indicate whether a DLT project has the potential to build a sustainable business case. If no indications are present for a sustainable business case, then decision-makers might reject the idea of initiating a DLT project in order to save time and money.

We investigate this research question through modeling a Peer-to-Peer (P2P) electricity trading case. Blockchain solutions exist for smart grids that enable P2P electricity trading [9]. The insights from modeling this case are used to define an abstract e^3value model fragment that indicates a potential sustainable business case for DLT. We test the model fragment on a second case concerning image rights management.

Section 2 provides background information on requirements for successful DLT implementations aimed at disruptive business cases and e^3value as an early RE technique. Section 3 presents the first case-study (i.e., smart grid), its modeling using e^3value, the abstraction of the case-study insights in an e^3value model fragment indicating a potential DLT business case, and the proof-of-concept application on the second case (i.e., image rights management). Section 4 discusses our results so far and the limitations of the research. Finally, Sect. 5 states our contribution and presents our future research.

2 Background

2.1 Requirements for Sustainable DLT Business Cases

Gordijn et al. [5] explain that most DLT projects do not survive the proof-of-concept phase as they expose business cases for DLT that are not sufficiently disruptive in the sense that they do not aim at replacing the middleman by a DLT-based system, i.e., a Decentralized Autonomous Organization (DAO)[1]. A first requirement for a sustainable

---

[1] The idea of a Decentralized Autonomous Organization is attributed to Vitalik Buterin, one of the initiators of the Ethereum project.

business case is affecting the business ecosystem by removing the party that has the power to prescribe rules and regulations over other parties. Basically, the only value contributed to the ecosystem by such trusted third party is the intermediation of transactions between other parties. Removing the middleman is the most important reason to use DLT as this will disrupt the ecosystem (**requirement 1**).

As decentralization is expensive, two further requirements are elaborated [5]. First, the parties that need to share data or distributed computing should be peers in a market structure, meaning that these parties do not trust each other (**requirement 2**). Second, the transactional data stored should be immutable (**requirement 3**). Blockchain technology offers the capability to represent the full and immutable transaction history. Overall, we can say that a sustainable DLT business case requires transactional data storage and a computing environment in which trust, security and permanence are requirements, and in which the ecosystem is changed by replacing an intermediary (i.e., trusted third party) by a DAO.

2.2   Value-Based Requirements Engineering

The e³value modeling approach is a Value-Based Requirements Engineering (VBRE) technique [10]. VBRE techniques are early RE techniques, meaning that they are used early on in the process of eliciting, specifying and validating system requirements.

As an early RE technique, e³value modeling is used to analyze the business ecosystem in which a new IT system (e.g., a DLT-based system) is to be implemented. The analysis focuses on how an IT system will affect (i.e., enable, facilitate, automate, optimize, etc.) the creation and delivery of products/services within the ecosystem. The value model is subsequently operationalized by designing business processes and by developing a supporting IT system architecture.

Figure 1 shows an e³value model. The electricity supplier is an *actor* that requests electricity (a *value object*) from producers (a *market segment*) and offers this electricity to consumers (another *market segment*). The *value exchanges* of electricity are reciprocated by *value exchanges* of money (another *value object*). To deliver the electricity to consumers (the *value activity* of electricity supplying), distribution and metering services (*value objects*) are needed. These services are delivered by the operator of the distribution system to which the consumers are connected (a *market segment*).

For more information on the syntax and semantics of e³value models we refer to [7].

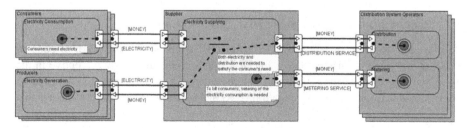

Fig. 1. Example e³value model

3 e³value Modeling of Potential DLT Business Cases

The DLT case that we explore is based on an analysis of the current and expected future Belgian electricity market [9]. In Belgium, a single transmission system operator (TSO) operates the high-voltage electricity transmission network and is responsible for grid balancing (i.e., equality of electricity injection and take-off). Belgium has eight regional distribution system operators (DSOs) that transmit electricity over medium- and low-voltage distribution systems to consumers. Producers generate electricity using different types of facilities and inject generated electricity into the high-voltage transmission system or directly into medium- and low-voltage distribution systems. Some consumers have evolved into prosumers which generate electricity for their own consumption (e.g., using solar panels), but which also inject excess production into the distribution system of the DSO of their region.

Apart from the physical electricity transmission, there is buying and selling of electricity. Electricity is sold by suppliers at retail price to customers. These suppliers buy electricity at (the lower) wholesale price on electricity exchange markets, through the intermediation of Access Responsible Parties (ARPs) which, based on forecasting methods, match buy orders and sell orders such that for every quarter-hour, electricity injection and take-off are balanced for the grid access point they are responsible of.[2]

Figure 2 shows an e³value model of the decentralized electricity market ecosystem. Indirectly, consumers and prosumers pay for transmission and distribution services via the bills paid to suppliers. Belgium is in the process of introducing digital meters, which allow suppliers (and other parties) to directly read electricity consumption and (in case of prosumers) production. This new type of meters, in the future accompanied by IoT-based sensors in electricity-consuming devices, offers the advantage of 'smart' metering, allowing households and firms to better control their consumption and (if applicable) production patterns as well as allowing ARPs to better forecast consumption and production. It is expected that suppliers compensate excess electricity generation by prosumers at an export tariff (see red *value exchange* in Fig. 2), which is higher than the wholesale price but lower than the retail price.

Smart metering allows introducing, in the future, smart grids which allow Peer-to-Peer (P2P) trading of electricity between prosumers and consumers, and hence promote the increased use of renewable energy sources and the increased consumption of locally generated electricity. A smart grid is a geographically bounded perimeter of the grid (i.e., a microgrid),[3] that is served by a same DSO, in which a new role, the aggregator (see Fig. 3), balances consumption and local production (i.e., by prosumers) and, in

---

[2] ARP is a role assumed by suppliers, producers, major consumers as well as electricity traders – in June 13, 2019 there were 87 ARPs providing balancing services to Elia, the Belgian TSO (https:// www.elia.be/en/grid-data/lists-and-codes/list-of-arps). The models in this section abstract from the situation where an ARP fails in balancing, in which case the TSO needs to invoke (costly but effective) measures and charges the ARP an imbalance penalty fee.

[3] In principle, the microgrid can be virtual and not bound to a geographical area [9]. For our analysis, we assume that a microgrid falls within the perimeter of one DSO. As, for instance, the Flanders region in Belgium had more than 2.8 million households in 2018, with only 2 DSOs, this assumption will hold in almost all cases.

case of shortage or excess, trades electricity with suppliers or other parties in the role of ARP. The aggregator is responsible for metering (i.e., capturing information provided by the smart devices), billing, and balancing of the microgrid (i.e., the aggregator is the ARP for the microgrid).

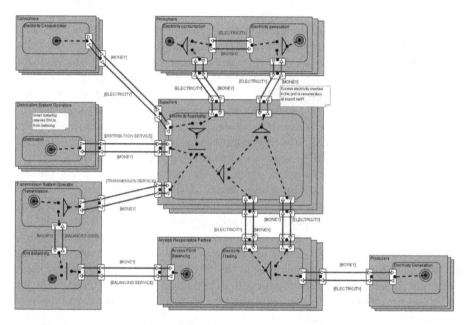

Fig. 2. Decentralized electricity market with smart metering (Color figure online)

It is expected that in a smart grid ecosystem, the price paid for excess local electricity produced is higher than the export tariff, hence stimulating more consumers to become prosumers. However, if the aggregator of a microgrid is an economic independent entity (i.e., an e³value *actor*), then the costs (i.e., variable, fixed and investment) of hosting the P2P market (i.e., an e³value *value activity*) need to be covered by the difference of incoming and outgoing cashflows, while this difference must also allow for a certain profit margin in order to convince parties to assume the aggregator role.[4] This means that microgrids will only be viable if they have some minimum scale, which contradicts the objective of stimulating consumption of locally produced electricity. Replacing the aggregator by a DAO is therefore an economical option to reduce the scale of microgrids and realize the objective of increasing the consumption of locally produced electricity. Hence the idea of implementing a DLT-based system to perform the hosting the P2P market *value activity*.

---

[4] Given that the aggregator is a role, which can be played by another party (e.g., a supplier, a large industrial prosumer), it can also be modelled as a *value activity* of that other party. This doesn't affect our analysis as value activities need to be profitable or provide utility for the actors performing them.

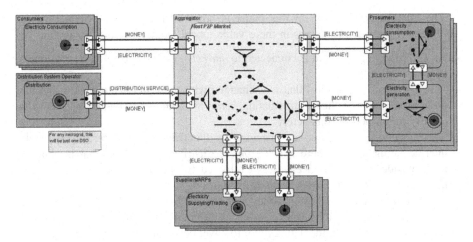

Fig. 3. Smart grid ecosystem with aggregator

In the smart grid ecosystem, the aggregator is a middleman between consumers, prosumers and suppliers. Within the microgrid, consumers and prosumers participate as peers in the electricity market. The aggregator is needed as trusted third party that intermediates between these consumers and the local producers (i.e., prosumers) of electricity. Also, there is a need to keep track of how much electricity is consumed (by consumers and prosumers) and how much electricity is produced (by prosumers) and, for the working of a fair market mechanism, this measuring (i.e., metering) must be accurate and reliable. Further, the aggregator trades electricity with suppliers and/or ARPs and distributes the expenses and revenues fairly amongst consumers and prosumers. Consequently, the suppliers and ARPs also participate as peers in the microgrid electricity market, without assuming a seller dominant position as in the current situation (Fig. 2), which is the disruption caused by the introduction of smart grids. Finally, the contracting of the DSO service is fully handled by the aggregator, who shares costs amongst consumers and prosumers.

Comparing this case to the three requirements for a sustainable DLT business case [5] (see Subsect. 2.1), we observe the following:

- **Requirement 1 – removing the middleman.** The aggregator is clearly a middleman. In a perfect balanced ecosystem, the consumers and prosumers would exchange electricity for money directly, but due to periodic imbalances and the need of a physical electricity distribution network, the services of an intermediary come in handy;
- **Requirement 2 – market structure.** In the smart grid ecosystem, consumers, prosumers and suppliers are peers. They do not need to trust each other, because the aggregator is a third party that establishes trust in the ecosystem;
- **Requirement 3 – immutable transaction history.** A traceable, secure and transparent account of 'who consumes and who produces what amount of electricity when' is needed for performing P2P market hosting.

The question we address in this paper is how to visually find evidence of the fulfillment of these requirements in the e³value model. Analyzing Fig. 3, we find

- An *actor* (<u>aggregator</u>) that is connected to *market segments* (<u>consumers</u>, <u>prosumers</u>, <u>suppliers/ARPs</u>);
- A *value object* (<u>electricity</u>) that is exchanged with these *market segments* and that flows in and out of the intermediating *actor*, without being altered by the *value activity* performed by this actor;
- Some evidence of the service provided by the *value activity* performed by the intermediating *actor* – here a *value object* (<u>distribution service</u>) that is obtained from outside and that is needed (as evidenced by the *AND-gates*)[5] for the *value transactions* with the *market segments*;
- Reciprocal *value exchanges* of money with the *market segments* – the money flows in exchange for electricity can be valuated differently for different *value transactions*, allowing the intermediating *actor* to cover costs (and possible realize profits).

If we now abstract from the particular case, the e³value model of Fig. 4 is obtained where the above observations are translated into an abstract value model fragment. The model shows an *actor*, referred to as intermediating actor, that passes on a *value object*, referred to as the focal value object, from one *market segment* to another,[6] without altering this *value object*. The *value exchanges* of this *value object* are reciprocated with money flows. The *value activity* of the actor that performs the work to pass on the focal value object, referred to as intermediating actor's primary value activity, obtains a *value object* from another *actor* (or *market segment*) which is needed to perform the work required to pass on the focal value object.

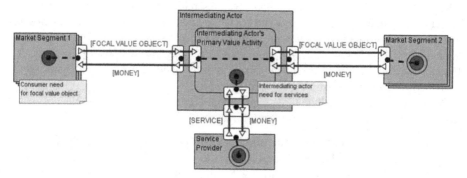

Fig. 4. Early indications of a potential DLT business case

---

[5] Alternatively, the value model can show a *start signal* inside the Host P2P market *value activity* that indicates the need for distribution services.

[6] A second *market segment* is strictly not needed as the focal *value object* can be passed on to another *actor* within the same *market segment* via another *value transaction*.

To test the e^3value model fragment and at the same time demonstrate its use, we applied it to the case of KodakOne (https://kodakone.com), which is a joint initiative of Eastman Kodak and WENN Digital to establish an online platform where professional and amateur photographers sell licenses for using their images to interested parties.

Figure 5 shows the envisioned business ecosystem enabled by DLT. KodakOne connects image providers and image users, allowing them to sell and buy the right to use an image. If not done before, the copyright of the image is registered with the US Copyright Office. These activities are performed by WENN Digital. KodakOne operates under the Kodak brand for which the license is obtained from Kodak Eastman. WENN Digital also performs a number of other value activities which are outside the scope of our analysis (e.g., AI-based web crawling to detect copyright infringement, image cataloguing and searching).

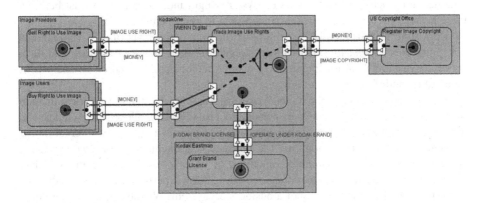

Fig. 5. KodakOne ecosystem for trading image rights

If we compare Fig. 5 to Fig. 4, then we discover an *actor* (WENN Digital) that passes on a *value object* (image use right) from one *market segment* (image providers) to another *market segment* (image users), without altering the *value object*. The *value exchanges* of image use rights are reciprocated with money flows and the primary *value activity* of the intermediating actor (trade image use rights) needs other *value objects* (image copyright, Kodak brand license) to perform the work. Hence, a potential business case for implementing the trading of image use rights using DLT is identified.

In reality, the online image use rights trading platform has being implemented using blockchain technology and a digital currency, the KodakCoin, was introduced for buying image use rights. KodakOne was launched in June 2019.

4 Discussion

Further research is required to investigate whether the e^3value model fragment shown in Fig. 4 effectively suggests potential DLT business cases. The fulfillment of **requirement 1** seems to be indicated by an *actor* that passes on a *value object* from one party to another where these *value exchanges* are reciprocated by *value exchanges* of money. Further, this *actor* has a *value activity* that needs to perform some work for passing on the *value object*, as evidenced by the sourcing of at least one other *value object*. We acknowledge that work performed by an intermediating actor's primary value activity might not always be visible in the e3value model. We assume, however, that for performing work, resources are needed which need to be sourced from another value activity performed by the same actor or from other actors or market segments. Whether such sourcing is visible depends of course on the level of granularity at which the intermediating actor's primary value activity is modelled.

The parties that exchange the focal value object with the intermediating actor are modelled as *market segments*. Each individual *actor* in a *market segment* ascribes the same value to the *value objects* that are exchanged, which signifies that the parties represented through these *market segments* are peers. The mere existence of the intermediating actor in the business ecosystem might indicate a lack of trust between these peers, which is exactly what is expressed in **requirement 2**.

Regarding **requirement 3** we admit that the granularity level of an e^{3}value model does not allow representing requirements regarding the storage of transactional data, hence the fulfillment of this requirement cannot be concluded based on an analysis of an e^{3}value model.

We also acknowledge three other types of limitations. First, the early identification of potential DLT business cases is performed visually. This allows for a 'quick and dirty' analysis, however, the e^{3}value approach also permits to quantify different model elements. Adding information on, for instance, cardinalities of *market segments*, occurrences of *value transactions*, valuation of *value objects*, and adding variable, fixed and investment costs to *value activities*, allows performing a net cash flow analysis to evaluate the viability of a business ecosystem. We did not yet explore how this aspect of the e^{3}value approach can be used to identify DLT business cases.

Second, our approach only identifies DLT business cases based on the removal of the middleman, which involves a disruptive application of DLT – not in the least for the trusted third party that acts as middleman. The approach therefore strongly relies on the requirements for such cases stated in [5]. There are other use cases for DLT, which might not be disruptive but still offer benefits in terms of increased security, traceability or efficiency. For instance, blockchain-based coordination systems have been implemented for executing message-based collaborative processes. For identifying such cases a business process model is more interesting than a value model which is time-agnostic and does not show the exchange of messages that are needed for choreographing an ecosystem's value activities and included processes.

Third and most obvious, our approach identifies the ***potential*** for a DLT business case. After such identification, additional analyses need to be performed before the business case of implementing DLT is proven. For instance, the work performed in the intermediary actor's primary value activity needs to be automated using smart contracts, which requires an investigation of the technical feasibility of a DLT solution. Also, the specific type of DLT needs to be decided on, with respect to data structure (e.g., blockchain, non-block DLT, directed acyclic graph), network (e.g., Ethereum, IOTA, Hedera HashGraph), degree of privacy/publicness of the data, permissionless/permissioned, etc. Apart from such technical questions, also legal, governance, financial and sustainability aspects need to be considered. It is our position, however, that these aspects are not worth investigating if the potential for a DLT business case is not shown, which is exactly what our approach aims to accomplish.

5   Conclusion

The e^3value model fragment that we abstracted from the P2P electricity trading case is a first attempt at defining an e^3value model pattern for early identification of sustainable DLT business cases. As a proof-of-concept, we demonstrated the use of the model fragment regarding the online image rights trading platform KodakOne, which has been implemented using blockchain technology.

Patterns were popularized in software engineering as proven solutions to reoccurring problems, where a common heuristic to qualify a solution as a pattern are three occurrences. Hence, we cannot claim to have established the model fragment as a pattern yet. In future research, we will investigate additional cases of disruptive DLT implementation (i.e., replacing the middleman) and other proven or promising applications of DLT in order to refine our current solution, possibly extend it for other types of DLT use, evaluate it as a pattern, and design a method for verifying the occurrence of the pattern in e^3value models. Regarding the immutable transaction history and other requirements that might pop up in our further research (e.g., for other types of DLT use), we will identify the information that is needed to assess these requirements and investigate how it can be modelled, possibly using other modeling languages than e^3value.

References

1. Ølnes, S., Ubacht, J., Janssen, M.: Blockchain in government: Benefits and implications of distributed ledger technology for information sharing. Gov. Inf. Q. **34**(3), 355–364 (2017)
2. Greenspan, G.: Ending the bitcoin vs blockchain debate (2015). https://www.multichain.com/blog/2015/07/bitcoin-vs-blockchain-debate/
3. Christidis, K., Devetsikiotis, M.: Blockchains and smart contracts for the internet of things. IEEE Access **4**, 2292–2303 (2016)
4. Trujillo, J.L., Fromhart, S., Srinivas, V.: Evolution of blockchain technology. Insights from the GitHub platform. Deloitte Insights (2017)
5. Gordijn, J., Wieringa, R.J., Ionita, D., Kaya, F.: Towards a sustainable blockchain use case. Presented at the 13th International Workshop on Value Modelling and Business Ontologies (VMBO 2019). https://vmbo2019.blogs.dsv.su.se/files/2019/02/GordijnEtAl.pdf
6. Wieringa R.J., Engelsman, W., Gordijn, J., Ionita D.: A business ecosystem architecture modeling framework. Accepted for the 21st IEEE Conference on Business Informatics (CBI 2019). https://research.e3value.com/docs/bibtex/pdf/TEAM%20CBI%202019.pdf
7. Gordijn, J., Akkermans, H.: Value Webs. Understanding e-Business Innovation. The Value Engineers, Soest (2018)
8. Poels, G.: Enterprise modelling of digital innovation in strategies, services and processes. Accepted for the BPM 2019 1st Workshop on Value and Quality of Enterprise Modelling (VEnMo 2019)

9. Degraeve, H., Nys, J.: The potential of peer-to-peer trading and blockchain technology in a decentralized energy network. A value-based analysis. Unpublished Master dissertation, Ghent University (2018). http://www.mis.ugent.be/wp-content/uploads/2019/06/JornNys-FMEBENDA341-746856-1528185345-Degraeve_Nys_2018.pdf
10. Gordijn, J., Akkermans, H.: Designing and evaluating e-business models. IEEE Intell. Syst. **16**(4), 11–17 (2001)

Empirical Methods in Conceptual Modeling (EmpER) 2019

Preface

João Araujo[1], Jennifer Horkoff [2], and Sotirios Liaskos[3]

[1] Universidade Nova de Lisboa, Portugal
p191@fct.unl.pt
[2] Chalmers and the University of Gothenburg, Sweden
jenho@chalmers.se
[3] York University, Canada
liaskos@yorku.ca

Conceptual modeling continues to enjoy substantial attention in diverse fields such as Information Systems Analysis, Software Engineering, Enterprise Architecture, Business Analysis and Business Process Engineering. A variety of conceptual modeling languages, frameworks and systems have been proposed, promising to facilitate activities such as communication, design, documentation or decision-making.

Success in designing a conceptual modeling system is, however, predicated on demonstrably attaining such goals through observing their use in practical scenarios. At the same time, the way individuals and groups produce and consume models gives raise to cognitive, behavioral, organizational or other phenomena, whose systematic observation may help us better understand how models are used in practice and how we can make them more effective.

The 2nd International Workshop on Empirical Methods in Conceptual Modeling (EmpER'19), co-located with the 38th International Conference on Conceptual Modeling (ER 2019), aimed at bringing together researchers with an interest in the empirical investigation of conceptual modeling languages, frameworks and practices. The workshop invited three kinds of papers: finished empirical studies, proposed empirical studies and theoretical, review or experience papers on the topic of empirical research in conceptual modeling. The workshop particularly welcomed negative results as well as proposed empirical studies that are in their design stage so that authors can benefit from early feedback and adjust their designs prior to a potentially effort- and resource-intensive administration. A total of twenty-one (21) reviewers were invited to serve the program committee of the workshop based on their record of past contributions in the area of empirical conceptual modeling.

Overall, a total of three (3) papers were accepted out of the five (5) that were reviewed. All papers describe empirical studies already conducted. The workshop involves presentations of the papers followed by discussion and audience feedback to the authors.

Exploiting Conceptual Modeling for Searching Genomic Metadata: A Quantitative and Qualitative Empirical Study

Anna Bernasconi[✉], Arif Canakoglu, and Stefano Ceri

Dipartimento di Elettronica, Informazione e Bioingegneria,
Politecnico di Milano, Milan, Italy
{anna.bernasconi,arif.canakoglu,stefano.ceri}@polimi.it

Abstract. Providing a common data model for the metadata of several heterogeneous genomic data sources is hard, as they do not share any standard or agreed practice for metadata description. Two years ago we managed to discover a subset of common metadata present in most sources and to organize it as a smart genomic conceptual model (GCM); the model has been instrumental to our efforts in the development of a major software pipeline for data integration.

More recently, we developed a user-friendly search interface, based on a simplified version of GCM. In this paper, we report our evaluation of the effectiveness of this new user interface. Specifically, we present the results of a compendious empirical study to answer the research question: *How well is such a simple interface understood by a standard user?* The target of this study is a mixed population, composed by biologists, bioinformaticians and computer scientists.

The result of our empirical study shows that the users were successful in producing search queries starting from their natural language description, as they did it with good accuracy and small error rate. The study also shows that most users were generally satisfied; it provides indications on how to improve our search system and how to continue our effort in integration of genomic sources. We are consequently adapting the user interface, that will be soon opened to public use.

Keywords: Conceptual model · Data integration · Genomics · Next generation sequencing · Open data · Evaluation · Usability

1 Introduction

With progress of DNA sequencing technology, many international consortia are providing public, open datasets that can be used for answering research questions, from biological (e.g. what are the basic mechanisms for explaining DNA organization and gene activation) to clinical (e.g., finding gene panels that can be

© Springer Nature Switzerland AG 2019
G. Guizzardi et al. (Eds.): ER 2019 Workshops, LNCS 11787, pp. 83–94, 2019.
https://doi.org/10.1007/978-3-030-34146-6_8

used for effectively separate cancer patients into classes by observing their expression). In most cases, public datasets must be assembled from several sources, each providing specialized information (e.g., genome annotations, mutations, gene expression, protein bindings to DNA, and so on). Thus, researchers must be able to inspect metadata that describe experimental conditions, so as to ascertain their relevance with respect to the research question and how many instances of compatible data are available for supporting their study.

To facilitate this task, we started two years ago a large data integration project, with the ambitious objective of collecting the open source content of many important genomic sources into a single repository, with integrated and normalized metadata. The integrated repository offers to users a single data organization that can be inspected with a single search query. Before integration, metadata at the various sources were understood and translated to a standard conceptual model, designed at the start of our project, and discussed in [3].

The conceptual model drives the periodic integration process of genomic data, as it allows to recognize and periodically extract non-overlapping portions of datasets at each source; a software pipeline is used for data injection from each source to an integrated repository. For what concerns metadata in particular, the pipeline includes value normalization and enrichment steps that improve the ability to compare metadata from different sources. Currently, we have integrated experimental genomic data from Encyclopedia of DNA Elements (ENCODE), The Cancer Genome Atlas (TCGA), Roadmap Epigenomics, subsets of Gene Expression Omnibus, Cistrome, and annotations from GENCODE and RefSeq (see references in companion paper [2]); we plan to add many other sources.

For searching metadata, we provided two very different user interfaces. One interface, described in [2], is focused on explaining the inference process that we can perform on metadata in order to do data matching. Such interface is made available to expert users (and to us) to clarify the process of query and inference, with a diagrammatic representation of inference results, where all the connections are extensively shown. We soon realized that such interface is too complex for most of our generic users, who are biologists or bioinformaticians with no experience of knowledge graph matching. We then developed a user-friendly interface, which actually hides not only the inference steps, but also the complexity of the conceptual model. We translated the ER model into a much simpler denormalized structure consisting of a star with four related dimensions, which can be queried by using a structured form; the complexity of ontological inference was implemented in the user-friendly interface as just a *check-board*, by means of which the user can augment or reduce the inference process, hence the number of choices that are made available for satisfying a search query.

In principle, we were uncertain that this transformation could capture at the same time the original semantics and the user understanding. The main focus of this paper is to report our evaluation of the effectiveness of the user interface and henceforth of our data transformation. Specifically, we report the results of a compendious empirical study to answer our research question: *How well is such a simple interface understood by a standard user (i.e., students, biologists, interdisciplinary user base)? In how many cases it fulfills the data integration needs without errors?*

The target of this study is a mixed population, composed by biologists, bioinformaticians and computer scientists, who participated to the empirical study; most of them were totally unaware of conceptual modelling guidelines and, as such, well represented our target users. We are currently considering their feedback and adapting the user interface, that will be soon opened to public use.

Related Work. In the last few years, the focus of empirical studies dedicated to conceptual modelling has ranged from works on tools based on CM [10], to process mining [1] and to artifact sampling [5]. A broad study has compared traditional conceptual modeling with ontology-driven conceptual modeling [9]. Some recent works employ conceptual models to explain biological entities and their interactions [6,8], or to characterize the objects during analysis workflows [7]. Our use of conceptual modeling is aimed at data integration for the purpose of building a new resource and make it publicly available.

Paper Organization. In Sect. 2 we describe the CM and explain its reduction to four simple views, which drive the user-friendly search system; we also explain how search is performed. In Sect. 3 we illustrate how we designed our study, by first providing instructional material and then asking to provide answers to an online questionnaire, whose questions test specific aspects of our system; in Sect. 4 we discuss the study results and in Sect. 5 we conclude.

2   Genomic Conceptual Model: Original and Simplified

We report here a synthetic description of the Genomic Conceptual Model [3] and then we explain its simplification operated to support the user-friendly interface.

Genomic Conceptual Model. GCM is a star-like entity-relation model that summarizes the common organization of a limited set of concepts supported by most genomic data sources, although originally with different formats and names. In the upper part of Fig. 1 we show its sketch from [3] (this conceptual representation is also used for the advanced user interface, see [2]); with respect to the original GCM one can note some small changes, which are due our experience of use of the model. The ITEM represents the central entity of the schema: a single experimental (or annotation) file of genomic regions with their properties. The schema includes four dimensions (or views) that describe the biological phenomena observed in the experiment (entities DONOR, BIOSAMPLE and REPLICATE), the management aspects of the experiment (entities PROJECT and CASESTUDY), the technological process used for the production of the item (entity EXPERIMENTTYPE), and the extraction parameters used for internal selection and organization of items (entity DATASET). One-to-many relationships connect the various entities to the ITEM; two many-to-many relationships are needed for the relationships between ITEM and REPLICATE (as the same item can be used in replicated experiments) and between ITEM and CASESTUDY (as the same item can be used in several use cases).

The GCM schema is extended by two sub-models representing, respectively, the original unstructured metadata and the semantic enrichment for specific attributes. Many attributes and their respective values discovered within sources

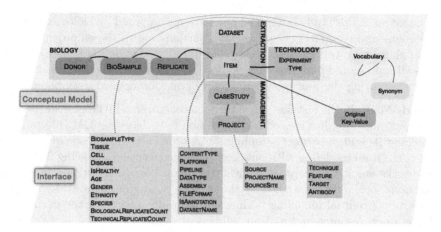

Fig. 1. Upper part: the genomic conceptual schema, which includes 8 entities connected by 5 one-to-many relationships and 2 many-to-many relationships. Lower Part: the simplified conceptual model used for our user-friendly search interface, which is based on 4 denormalized views; the figure includes the attributes selected in each view.

cannot be mapped to the same conceptual model. Thus, these metadata are directly downloaded from the original sources and transformed into key-value pairs. Moreover, as result of a normalization and enrichment phase, we associate specific values of the GCM with controlled terms (see [4]). Out of all GCM attributes, we selected ten of them as worthy of enrichment. We selected one or two preferred bio-ontologies for each attribute, and linked to each value a term from the chosen ontology, equipped with its synonyms and a small hierarchy of hypernyms and hyponyms, connected though *is_a* and *part_of* relationships.

Design of a Simplified View Supporting the User-Friendly Interface. As the start point for a user-friendly interface we opted for a drastic simplification of the model. We merged the ITEM entity with the extraction dimension and we denormalized all many-to-many relationships; denormalization was applied to items having multiple replicas and to items appearing in the same case study. We also selected some of the attributes from the entities of each dimension (26 out of 38 attributes in the current GCM) based on typical use, while the other attributes were re-inserted as key-value pairs. The bottom part of Fig. 1 illustrates the resulting schema, with the four dimensions connected to each ITEM and the 26 attributes selected from the entities of each dimension that were chosen to appear in the interface.

Items are implicitly gathered within a folder or dataset; the simplified *Extraction View* includes: DATASETNAME, denoting the folder gathering the items; CONTENTTYPE, type of genomic regions in the file (such as gene segments, introns, transcripts); PLATFORM, instrument used to sequence the raw data related to the item; PIPELINE, list of methods used for processing phases, from raw data to processed data; DATATYPE (e.g., peaks, expression quantifications, methylation levels); ASSEMBLY, reference genome such as hg19 or GRCh38;

FILEFORMAT, standard data format of the items, dictating region schema, number and semantics of columns, and a Boolean variable ISANNOTATION, indicating if the dataset includes experimental data or genome annotations. The *Biology View* is centered on the description of biological samples, i.e. material sample taken from a biological entity and used for the experiment, with information on: TISSUE, a multicellular component in its natural state; CELL, denoting single cells in natural state, immortalized cell lines, or cells differentiated from specific cell types; DISEASE, possibly carried by the sample, with the Boolean health status (ISHEALTHY). Biological material is possibly provided by a donor, described by: AGE (in number of days), GENDER, ETHNICITY, and SPECIES. Finally, when an assay is performed multiple times on separate biological samples (or on the same one), multiple replicates of the experiment are generated. To keep track of the replication process, we store the BIOLOGICALREPLICATECOUNT and the TECHNICALREPLICATECOUNT. The *Management View* describes the project producing the item, and includes: SOURCESITE where the material is analyzed and the item produced (e.g., universities, biobanks, hospitals, research centers, or laboratories); PROJECTNAME, particularly relevant in the context of cancer Fenomics (e.g., TCGA-BRCA is the study for Breast Invasive Carcinoma of The Cancer Genome Atlas); SOURCE, the program or consortium responsible for the production of genomic items (e.g, ENCODE/TCGA/...). The *Technology View* describes the technology producing the itiem; it includes: TECHNIQUE, the procedure conducted to produce the items; FEATURE, the specific genomic aspect studied with the experiment (such as gene expression, mutations...); then, for epigenomic experiments such as ChIP-Seq: ANTIBODY, a protein employed against the TARGET proteins.

User Interface. The user interface presents to users the possibility of opting for structured search (based on the described 25 attributes) or unstructured search (based on key-value pars). In both cases, it extracts matching items; the number of matching items is dynamically provided while the user enters search values. In the case of structured search, possible matching values are shown in a drop-down list; the list is dynamically updated while the search proceeds. The search query is a conjunction over its structured and semi-structured search steps; within structured search, it is a conjunction of the search clauses which are progressively built by selecting attributes, while every selected search value provides a disjunctive option. Abstract examples of queries are shown in Fig. 2, in the next section.

3   Experiment Description

Study Rationale. For evaluating the usability and usefulness of our interface, we planned an empirical study consisting of presenting a questionnaire to a group of biologists, bioinformaticians, and computer scientists/software developers with interest in Genomics. Before being engaged with the search system, we provided users with WIKI documentation and video tutorials. We planned questions of progressive levels of difficulty; each question presents a specific research scenario and participants are asked to use our interface for extracting items, thereby simulating the typical search task (i.e., checking that our repository stores sufficient information for addressing the needs of each scenario). After the submission of answers, we show the right answers to users, and provide explanations of each answer; we expect that during the process users can develop a better understanding and progressively master the search system. After such training, we ask the users to evaluate the overall experience and specify the degree of expertise in the domain.

Table 1. Proposed survey questions.

Q1. How many datasets do we provide from the source TCGA with assembly GRCh38?

Q2. How many items do we provide for TCGA, assembly GRCh38, in the normal (**a**)/tumoral (**b**) cases?

Q3. Which TCGA GRCh38 project among COAD (Colon adenocarcinoma), LUAD (Lung adenocarcinoma), and STAD (Stomach adenocarcinoma) has more gene expression data?

Q4. How many sources contain data annotated with the human fetal lung cell line IMR-90 (both using original spelling (**a**) and alternative syntaxes (**b**))?

Q5. How many sources contain data annotated with the tissue uterus (both using original spelling (**a**) and the broadest possible intepretation (**b**))?

Q6. In ENCODE, how many items of ChIP-Seq can you find for the histone modifications H3K4me1, H3K4me2, and H3K4me3?

Q7. Assume you want to retrieve items from the TADs source that correspond to combined replicates (i.e., they belong to at least 2 biological replicates). How many items can you find?

Q8. We would like to retrieve items of hg19 assembly from healthy brain tissue (and possibly its subparts) of male gender, up to 30 years old. How many items can you find with these characteristics in the sources ENCODE (**a**) and TCGA (**b**)?

Q9. We are interested in ovarian cancer patients at clinical Stage III and IV. Select TCGA-OV project data. Then, select pairs with the key 'clinical_patient_clinical_stage' corresponding to the stage iii and iv (e.g., stage iiia, stage iiib, ...). How many items can you retrieve?

Q10. Suppose you need to identify DNA promotorial regions bound by the MYC transcription factor that present somatic mutations in breast cancer patients. For each of the following steps, provide the number of retrieved items. First, get from ENCODE source, ChIP-seq narrowpeak data from the cell line MCF-7, regarding MYC binding sites (**a**). Second, DNA-seq data is needed from TCGA BRCA patients which encountered a new tumor occurrence (**b**). Third, genomic region annotations describing promoters locations should be retrieved from RefSeq (**c**).

Experiment Design. During the conception of the survey, we followed a number of study design principles. We attempted to lower the ambiguity of the questions and to provide some guidance to the users; we used questions that could have exact answers (i.e., numbers), to lower the possible interpretation biases; we stratified questions by complexity, to capture different levels of understanding of the interface and its structure; we diversified the challenges addressed in the questions, to overview all search possibilities encompassed by our system.

Table 2. Input features tested in the survey. Desired output column contains numbers of items (#I), datasets (#D), or sources (#S).

Group	Question	Sub-questions	Desired output	Cross-dimension attributes	Logical disjunction	Semantic enrichment	Combination original/integr.	Complete study
1	Q1	1	#D	×				
	Q2	2	#I	×				
	Q3	1	#I	×				
2	Q4	2	#S			×		
	Q5	2	#S			×		
	Q6	1	#I	×	×			
	Q7	1	#I	×				
3	Q8	2	#I	×		×		
	Q9	1	#I		×		×	
	Q10	3	#I	×			×	×

In Table 1 we show the complete list of 10 proposed questions (some of which contain two or three sub-questions). We divided the questionnaire according to three groups of questions, in order of complexity: the first provides a simple scenario with incremental addition of filters: first a source with the assembly (Q1), then selection of normal/tumor patients (Q2) and of specific disease projects (Q3); the second explores peculiar (i.e., less standard) features of the search, e.g., semantic enrichment with synonyms (Q4), ontological hierarchies (Q5), disjunction of attribute values (Q6), and aggregate attributes (Q7); the third builds three more complex cases: combination of many filters (Q8), joined use of original metadata (in key-value format) and structured metadata (Q9), composition of three selections from data sources to simulate a complete study (Q10). Figure 2 visually explains the process of attribute selection and value provisioning required by questions Q2, Q5, and Q9.

As shown in Table 2, in different questions, we tested: the ability to compose queries by combining attribute filters coming from different dimensions, the use of value filters in disjunction one with the other, the understanding of semantic enrichment options, the combined used of original metadata filters (using a key-value-based interface) with structured integrated metadata (based on the GCM). With respect to the interplay between original and structured metadata: the query interface must enable interaction with both (in the key-value pairs it is important that people can ask separately what are the key—typically defining the property associated to the item—and what are the values—associated to

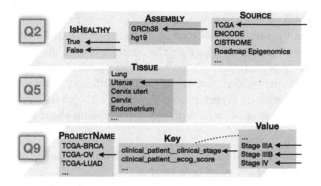

Fig. 2. Q2 describes a case in which the user selects from the IsHEALTHY attribute list first the value "True" and then the value "False", corresponding to two sub-questions. Then, she selects "GRCh38" among the possible values in the ASSEMBLY attribute list and "TCGA" as a SOURCE. Q5 presents an enriched list of values for the attribute TISSUE—note that "Cervix uteri" and "Cervix" are synonyms and, together with "Endometrium", they are hyponyms of uterus. For Q9, after selecting the PROJECT-NAME, the user explores keys and values through a specific interface.

the specific property). In different questions we alternatively asked to report the number of items, datasets, or sources.

Study Execution. The experiment target users were sourced from within our research group (GeCo) and from several collaborating institutions (such as Politecnico di Torino, Istituto Nazionale dei Tumori, Università di Torino, Università di Roma Tre, Istituto Italiano di Tecnologia, Radboud Universiteit Nijmegen, Freie Universität Berlin, Harvard University, Broad Institute, National University of Singapore, University of Toronto), including researchers with different backgrounds (computational and molecular biology, bioinformatics, and computer science) but also students and pure software developers with interest in Genomics. Out of about 60 invitations, we received 40 completed responses.

4   Results

We first describe how many answers were correctly provided, then how the users evaluated their experience with our system.

Correct Answers. In Table 3 we report: the required semantic level to set at the beginning of the query, the numbers of dimensions, integrated attributes and original keys involved in the query. Then we show percentages of correct answers (scores) of each specific sub-question and aggregated by group. Note that, if we consider together the performances of each group, as expected, group 1 reached a high percentage of correct answers (93.33%), group 2 a little less (75.94%), while group 3 had the worse score (68.47%). Some typical errors spotted in many answers are also reported. Question 8 had a low rate of correct answers

Table 3. Result features. Semantic levels include original values (O), synonyms and vocabulary terms (S), or the expanded option, with also hierarchical hyponyms (E).

Question	Semantic level	#dim.	#integr. attributes	#orig. keys	Scores	Group score	Typical errors
Q1	O	2	2	0	97.50%	93.33%	#items instead of datasets
Q2a	O	3	3	0	97.50%		
Q2b	O	3	3	0	92.50%		
Q3	O	3	2	0	87.50%		
Q4a	O	1	1	0	72.50%	75.94%	#items instead of sources and wrong spelling
Q4b	S	1	1	0	82.50%		#items instead of sources
Q5a	O	1	1	0	82.50%		#items instead of sources
Q5b	E	1	1	0	70.00%		#items instead of sources
Q6	O	2	3	0	67.50%		
Q7	O	2	2	0	82.50%		Wrong use of replicate count
Q8a	E	3	6	0	50.00%	68.47%	Wrong use of age selector
Q8b	E	3	5	0	52.50%		Wrong use of age selector
Q9	O	1	1	1	75.00%		
Q10a	O	4	5	0	82.50%		
Q10b	O	2	2	1	70.00%		
Q10c	O	2	3	0	85.00%		

(50% and 52.63%); we asked to retrieve the number of items in two sources for a specific assembly from a healthy tissue (using the semantic option that includes ontological hierarchy) of one gender in a restricted age range. Such question combined many elements (six data search filters, use of semantic expansion, age feature).

Overall, users replied correctly to 78.92% of the questions (grouping together the sub-questions of a same entry). Five users answered correctly to all questions. On average, it took them less than 44 min to answer all the 10 questions.

Lessons Learned. In retrospective, we made mistakes in the formulation of some of our queries. Users were confused when we asked them to count the containers (e.g. sources and datasets) instead of the data items, probably because they do not understand the notions of sources and of datasets. Distinguishing the dataset and data source storing the items probably requires a computer science background that was not present in many users. As in these cases users made the exact choices of attributes and values and just provided a wrong numerical answer, we considered their answers as valid. In one question (Q8) users did not reach a satisfying percentage, probably due to the misinterpretation of some filters.

In spite of these mistakes, our user study provided us with an important feedback. We were forced to denormalize and simplify the conceptual schema, but the logical organization of our simplified schema, centered on the item with selected attributes and organized along four dimensions, still proved to be effective; it facilitated both the training and the search interface organization. Clustering attributes along the four dimensions allowed us to explain them first collectively and then individually; users understood well their meaning and in most cases were able to translate narrative questions into the correct choice of attributes embedding the questions' semantics.

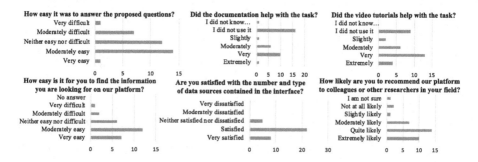

Fig. 3. Histograms showing the user's evaluations of the search system.

Qualitative Results. After filling the first part of the questionnaire, we asked users if they learned from the system and if they liked it, and to give us hints on how to proceed in our work (possibly with open suggestions to improve it). Answers to this part of the questionnaire are shown in Fig. 3.

Two thirds of users declared that answering to the proposed questions was "Moderately easy" or "Neither easy nor difficult". Most users either did not use the documentation or found it moderately/very useful, while users who watched the video tutorials were generally satisfied with them. When asked to perform a query to reach items useful to their own research, most users declared it was moderately easy. The majority was satisfied with the data sources available in the interfaces and was quite likely to recommend the platform to colleagues and researchers in the field.

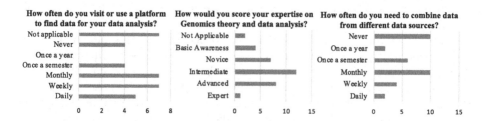

Fig. 4. Histograms showing the user's expertise on genomic data analysis.

Figure 4 shows histograms on the self-assessment of users about their experience in the field of genomic data analysis. Users present expertise scores that range from "None" to "Expert". When asked about their use of platform to find data for analysis and about their need to combine inter-sources data, answers ranged from "Never" to "Daily", confirming that our users' test-set was well-assorted. Users also provided interesting suggestions, including a number of relevant sources to add to the framework and particular features that could be useful for practitioners.

5   Conclusions

Although we were forced to denormalize and simplify the conceptual schema, still its logical organization helps the users in translating a natural language question into the right choice of attributes, keys and values for querying our search interface; thus, we conclude that the most important aspects of attribute semantics are conveyed to users also in the context of the simplified conceptual schema. Some specific feedback and the observation of users' mistakes allowed us to improve the instructions for learning how to best use the search interface, as we eliminated some sources of ambiguities that could have created some of the misunderstanding. We also received important indications about missing data sources according to users' experience; this information will drive us in selecting the next sources to be integrated to our repository.

Acknowledgement. This research is funded by the ERC Advanced Grant 693174 GeCo (Data-Driven Genomic Computing), 2016–2021.

References

1. Back, C.O., Debois, S., Slaats, T.: Towards an empirical evaluation of imperative and declarative process mining. In: Woo, C., Lu, J., Li, Z., Ling, T.W., Li, G., Lee, M.L. (eds.) ER 2018. LNCS, vol. 11158, pp. 191–198. Springer, Cham (2018). https://doi.org/10.1007/978-3-030-01391-2_24
2. Bernasconi, A., Canakoglu, A., Ceri, S.: From a conceptual model to a knowledge graph for genomic datasets. In: Laender, A.H.F., Pernici, B., Lim, E., de Oliveira, J.P.M. (eds.) ER 2019, LNCS, vol. 11788, pp. 352–360, 2019. Springer, Cham (2019)
3. Bernasconi, A., Ceri, S., Campi, A., Masseroli, M.: Conceptual modeling for genomics: building an integrated repository of open data. In: Mayr, H.C., Guizzardi, G., Ma, H., Pastor, O. (eds.) ER 2017. LNCS, vol. 10650, pp. 325–339. Springer, Cham (2017). https://doi.org/10.1007/978-3-319-69904-2_26
4. Bernasconi, A., et al.: Ontology-driven metadata enrichment for genomic datasets. In: International Conference on Semantic Web Applications and Tools for Life Sciences, vol. 2275. CEUR-WS (2018)
5. Lukyananko, R., Parsons, J., Samuel, B.M.: Artifact sampling in experimental conceptual modeling research. In: Woo, C., Lu, J., Li, Z., Ling, T.W., Li, G., Lee, M.L. (eds.) ER 2018. LNCS, vol. 11158, pp. 199–205. Springer, Cham (2018). https://doi.org/10.1007/978-3-030-01391-2_25

6. Palacio, A.L., López, Ó.P., Ródenas, J.C.C.: A method to identify relevant genome data: conceptual modeling for the medicine of precision. In: Trujillo, J.C., Davis, K.C., Du, X., Li, Z., Ling, T.W., Li, G., Lee, M.L. (eds.) ER 2018. LNCS, vol. 11157, pp. 597–609. Springer, Cham (2018). https://doi.org/10.1007/978-3-030-00847-5_44

7. Rambold, G., et al.: Meta-omics data and collection objects (MOD-CO): a conceptual schema and data model for processing sample data in meta-omics research. Database **2019**, baz002 (2019)

8. Reyes Román, J.F., Pastor, Ó., Casamayor, J.C., Valverde, F.: Applying conceptual modeling to better understand the human genome. In: Comyn-Wattiau, I., Tanaka, K., Song, I.-Y., Yamamoto, S., Saeki, M. (eds.) ER 2016. LNCS, vol. 9974, pp. 404–412. Springer, Cham (2016). https://doi.org/10.1007/978-3-319-46397-1_31

9. Verdonck, M., et al.: Comparing traditional conceptual modeling with ontology-driven conceptual modeling: an empirical study. Inf. Syst. **81**, 92–103 (2019)

10. Zhang, H., Li, T., Wang, Y.: Design of an empirical study for evaluating an automatic layout tool. In: Woo, C., Lu, J., Li, Z., Ling, T.W., Li, G., Lee, M.L. (eds.) ER 2018. LNCS, vol. 11158, pp. 206–211. Springer, Cham (2018). https://doi.org/10.1007/978-3-030-01391-2_26

What Are Real JSON Schemas Like?
An Empirical Analysis of Structural Properties

Benjamin Maiwald, Benjamin Riedle, and Stefanie Scherzinger[(✉)]

OTH Regensburg, Regensburg, Germany
bennymaiwald@googlemail.com, riedle.benjamin@gmail.com,
stefanie.scherzinger@oth-regensburg.de

Abstract. Recently, the semantics of the JSON Schema format, a de-facto standard for JSON schema declarations, has been formalized. It turns out that JSON Schema is a surprisingly complex schema language based on an open document semantics. In this paper, we present a first empirical analysis of a curated collection of real-world JSON Schemas. Knowing what real JSON Schemas are like (to borrow from a title of a related study on DTDs) helps practitioners and researchers in making realistic assumptions when building tools for JSON Schema processing.

1 Introduction

The JavaScript Object Notation (JSON) is gaining in popularity, and so is JSON Schema[1] for declaring schemas for JSON documents. For instance, let us consider the JSON document, {"City": "Regensburg", "Country": "Germany"}, representing an object with two key value pairs, and declaring the City to be Regensburg and the Country to be Germany. Figure 1a shows a matching JSON Schema declaration (also in JSON format). It declares that all documents valid w.r.t. this schema must contain an object with two string-typed properties Country and City, and that any additional properties are not allowed.

At the time of writing this paper, the JSON Schema Test Suite[2] lists over 40 JSON Schema validators, implemented for 18 programming languages, a clear sign of the adoption of this schema language. Recently, the database research community has started to focus on JSON Schema. In [4] and [10], the language has been formalized, capturing its syntax, semantics, and its expressive power. This has shown that the language is complex.

In this paper, we present the first empirical study on JSON Schema, based on a curated collection of real-world documents. This is in the tradition of empirical studies on XML schema languages [2,5,7,8,11]. Knowing what real JSON Schemas are like (to borrow from a title of earlier, related work [5] on Document Type Definitions, commonly abbreviated as DTDs), helps make realistic assumptions, both for researchers and practitioners dealing with this language. In our analysis, we focus on practical aspects, such as the lengths of documents

---

[1] https://github.com/json-schema-org.
[2] https://github.com/json-schema-org/JSON-Schema-Test-Suite, as of July 2019.

© Springer Nature Switzerland AG 2019
G. Guizzardi et al. (Eds.): ER 2019 Workshops, LNCS 11787, pp. 95–105, 2019.
https://doi.org/10.1007/978-3-030-34146-6_9

```
{                              {                                     {
  "type": "object",              "Person": {                          "type": "object",
  "properties": {                  "name": "Johannes Kepler",         "string_def":   {"type": "string"},
    "Country": {"type": "string"},  "born": "27-DEC-1571"             "properties": {
    "City":    {"type": "string"},  },                                 "Country": {"$ref": "#/string_def"},
  },                               "City": "Regensburg",               "City":    {"$ref": "#/string_def"},
  "required": ["Country", "City"],  "Country": "Germany"              },
  "additionalProperties": false  }                                    "required": ["Country", "City"],
}                                                                     "additionalProperties": false
                                                                    }
```

(a) Schema S.   (b) Document D_b.   (c) Schema $S_{\$ref}$.

Fig. 1. The JSON documents D_b is not valid w.r.t. JSON Schemas S and $S_{\$ref}$.

and the usage of types, but also on essential graph-theoretic properties, such as recursion and the specified nesting depth. Similar characteristics have been studied in the context of XML schemas. As a feature specific to JSON Schema, we study how schema authors deal with the *open document assumption*: with JSON Schema, undeclared properties are allowed, unless explicitly ruled out. In the upcoming example, we illustrate this idea.

Example 1. The JSON Schema document S from Fig. 1 originates from [10]. It declares that any JSON document D valid w.r.t. schema S is an object with two key-value pairs. The keys are Country *and* City, *and both values are string-typed. As additional properties are not allowed (see the declaration in S), yet the JSON document D_b contains an object* Person, D_b *is not valid w.r.t. schema S.*

If the instruction additionalProperties *were omitted, document D_b would be valid w.r.t. S, as it contains (at least) the required properties.*

In our analysis, we specifically determine whether a JSON Schema declaration is *schema-full*, meaning no additional properties are allowed, or whether it is *schema-mixed*, allowing for additional properties. For schema-full declarations, the authors must rigorously rule out additional properties at every level.

Contributions. Overall, this paper makes the following contributions.

- We downloaded and analyzed over 150 real-world schema declarations from SchemaStore[3], a curated collection of JSON Schemas.
- We manually categorized these schemas into groups, based on their purpose.
- We found evidence that JSON Schema documents can become large (as in several megabytes), which can be a challenge for parsing and validation.
- We analyzed the documents regarding key characteristics, such as recursion, as well as the maximum nesting depth imposed on valid JSON documents.
- We investigated how schemas behave w.r.t. the open document assumption. Interestingly, most schemas allow for great degrees of freedom.

Structure. In Sect. 2, we describe the methodology of our empirical study and state our research questions. Section 3 presents the results, which we discuss in Sect. 4. In Sect. 5, we discuss threats to the validity of our work. Section 6 reviews related work. We conclude with Sect. 7.

---

[3] www.schemastore.org/json.

2   Methodology

2.1   Context Description

We have identified 168 JSON Schema documents from SchemaStore[4] on February 25, 2019. Three files could not be downloaded due to broken weblinks, 5 files could not be processed due to document-internal references that could not be resolved. One further file was recognized as invalid by the JSON Schema validators used (see Sect. 2.3).[5] Altogether, we continue with 159 documents as the basis of our study. Our Python analysis scripts are available online.[6]

2.2   Research Questions

RQ1: How large are real-world JSON Schema documents? We ask how large files are in practice, as large files are a challenge for most processing tasks. For instance, when schema validators process all data in main memory, they may not be able to handle overly large files.

RQ2: What is the distribution of types? The JSON Schema language offers a rich set of types. We ask which types are commonly used.

RQ3: Are schema declarations schema-full or schema-mixed? Declaring schema-full JSON Schema documents requires considerable effort. We ask whether authors "go the extra mile" in specifying tight schemas.

RQ4: How common is recursion? The JSON Schema format allows for recursive schemas. Studies on schemas for XML have shown that recursion is rather common, and we ask whether this transfers to JSON Schemas.

RQ5: Do schemas impose maximum nesting depths? JSON documents can be deeply nested. We are interested in the maximum depths of valid non-recursive documents, as a proxy for schema complexity.

2.3   Analysis Process

Validation. We processed all documents with three validators[7], to ensure they are valid JSON Schema documents. Two validators flagged `nodemon.json`[8] because of an invalid regular expression pattern. Document `asmdef`[9] missed the prefix symbol "$" in keyword `$schema`, but this raised no validation error.

---

[4] While there are daily updates to this collection, our analysis can be reproduced, as the site is managed on GitHub at https://github.com/SchemaStore/schemastore.

[5] The fact that not all files are available or can be processed matches the reports of earlier studies on XML and XML schema languages, e.g. [5].

[6] https://github.com/miniHive/schemastore-analysis.

[7] https://github.com/everit-org/json-schema (Java), https://www.npmjs.com/package/ajv-cli (command-line), https://github.com/Julian/jsonschema (Python).

[8] https://github.com/SchemaStore/schemastore/commits/master/src/schemas/json/nodemon.json, currently in the version committed back in January 2019.

[9] https://github.com/SchemaStore/schemastore/commits/master/src/schemas/json/asmdef.jsonf, currently in the version committed back in July 2018.

Manual Classification. We have manually classified all JSON Schema files into one of four categories. In doing so, we lean on an earlier categorization for DTDs [5], based on the intuition proposed there that the schema structure depends on the use case that the schema is intended for: The notion of *data* schemas is only natural, as JSON is a data-exchange format. Category *meta* reflects schemas that define markup for other schemas. For instance, there are JSON *meta* schemas for every JSON schema draft, for validating whether a JSON Schema document adheres to a given draft. Category *conf* is added by us. It declares JSON documents that hold configurations for services. *app* schemas are used in data exchange between applications. As stated in [5], the boundaries are not always clear. For instance, the Avro schema definition[10] could be seen as a *meta* schema, since Avro is itself a schema language. However, Avro is also the wire format for communication between Hadoop nodes, so we classify this document as an *app* schema.

Figure 2 shows the distribution of documents across the four categories. Most documents fall into category *conf.* The second largest category *data* contains only about half as many documents. The smallest group is *app*, a finding that is in line with related work on DTDs [5].

Formatting. We normalized all documents by pretty-printing them with the command-line tool `json_pp`. This allows us to compare lines of code.

Resolving References. JSON Schema documents may contain references, as illustrated in the following example.

Example 2. Document $S_{\$ref}$ in Fig. 1c is an equivalent refactoring of S in Fig. 1a: It uses references to refer to a central `string` *type declaration. Here, the effect is similar in spirit to introducing a type alias in C++ programming.*

Across all documents, 46 contain no references. Among the remaining are cases where external schemas are referenced. To be able to work on self-contained documents, in *resolving external references*, we replace references to external schemas by their targets. We refer to the result as the *resolved schema*.

For non-recursive schemas, this yields a DAG and we can determine the longest path from the root to a leaf, the *resolved depth*. Due to the open document assumption, the resolved depth is not necessarily an indicator how deeply nested the documents declared by the schema may become, as illustrated next.

Example 3. Let us consider Fig. 1 and assume that JSON Schema document S misses the `additionalProperties` *restriction and is therefore schema-flexible. Then D_b is valid w.r.t. schema S, yet the nesting depth of D_b is not constrained by S, as additional properties such as object* `Person` *can be deeply nested.*

---

[10] http://json.schemastore.org/avro-avsc.

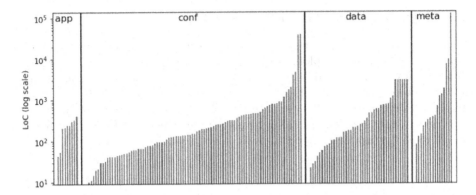

Fig. 2. Distribution of documents over the categories and their file sizes in LoC.

Expanding References. Using references, schemas can be declared more succinctly. This has an effect when we count the occurrence of types.

Example 4. In the schema from Fig. 1a, there are two occurrences of type string, *in the equivalent schema from Fig. 1c, there is only one.*

For non-recursive schemas, it is straightforward to expand all references (even document-internal references) by repeatedly inlining the targets of references.

3   Detailed Study Results

3.1   RQ1: How Large Are Real-World JSON Schema Documents?

In Fig. 2, we capture JSON Schema documents by their lines of code (LoC), in a visualization inspired by [5]: Vertical lines show the partitioning of schemas into categories (*app, conf, data,* and *meta*). Each bar represents a JSON Schema document. We show the LoC of schemas (sorted by size) after pretty-printing, but before external references are resolved. *data* schemas have only 692 LoC on average. The average LoCs for category *app* is even smaller with only 228, though this may be an effect of the small batch size for this category. In contrast, the average LoC for category *meta* is 8,963 (1,588 without the Ansible2.5 schema[11], which is an outlier in size) as well as 1,209 for category *conf.*

Results. It turns out that there are comparatively large files. The largest document (Ansible2.5) is generated. It has over 119K LoC, and in its raw format requires over 5 MB when stored on disk.

3.2 RQ2: What Is the Distribution of Types?

We counted the type declarations in resolved schemas. Figure 3 shows the distribution of types using box-plots, broken down by document category. We aggregate type keywords into groups, using a classification introduced in [4] for string, number, object, and array schemas, and further one group for Boolean combinations and comparisons. For example, the string schema groups the keywords `string` and `pattern` (for declaring regular expressions). We further introduce an additional group for `null` values.

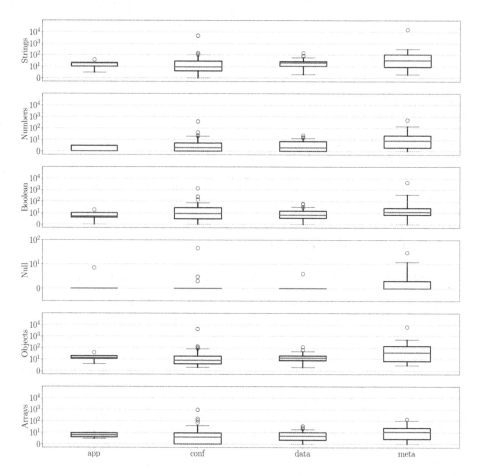

Fig. 3. Type distribution, broken down by keyword schemas (c.f. [4]).

The box-plot whiskers show the 0%–95% quantiles with a logarithmic scale on the vertical axis, to enable our readers to see the outliers. The minor grid, with a horizontal line every power-of-10 ticks, helps to calibrate the eye w.r.t. the different scaling of the vertical axes.

Note that the result of simply counting the occurrences of type keywords depends on how compactly schemas are declared, as discussed in Sect. 2.3. For non-recursive schemas, we can compute the ratio of the number of nodes in the expanded (and resolved) versus the resolved schemas. The median ratio is 1.43, the highest ratio of over 9 is evidenced by lsdlschema[12]. Thus, references lead to more compact schemas in general.

Results. As can be seen, the document categories differ in their characteristics. Documents in *meta* make extended use of nulls, as well as objects, which seems natural when declaring meta languages. At the same time, *conf* and (in particular) *meta* documents tend to be larger, which drives up the occurrence counts. Overall, *data* and *app* display similar characteristics.

3.3   RQ3: Are Schema Declarations Schema-Full or Schema-Mixed?

In 116 out of 156 documents, the keyword additionalProperties occurs (either set to true or false). However, there are only 8 schemas that are actually schema-full declarations. Among *conf* documents, only two are schema-full and contain very tight specifications up to the point where not even variable-length arrays are allowed. Thus, most declarations are schema-mixed.

On a related issue, the required tag occurs in 102 documents. Thus, in about a third of the documents, all properties are optional. Notably, Ansible2.5 has over 2K occurrences of required, but not a single AdditionalProperties.

Results. Over 70% of all documents contain the keyword additionalProperties at least once. Thus, schema authors actively control the degree of schema-flexibility, yet few declare schema-full documents (in less than 5% cases).

3.4   RQ4: How Common Is Recursion?

Out of all schemas analyzed, only 26 are recursive. About 62% of the schemas in *meta* are recursive, whereas the other categories do not contain more than a third of recursive schemas. The maximum cycle length is 20.

Results. This ratio of approx. 16% of recursive schemas is in stark contrast to an earlier finding on DTDs, where 60% of documents were recursive [5]. There, it was reported that *data* DTDs are usually non-recursive, which is not the case for JSON Schema documents of this category, where it is nearly 30%. It is plausible that recursion is more common in *meta* schemas, as they declare languages. For instance, JSON Document Transform[13] declares a transformation language for JSON documents, so it is naturally recursive.

---

[12] See https://github.com/SchemaStore/schemastore/commits/master/src/schemas/ json/lsdlschema.json in the version of March 2018.

[13] http://json.schemastore.org/jdt.

3.5   RQ5: Do Schemas Impose Maximum Nesting Depths?

The bar chart in Fig. 4 shows the resolved depths for non-recursive schemas. For recursive schemas, we leave a placeholder, to convey a sense of quantity. For non-recursive schemas, we show a bar indicating the resolved depth. Bars for documents that are schema-full are colored black, documents that are schema-mixed are colored blue. As discussed in Sect. 2.3, only the combination of non-recursive schemas that are schema-full imposes a limit on nesting depth: Only five JSON Schema documents limit the maximum nesting depth of JSON documents that are valid w.r.t. them (three of the schema-full documents are recursive and thus not shown here). Overall, the minimum resolved depth is 3. The average resolved depth of approx. 11 is much lower than the maximum of 43.

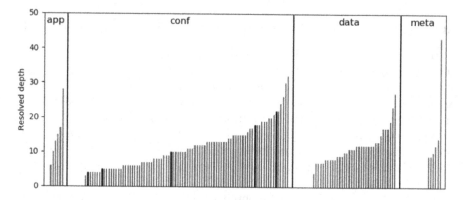

Fig. 4. Resolved depth in non-recursive schemas. Gaps denote recursive schemas. Black bars highlight schema-full declarations (chart best viewed in color).

Results. A depth of 10 may be conceptually still manageable for humans (who are said to be able to recall up to seven items in their working memory), while a depth of 40 seems daunting (to provide perspective, in the DTDs analyzed by [5], the resolved depth was 20 at most). Yet inspecting the outlier document lsdlschema[14] reveals that it is part of Microsoft Power BI. Users of this product can specify natural language queries over relational data, such as searching for the oldest customer. lsdlschema describes the linguistic annotations derived in parsing and processing these queries. It is plausible that a professional linguistic model requires a deeply nested schema.

4   Discussion

We have found some JSON Schema documents to be comparatively large. As JSON Schema documents themselves are specified in JSON, large files incur an overhead for parsing [9] and validation [10].

---

[14] See footnote 16.

In contrast, let us compare this with schemas from the JSON Schema Test Suite. As of July 8th, 2019, this collection contains 733 schemas for unit testing. The largest test schema spans only 38 LoC (after pretty printing). This is not representative of our observations from real-world schemas. As these tests are the basis for the JSON Schema Benchmark[15], this reveals a gap in the benchmark setup, and calls for extensions.

We have found that recursion is not as common as in schemas for the related format XML. Assuming that this result can be generalized (e.g., by a follow-up study on a larger document collection), this can be valuable information for researchers and practitioners who build tools that process JSON Schema.

Further, we have found that most declarations in JSON Schema documents are schema-mixed. This makes for easy backwards compatibility when schemas evolve: Assuming that new property declarations are added to the schema over time, this won't break interfaces that validate new JSON documents against a legacy schema. Yet without an extended, qualitative survey, we can only speculate as to the authors' reasons for not declaring tighter schemas.

5   Threats to Validity

Construct Validity. Our analysis is based on a specific document collection. Our biggest threat to validity is that this collection is small. In future work, we would thus like to analyze additional documents hosted on GitHub. As of June 25th 2019, we searched GitHub for JSON Schema documents using BigQuery[16], in particular, files ending in .json which contain the property $schema. This simple search revealed over 400K candidates. Thus, there is a larger document collection for exploration. Nevertheless, schemas on SchemaStore are a good starting point, as they are curated (some files have undergone more than 60 revisions). In contrast, repositories on GitHub are popular for personal and experimental development [6], and the schemas hosted there may not all be up to standard.

A minor threat is that we may have misclassified JSON Schema documents into categories. After all, this was done manually, and as pointed out in [5], the boundaries between categories are not always perfectly clear.

External Validity. It is a fundamental question whether results of studies on open source code generalize to commercial settings [3].

6   Related Work

The JSON Schema language has recently come to the attention of researchers. In [4] and [10], its syntax and semantics are explored from a language-theory point-of-view. While the authors of [10] impressively validate 18 million JSON documents from Wikidata against a (single) JSON Schema, their goal is not to study

---

[15] https://github.com/ebdrup/json-schema-benchmark/.

[16] Google BigQuery allows for querying the GitHub open data collection, mostly non-forked projects with an open source license: https://cloud.google.com/bigquery/.

the properties of real-world JSON Schema documents. To the best of our knowledge, there are no systematic empirical studies of real-world schemas yet.

Our work is strongly inspired by Byron Choi's study on DTDs [5]. There are various other works on profiling DTDs or XML Schema [2, 5, 7, 8, 11]. In hindsight, these studies have really helped the database community to better understand the proliferation and adoption of these schema languages and their features.

7 Conclusion

In this paper, we present a first analysis over a curated collection of JSON Schema documents. We see plenty of opportunity for follow-up studies. For instance, JSON Schema documents may actually be unsatisfiable, so no valid documents exist. This is possible in theory [4], yet whether this actually occurs in real-world schemas (and is thus a practical problem) is an open issue.

Also, the best practices as to how schema authors express constraints have not been systematically explored. Yet already, we have gained insights that indicate that existing JSON Schema benchmark might have to be extended, for instance, by larger documents that stress-test schema parsing and validation. Also, we are surprised that authors tend to write schema-flexible declarations, which is a mind-shift when coming from XML schema languages, such as DTDs.

Acknowledgements. This project was supported by the *Deutsche Forschungsgemeinschaft* (DFG, German Research Foundation), grant #385808805. We thank Mohamed-Amine Baazizi, Dario Colazzo, Giorgio Ghelli, and Carlo Sartiani for their comprehensive EDBT tutorial [1]. We thank Meike Klettke and Uta Störl for their feedback, and Sebastian Sidortschuck for computing statistics on the JSON Schema Test Suite.

References

1. Baazizi, M.A., Colazzo, D., Ghelli, G., Sartiani, C.: Schemas and types for JSON data (Tutorial). In: Proceedings of EDBT (2019)
2. Bex, G.J., Neven, F., den Bussche, J.V.: DTDs versus XML schema: a practical study. In: Proceedings of WebDB 2004 (2004)
3. Bird, C., Menzies, T., Zimmermann, T.: The Art and Science of Analyzing Software Data, 1st edn. Morgan Kaufmann Publishers Inc., San Francisco (2015)
4. Bourhis, P., Reutter, J.L., Suárez, F., Vrgoč, D.: JSON: data model, query languages and Schema specification. In: Proceedings of PODS (2017)
5. Choi, B.: What are real DTDs like? In: WebDB (2002)
6. Kalliamvakou, E., Gousios, G., Blincoe, K., Singer, L., et al.: The promises and perils of mining GitHub. In: Proceedings of MSR (2014)
7. Laender, A.H., Moro, M.M., Nascimento, C., Martins, P.: An X-ray on web-available XML schemas. SIGMOD Rec. **38**(1), 37–42 (2009)
8. Martens, W., Neven, F., Schwentick, T., Bex, G.J.: Expressiveness and complexity of XML schema. ACM Trans. Database Syst. **31**(3), 770–813 (2006)
9. Palkar, S., Abuzaid, F., Bailis, P., Zaharia, M.: Filter before you parse: faster analytics on raw data with sparser. Proc. VLDB Endow. **11**(11), 1576–1589 (2018)

10. Pezoa, F., Reutter, J.L., Suarez, F., Ugarte, M., Vrgoč, D.: Foundations of JSON schema. In: Proceedings of WWW (2016)
11. Sahuguet, A.: Everything you ever wanted to know about DTDs, but were afraid to ask. In: Proceedings of WebDB (2000)

Getting to Win-Win in Inter-organizational Relationships Through Customer Segmentation

Vik Pant[1(✉)] and Eric Yu[1,2]

[1] Faculty of Information, University of Toronto, Toronto, Canada
vik.pant@mail.utoronto.ca, eric.yu@utoronto.ca
[2] Department of Computer Science, University of Toronto, Toronto, Canada

Abstract. Coopetition describes a phenomenon in which actors simultaneously cooperate and compete with each other. A stable and sustainable coopetitive relationship is predicated on the presence of one or more win-win strategies. In this paper, we demonstrate the generation of a win-win strategy by two startup companies in a business relationship in the real-world. Originally, these startup companies regarded each other as rivals. In the course of our Action Research engagement, conceptual modeling revealed that, contrary to their original assumptions, the two companies operated in different input and output markets. Therefore, instead of engaging in adversarial behavior, they could benefit from cooperation. We use $i*$ strategic actor modeling, with actor specialization, to differentiate customer segments, in combination with game-theoretic analysis. The resulting artefacts, our conceptual models, are being used by the founders of these startup companies to inform their decision-making.

Keywords: Coopetition · Win-win · Strategy · $i*$ · Actor specialization

1 Introduction

Strategic coopetition describes a relationship in which actors compete and cooperate simultaneously [1]. It is observed widely in economic, political, civic, and social contexts. The sustainability of a coopetitive relationship is predicated on the existence of a win-win outcome for all the stakeholders [1]. Win-win refers to a condition in which all members in a relationship are better off as a result of being in that relationship. Conversely, lose-lose refers to a condition in which all members are worse off as a result of being in that relationship. Win-lose characterizes a relationship in which some members are better off while others are worse off by participating in that relationship. Lose-lose and win-lose relationships are unsustainable because in such relationships, definitionally, some players are worse off by participating than abstaining.

In this paper, we attempt the generation of a win-win strategy through the application of conceptual modeling. Our modeling is used to analyze the relationship between two startups in data science professional development market in Toronto. We show that by adopting a purely competitive orientation these organizations create a zero-sum relationship. We apply conceptual modeling to assist these startups in

© Springer Nature Switzerland AG 2019
G. Guizzardi et al. (Eds.): ER 2019 Workshops, LNCS 11787, pp. 106–119, 2019.
https://doi.org/10.1007/978-3-030-34146-6_10

adopting a non-competitive and pre-cooperative stance, with the potential of yielding a positive-sum outcome. Our research shows that ad hoc decision-making leads to faulty assumptions that can impede organizational progress and growth. Without modeling, founders of these startups erroneously assumed that they were competitors in input and output markets. Conversely, conceptual modeling can support organizational advancement and development by assisting decision-makers to secure a deeper decision rationale. Conceptual modeling allowed the founders of these startups to realize that they operate in different markets. This motivated them to eschew competitive positions that were yielding their zero-sum outcomes.

2   Empirical Study: Startups in the Market of Data Science Professional Development

The global demand for data science talent has grown significantly because it is regarded as a source of competitive advantage in many industries. This growth in demand for data science talent has spawned a booming market for professional development programs. Entrepreneurs have launched new startups that provide such programs in the same market as traditional education institutions such as universities and colleges. These startups include training bootcamps and mentorship academies that offer professional development programs either online, on-premise, or through a blended channel. This market is extremely lucrative for startups due to high and rising demand for data science professional development programs in Toronto.

Our empirical study focuses on two professional development startups in the Toronto market. One startup, referred to as Training Bootcamp (TB), offers classroom-based instruction to cohorts of students. Students apply to this program and, upon acceptance, undertake a twelve-week program of study that includes multiple courses that are taught by professional data scientists from the industry. Another startup, referred to as Mentorship Academy (MA), offers personalized one-on-one coaching to mentees by pairing them up with a mentor that is a seasoned data scientist from the industry. The mentor and the mentee develop a customized learning plan that spans twelve weeks and entitles the mentee to an allocation of their mentor's time. TB and MA also offer employment services to their graduates by referring them to job placement opportunities.

3   Research Methodology and Modeling Approach

3.1   Research Methodology: Action Research

We adopted action research [2] methodology to perform this empirical study. Action research refers to a portfolio of techniques in which researchers participate actively to bring about changes in the domain that they are concomitantly studying [2]. It is used in business research wherein researchers apply critical reflection to link 'doing' with 'studying' [3]. A key element of action research is the notion of 'intervention' which is defined as: "purposeful action by an agent to create change" [3]. A co-author of this paper was known by the founders of these startups. He was invited separately and independently by these startup founders to provide business advice on a one-on-one basis. The data for our empirical study were gathered through five one-hour interactive and participatory sessions with founders of these startups (i.e., total of ten hours). After each session, models were constructed offline by one of the authors, then explained and discussed in the follow-up session, making revisions and adjustments where necessary. Our models and analyses were shared with these founders individually in verbal and diagrammatic form during subsequent advisory meetings.

3.2   Modeling Approach: Combining *i** and Payoff Matrices

Figure 1 presents a modeling methodology that combines *i** strategic actor modeling with Payoff Matrices from Game Theory. *i** supports early stage requirements engineering [4] and has been applied to analyze strategies [5–13] in the business context. This methodology is a variation of our methodology that combines *i** with Game Trees [11–13]. The difference between these methodologies is due to the relevance of sequence in the models and their analysis. In Game Theory, Game Trees are used to solve sequential move games (i.e., processual) while Payoff Matrices are used to solve simultaneous move games (i.e., structural) [14]. In [11–13], we combined *i** with Game Trees to study the phenomenon of reciprocality, which necessitates consideration of decision paths. However, in the empirical study presented in this paper we study the structural, rather than the processual, aspects of the relationship between these startups.

The methodology presented in Fig. 1 is divided into three phases: modeling, evaluation, and exploration. We operationalized this methodology in an iterative and interactive manner. Subjective qualitative assessments by subject matter experts (founders) and modeling specialists (authors) were used to collaboratively generate win-win strategies. The modeling phase encompasses the development of *i** SR models and their corresponding payoff matrices. The evaluation phase entails performing of label propagation in the *i** SR models and calculation of payoffs in the payoff matrix based on the results of label propagation in the *i** SR models. The exploration phase includes five non-deterministic steps for experimenting with additions and changes to the *i** SR models to generate one or more win-win strategies. In this way, the conceptual modeling methodology presented in Fig. 1 can be used in discriminative (i.e., assessing whether a win-win strategy exists) as well as generative (i.e., creating a new win-win strategy) modes.

A distinctive step in this engagement, not explored in previous applications of this methodology, was that in considering Adding or Removing Actors during the exploration phase (bolded in Fig. 1), a more general actor was refined into more specialized actors, thus allowing for analysis of customer segmentation.

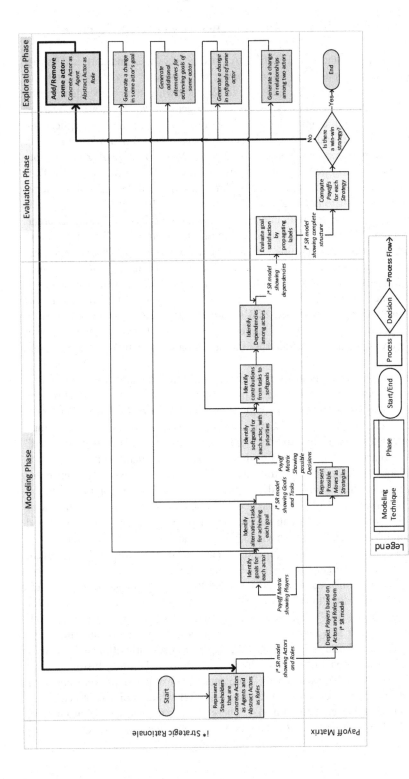

Fig. 1. Process steps for alternating between *i** and Payoff Matrix modeling to get to win-win (Introduction of new **actor** is highlighted in **bold**, *softgoal* and *tasks* in *italics*)

4   Conceptual Modeling of Data Science Instruction Startups

The key actors are the 2 startups (TB and MA), instructors (input market), and learner as well as client (output market). For readability, we present i* models separately for Learner (Fig. 2a), Instructor (2b), and Client (2c), showing their dependency relationships with the 2 startups. Figures 2a, 2b, and 2c depict *actors* that are relevant in the As-Is scenario of our empirical case study. Figures 2a, 2b and 2c depicts our interpretation of the input and output markets as perceived by TB and MA prior to our intervention. In the past (i.e., As-Is scenario), TB and MA did not analyze their input and output markets in a systematic or structured manner. TB and MA regarded their input and output markets to be comprised of three generic, undifferentiated, homogeneous, and monolithic customers: Learner (2a), Instructor (2b), and Client (2c).

Figure 2a includes the internal intentional structures of TB, MA, and Learner. Internal intentional structures of TB and MA are omitted from Figs. 2b and 2c due to page length constraints. The startups, TB and MA, possess certain *goals* which are states of affairs in the world that an *actor* wishes to achieve. TB has a *goal* "revenue be generated" while MA has a *goal* "market valuation be increased". A *goal* is achieved via the performance of a *task* which refers to the specific way of fulfilling that *goal* through the application of know-how. TB's *goal* of "revenue be generated" can be fulfilled by the performance of a task "charge course fees" while MA's *goal* of "market valuation be increased" can be fulfilled by the performance of a task "charge income share".

Tasks are compared by contrasting their impacts on *softgoals*. A *softgoal* is a quality objective that is not characterized by clear-cut and objective satisfaction criterion. *Contribution Links* are used to depict the impact of a *task* on a *softgoal* or a *softgoal* on another *softgoal*. For a Learner, the task "learn from training bootcamp" positively contributes (i.e., Helps) to the *softgoal* "team player skills be demonstrated" and negatively contributes (i.e., Hurts) to the *softgoal* "individuated skills be demonstrated". Conversely, the *task* "learn from mentorship academy" positively contributes to the *softgoal* "individuated skills be demonstrated" and negatively contributes to the *softgoal* "team player skills be demonstrated". A *softgoal* is regarded as satisfied or denied from the subjective and qualitative perspective of an *actor*. Satisfaction and denial of i* model elements is shown via checkmarks and crosses respectively.

Actors in strategic relationships depend on each other for *goals* to be achieved, *tasks* to be performed, *softgoals* to be satisfied, and *resources* to be obtained. A *resource* is a physical or informational entity needed to complete a *task*. In Fig. 2a, TB depends on the Learner for "tuition fees" (*resource*) and MA depends on Learner for "first year salary commission" (*resource*). The flat side of the 'D' in a dependency link points towards the *actor* that depends while the curved side points towards the *actor* that is depended upon. Figures 2a, 2b, and 2c, depict two scenarios (labeled 1 and 2) that correspond to the impact of a choice by a customer (i.e., Learner, Instructor, and Client) on TB and MA. Choices 1 and 2 are mutually exclusive wherein choice 1 indicates the decision by a customer to engage with TB while choice 2 indicates the decision by a customer to engage with MA. These choices are shown within Learner, Instructor, and Client *actors* as *tasks*. They are connected with the top-level goal of

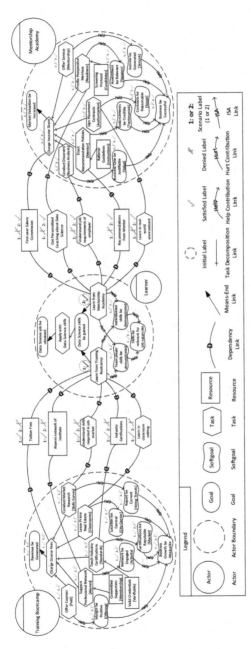

Fig. 2a. *i** SR diagram portraying relationship between TB, MA, and Learner in the past (i.e., As-Is scenario)

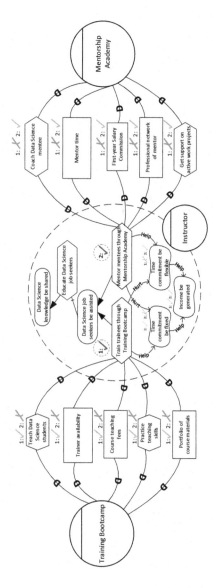

Fig. 2b. *i** SR diagram portraying relationship between TB, MA, and Instructor in the past (i.e., As-Is scenario)

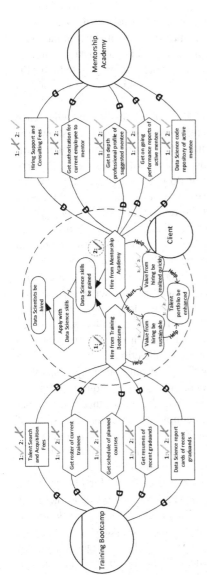

Fig. 2c. *i** SR diagram portraying relationship between TB, MA, and Client in the past (i.e., As-Is scenario)

		Training Bootcamp (TB)	
		(a) Recruit Learner (b) Hire Instructor (c) Engage Client	Do Not: (a) Recruit Learner (b) Hire Instructor (c) Engage Client
Mentorship Academy (MA)	(a) Recruit Learner (b) Hire Instructor (c) Engage Client	**M: 0** **T: 0**	M: 1 T: -2
	Do Not: (a) Recruit Learner (b) Hire Instructor (c) Engage Client	M: -2 T: 1	M: -2 T: -2

Fig. 2d. Payoff matrix that depicts the payoffs associated with each strategy available to TB and MA in the past (i.e., As-Is scenario)

each focal *actor* using *Means-Ends* links. *Means-Ends* links depict the relationship between a *goal* and any *task* that can be used to achieve it (i.e., OR decomposition).

In the past (depicted in the As-Is scenario), TB and MA, adopted a competitive stance towards each other because they assumed that their service offerings and value propositions were regarded as substitutes by their customers. This is shown via satisfaction labels attached to the subjects of the dependencies associated with scenarios 1 and 2. In Fig. 1, the evaluation phase involves the propagation of satisfaction labels on elements in *i** SR diagrams as well as the calculation of *payoffs* based on satisfaction of intentional elements. In Figs. 2a, 2b, and 2c satisfaction labels are propagated over the *softgoals* of the customers based on completion of the *task* associated with scenarios 1 and 2 respectively.

Figure 2d shows a payoff matrix that depicts the *payoffs* associated with each *strategy* available to TB and MA. Due to page length constraints, Fig. 2d shows the *strategies* that are available to TB and MA within the same payoff matrix. This combination is workable since the *strategies*, for dealing with customers, that are available to TB and MA are symmetrical (i.e., act or do not act). Three main *strategy* scenarios are possibilities: (i) TB and MA act, (ii) only TB acts or only MA acts, (iii) neither TB nor MA act. It must be noted that the numerical values of *payoffs* are relative and not absolute since they are meant to support the contrasting of *strategies* in terms their comparative gain or loss. In selecting a *strategy*, a rational *actor* is expected to prefer a *payoff* of 1 over a *payoff* of 0 and a *payoff* of 0 over a *payoff* of −2.

Payoffs associated with each of these *strategy* scenarios are calculated in the following way: (i) if both *players* act then they compete with each other to acquire and retain customers by lowering their prices (e.g., cheaper for learner and client) and raising their costs (e.g., more lucrative for Instructors). This scenario leads to a status quo payoff (0) since it puts downward pressure on each of their margins and depletes their profitability which is a contributor to their business objectives (TB: "revenue be generated" and MA: "market valuation be increased"), (ii) if only one player acts then the player that acts has a positive payoff (1) because it is able to acquire and retain customers thereby achieving its business objectives while the player that does not act has a negative payoff (−2) because it foregoes economic opportunity in spite of incurring fixed and overhead costs to run their business., (iii) if neither player acts then each of them earns a negative payoff (−2) by foregoing economic opportunities in spite of incurring fixed as well as overhead costs to run their businesses.

This payoff matrix shows that the *payoff* for not acting is −2 for either *player* irrespective of the *strategy* chosen by the other *player*. However, the *payoff* for acting is 0 if both *players* act and 1 if only one *player* acts. Therefore, acting is the dominant *strategy* for TB and MA since it guarantees a higher *payoff*, compared to not acting, regardless of the *strategy* chosen by the other *player*. This analysis suggests that both TB and MA are expected to act (i.e., recruit Learners, retain Instructors, and engage Clients) leading to a *payoff* of 0 for both TB and MA. This absence of a win-win *strategy* in the As-Is scenario triggered the exploration phase (depicted in Fig. 1). The intended outcome of this exploratory phase was a *strategy* that would support the attainment of positive non-zero *payoffs* by both TB and MA. Figures 3a, 3b, 3c and 3d presents models depicting the To-Be scenario that resulted through the iterative and interactive application of the methodology presented in Fig. 1.

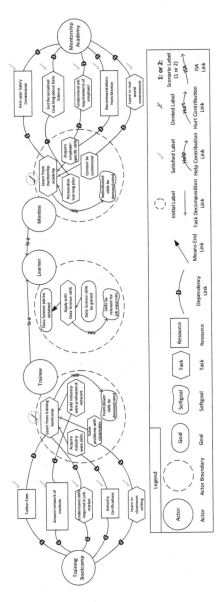

Fig. 3a. *i** SR diagram portraying relationship between TB, MA, Trainee, Mentee, and Learner in the future (i.e., To-Be scenario)

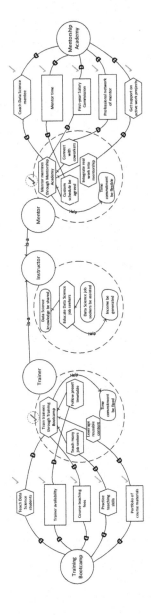

Fig. 3b. *i** SR diagram portraying relationship between TB, MA, Trainer, Mentor, and Instructor in the future (i.e., To-Be scenario)

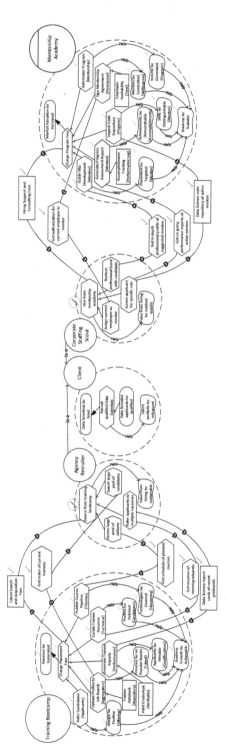

Fig. 3c. *i** SR diagram portraying relationship between TB, MA, Agency Recruiter, Corporate Staffing Scout, and Client in the future (i.e. To-Be scenario)

		Training Bootcamp (TB)	
		(a) Recruit Trainee (b) Hire Trainer (c) Engage Recruiter	Do Not: (a) Recruit Trainee (b) Hire Trainer (c) Engage Recruiter
Mentorship Academy (MA)	(a) Recruit Mentee (b) Hire Mentor (c) Engage Scout	**M: 1** **T: 1**	*M: 1* *T: -2*
	Do Not: (a) Recruit Mentee (b) Hire Mentor (c) Engage Scout	M: -2 *T: 1*	M: -2 *T: -2*

Fig. 3d. Payoff matrix that depicts the payoffs associated with each strategy available to TB and MA in the future (i.e., To-Be scenario)

The exploration phase in Fig. 1 presents five non-deterministic steps for generating a win-win *strategy* by adding or changing some elements in a relationship. In the case of TB and MA, we encouraged the founders of each startup to reconsider their assumptions of treating their three customers in a generic, undifferentiated, homogeneous, and monolithic manner. Our conceptual modeling methodology allowed TB and MA to think about different and specific types of customers: Learner, Instructor, and Client. We followed the technique presented in [15] to represent specializations of the Learner, Instructor, and Client entities.

Modeling assisted the founders of TB and MA to perform a deeper examination of their input and output markets. Analysis of the models revealed that TB and MA had different customers even though those customers shared certain aspects in common. Figures 3a, 3b, and 3c show that TB dealt with Trainees, Trainers, and Agency Recruiters while MA dealt with Mentees, Mentors, and Corporate Staffing Scouts. Trainees, Mentees, Instructors, Mentors, Agency Recruiters, and Corporate Staffing Scouts possessed different intentional structures. However, the commonalities in the intentional structures of Trainees and Mentees, Instructors and Mentors, as well as Agency Recruiters and Corporate Staffing Scouts is depicted in the Learner, Instructor, and Client actors respectively. Actor association to relate specialized entities with generalized entities is depicted via *is-a* links [15].

Applying the evaluation phase of Fig. 1 over the models of the To-Be scenario shows that TB and MA are not in a competitive relationship since they deal with different customers. This means that it is possible for the *goals* of TB and MA to be fulfilled independently of each other. The payoff matrix in Fig. 3d shows that the *strategies* available to TB and MA do not involve the same customers. The *payoffs* in the To-Be scenario are only different from the As-Is scenario when both TB and MA act. This is because TB and MA do not regard each other as competitors and they do not conflict over common customers. In the As-Is scenario, a payoff of 0 resulted (Fig. 2d) for TB and MA when both *players* act, however, in the To-Be scenario, a *payoff* of 1 results (Fig. 3d) for TB and MA when both *players* act. This demonstrates the application of the methodology presented in Fig. 1 to generate a win-win *strategy*. Our models and analyses were favorably received by the founders of these startups. They are incorporating our recommendations and suggestions in their strategic planning processes.

5 Related Work

i* modeling has been used to analyze inter-organizational relationships. In [5–7] we analyzed strategic pivots and directional shifts in startups and large enterprises. In [8–10] we analyzed organizations in terms of their simultaneously cooperative and competitive strategies. *i** modeling and game-theoretic modeling techniques have also been combined to analyze coopetitive strategies of organizations. In [11–13] we proposed a method for complementarily applying *i** with Game Trees to discriminate and generate win-win strategies. The work presented in this paper builds upon this corpus by offering empirical support for utilization of *i** modeling to analyze real-world coopetitive strategies. Our work is also related to the body of scholarly literature related to the application of action research for the generation of business strategies [2, 3].

6   Conclusion and Future Work

In this paper, we demonstrated the application of action research to generate win-win strategies in inter-organizational relationships. We proposed a variation of the methodology presented in [11–13], for performing processual analysis, to accommodate structural analysis. Our future work aims to address the challenges identified in applying this methodology in the empirical case. We developed two sets of *i** models (i.e., As-Is, To-Be) because *i** does not support conditional reasoning. A future step in our research involves experimenting with alternate mechanisms for depicting model configurations at different times. We also extended the notation of *i** slightly by including scenario labels (i.e., checks and crosses for scenarios 1 and 2) in our diagrams because *i** does not support conditional reasoning. Another future step in our research involves experimenting with alternate mechanisms for representing if-then associations in *i** models. Improving the visual scalability of *i** models is also a future step in our research.

References

1. Brandenburger, A.M., Nalebuff, B.J.: Co-opetition. Doubleday, New York (1996)
2. Eden, C., Huxham, C.: Action research for management research. Br. J. Manag. 7(1), 75–86 (1996)
3. Midgley, G.: Systemic intervention. In: Midgley, G. (ed.) Systemic intervention, pp. 113–133. Springer, Boston (2000). https://doi.org/10.1007/978-1-4615-4201-8_6
4. Yu, E.S.: Towards modelling and reasoning support for early-phase requirements engineering. In: Proceedings of the Third IEEE International Symposium on Requirements Engineering (RE), pp. 226–235. IEEE, January 1997
5. Pant, V., Yu, E., Tai, A.: Towards reasoning about pivoting in startups and large enterprises with i*. In: Poels, G., Gailly, F., Serral, A.E., Snoeck, M. (eds.) PoEM 2017. LNBIP, vol. 305, pp. 203–220. Springer, Cham (2017). https://doi.org/10.1007/978-3-319-70241-4_14
6. Pant, V., Yu, E.: Conceptual modeling to support pivoting – an example from Twitter. In: Woo, C., Lu, J., Li, Z., Ling, T., Li, G., Lee, M. (eds.) ER 2018. LNCS, vol. 11158, pp. 260–270. Springer, Cham (2018). https://doi.org/10.1007/978-3-030-01391-2_31
7. Pant, V., Yu, E.: Conceptual modeling to support the "larger goal" pivot – an example from netflix. In: Buchmann, R., Karagiannis, D., Kirikova, M. (eds.) PoEM 2018. LNBIP, vol. 335, pp. 394–403. Springer, Cham (2018). https://doi.org/10.1007/978-3-030-02302-7_26
8. Pant, V., Yu, E.: Modeling Simultaneous cooperation and competition among enterprises. Bus. Inf. Syst. Eng. 60(1), 39–54 (2018)
9. Pant, V., Yu, E.: Coopetition with frenemies: towards modeling of simultaneous cooperation and competition among enterprises. In: Horkoff, J., Jeusfeld, M., Persson, A. (eds.) PoEM 2016. LNBIP, vol. 267, pp. 164–178. Springer, Cham (2016). https://doi.org/10.1007/978-3-319-48393-1_12

10. Pant, V., Yu, E.: Modeling strategic complementarity and synergistic value creation in coopetitive relationships. In: Holmström Olsson, A., Olsson, H., Werder, K. (eds.) ICSOB 2017. LNBIP, vol. 304, pp. 82–98. Springer, Cham (2017). https://doi.org/10.1007/978-3-319-69191-6_6

11. Pant, V., Yu, E.: Getting to win-win in industrial collaboration under coopetition: a strategic modeling approach. In: Zdravkovic, J., Grabis, J., Nurcan, S., Stirna, J. (eds.) BIR 2018. LNBIP, vol. 330, pp. 47–66. Springer, Cham (2018). https://doi.org/10.1007/978-3-319-99951-7_4

12. Pant, V., Yu, E.: Generating win-win strategies for software businesses under coopetition: a strategic modeling approach. In: Wnuk, K., Brinkkemper, S. (eds.) ICSOB 2018. LNBIP, vol. 336, pp. 90–107. Springer, Cham (2018). https://doi.org/10.1007/978-3-030-04840-2_7

13. Pant, V., Yu, E.: A modeling approach for getting to win-win in industrial collaboration under strategic coopetition. Complex Syst. Inform. Model. Q. **19**, 19–41 (2019)

14. Dixit, A.K., Nalebuff, B.: The Art of Strategy: A Game Theorist's Guide to Success in Business & Life. WW Norton & Company (2008)

15. López, L., Franch, X., Marco, J.: Specialization in i* strategic rationale diagrams. In: Atzeni, P., Cheung, D., Ram, S. (eds.) ER 2012. LNCS, vol. 7532, pp. 267–281. Springer, Heidelberg (2012). https://doi.org/10.1007/978-3-642-34002-4_21

Modeling and Management of Big Data (MoBiD) 2019

Preface

Alejandro Mate[1] ⓘ, Miguel A. Teruel[2] ⓘ, Juan Trujillo[1] ⓘ,
and Il-Yeol Song[3] ⓘ

[1] Lucentia Research Group, Department of Software and Computing Systems,
University of Alicante, Alicante, Spain
{amate,jtrujillo}@dlsi.ua.es
[2] Lucentia Lab, Av. Pintor Pérez Gil, 16, 03540 Alicante, Spain
mteruel@lucentialab.es
[3] College of Computing and Informatics, Drexel University, Philadelphia, PA
19104, USA
song@drexel.edu

In the last decade, technology has advanced tremendously. Currently, a wide variety of devices, including sensor-enabled smart devices, and all types of wearables, connect to the Internet and power newly connected applications and solutions. On the one hand, the cost of technology has sharply decreased, making it possible for everybody to engage in sensing data. The vast amount of real time information can be accessed across the Internet. Furthermore, some of the environments are just online, like social media, where all the information is in the Cloud. As a result, new words as well as new expressions have appeared such as Big Data, Cloud Computing or Internet of Things, among others.

Due to all of these enormous amounts of data generated, there is an increasing interest in incorporating them, usually referred to as Big Data, into traditional applications. This new era of Big Data requires conceptualization and methods to effectively manage big data and accomplish intended business goals. Thus, the objective of MoBiD'19 is to be an international forum for exchanging ideas on the latest and best proposals for modeling and managing big data in this new data-drive paradigm. The workshop is a forum for researchers and practitioners who are interested in the different facets related to the use of the conceptual modeling approaches for the development of next generation applications based on Big Data. The 8th Workshop on Modeling and Management of Big Data has attracted 9 high quality submissions centered around the modeling and analysis of Big Data and IoT. From these submissions, 4 high quality papers have been selected after a blind review process that involved at least 3 experts from the field for each submission, resulting in an overall acceptance rate of 44%. We also have invited the keynote "From Big Data to Smart Data in the Context of Genomic Information Systems" by Ana León Palacio.

Regarding the accepted papers, the first one presents an empirical study of complex value relations in Hive, using data from open source repositories. The study effectively identifies scarce use of non-atomic values and potential issues in existing schemas and suggests future areas of study. The second paper focuses on conversational data, analyzing the use of Amazon Echo by elderly people. The paper classifies the data collected and shows how precise understanding of the commands is needed for an effective use and longer conversations are not supported at the moment. The third paper analyzes aggressive behavior patterns in residential care facilities. The study applies pattern mining techniques to identify and investigate the factors that contribute most to aggressive behavior from patients. The fourth paper is centered on Industry 4.0. The authors propose an ontology-based method to allow domain experts to adapt information dashboards that extract information from different sensors within factories and visualize only the information that is relevant according to their own particular needs.

Acknowledgments. We would like to express our gratitude to the Program Committee members for their hard work in reviewing papers, the authors for submitting their papers, and the ER 2019 organizing committee for supporting our workshop. We also thank ER 2019 workshop chairs Giancarlo Guizzardi, Frederik Gailly and Rita Suzana Pitangueira Maciel for their direction, guidance and support. MoBiD'19 was organized within the framework of the following project ECLIPSE (RTI2018-094283-B-C32) from the Spanish Ministry of Science, Innovation and Universities.

Facilitating Data Exploration
in Industry 4.0

Idoia Berges⬤, Víctor Julio Ramírez-Durán(✉)⬤, and Arantza Illarramendi⬤

University of the Basque Country UPV/EHU, 20018 Donostia - San Sebastián, Spain
{idoia.berges,victorjulio.ramirez,a.illarramendi}@ehu.eus

Abstract. Industrial Internet of Things (IIoT) devices operating in manufacturing plants allow capturing raw data generated by machines, regarding some indicators of interest. Multi-purpose dashboards facilitate a real-time visualization of all those raw data captured, and thus provide knowledge of each indicator. However, sometimes, domain experts interested in analyzing data belonging to specific domains find those dashboards too rigid. In this paper, we present a proposal that we have developed in a real Industry 4.0 scenario. Due to the customized visualizations that it provides, it enables domain experts to gain a greater value and insights out of the captured data. The core of the system is a new ontology that we have built, where, among others, the sensors used to capture indicators about the performance of a machine have been modeled. This semantic description allows to provide customized representations of the manufacturing machine, query formulation at a higher level of abstraction and customized graphical visualizations of the results.

Keywords: Data exploration · Industry 4.0 · Ontologies

1 Introduction

The deployment of Industry 4.0 approaches faces diverse research and innovation challenges including, among others, the development of tools for visualizing raw data to provide right information, to the right person at the right time.

Regarding visualization, in [16] a survey of visualization technologies tailored for smart manufacturing scenarios can be found. Focusing on visual surveillance of all raw data captured from monitored indicators, many proposals rely on the use of multi-purpose dashboards[1] that allow experts in the manufacturing process to find relevant information. However, sometimes, domain experts of Industry 4.0 scenarios interested in analyzing data belonging to particular domains, find those dashboards too rigid (visualizing metrics that are not relevant for

---

[1] https://logz.io/blog/grafana-vs-kibana/.

Supported by the Spanish Ministry of Economy and Competitiveness (MEC) under Grant No.: FEDER/TIN2016-78011-C4-2-R. The work of Víctor Julio Ramírez is funded by the contract with reference BES-2017-081193.

G. Guizzardi et al. (Eds.): ER 2019 Workshops, LNCS 11787, pp. 125–134, 2019.
https://doi.org/10.1007/978-3-030-34146-6_11

them and extremely complicated to set up new ones), having to create tailored solutions (e.g., the NILM dashboard presented in [1]). As an alternative, we propose the use of Visual Query Systems (VQSs). VQSs use visual representations to depict the domain of interest, and manipulation interaction mechanisms in order to formulate requests to the data sources by means of visual expressions [6]. Thus, the main goal of this paper is to present a semantic-based VQS tailored to Industry 4.0 scenarios. The system facilitates domain experts the data exploration task by allowing them to formulate queries through a digital representation of a machine and dynamically generated forms, which are customized by reasoning with the knowledge available in a domain specific ontology[2]. The use of an ontology-based approach instead of a database-based one allows taking advantage of the reuse, reasoning and interoperability capabilities [14].

The proposed system provides the following benefits in the data exploration process: **1. Possibility of querying the monitored data at a higher level of abstraction**. The user selects the sensors by clicking on them at the digital representation of the machine and inputs the desired constraints (e.g date, hour, limits of values, aggregation functions) in a form. Those forms are dynamically customized by reasoning with the annotated knowledge about the characteristics of the sensors that have been selected. **2. Possibility of incorporating on-the-fly semantic annotations in the visualization of results**. The results obtained for the queries are shown using tailored graphical representations customized according to the nature of the data domain. **3. Possibility of providing a customized visualization of a manufacturing machine**. Not all the machines of the same type (e.g. extruders) incorporate the same type of sensors. Visualizing a machine with its specific sensors, and thus, providing customized representations of machines is possible by consulting the ontology where the main components of the machine and its sensors have been described.

In the rest of this paper we present first some related works regarding ontologies in the manufacturing field and visual query systems. Next, we introduce a brief overview about the considered context. Then, we show briefly how the sensors that capture indicators values are described in the built ontology. Next, we present two functionalities provided by the proposed system: insertion of data and querying of data. We finish with some conclusions.

2   Related Work

In this section we revise works that are related with two main pillars of the proposal, visual query systems and ontologies in the Industry 4.0 scenario.

Visual Query Systems have been used for querying databases [6], for retrieving data from the Web [11], and also for exploring semantic web data e.g. Rhizomer [5]. However, few proposals can be found in the literature that provide visual query systems for industrial scenarios and even less that provide

---

[2] In this paper the term *ontology* refers to the knowledge base composed of the conceptual level (i.e., axioms for classes and properties) and the instance level (i.e., assertions about individuals).

semantic-based visual query systems. Among those last type of systems we highlight OptiqueVQS [15], a system that exploits ontology projection techniques to enable graph-based navigation over an ontology during query construction. In our case, we use a form-based approach but attached to a digital representation, described in an ontology, to facilitate querying at a higher level of abstraction. Moreover, the main differences with our proposal are: (1) OptiqueVQS shows all the classes defined in the loaded domain ontology. This forces domain experts to gather experience in the ontology before using the system. Our proposal focuses in a specific domain ontology, and thus presents an intuitive environment for those experts, facilitating the query formulation. (2) OptiqueVQS lacks of different result visualizations. Our proposal presents different visualizations of the results of the queries depending on the nature and format of the data.

Furthermore, ontologies are being used in different manufacturing scenarios ([10,12]). For example, the Manufacturing Service Description Language (MSDL) ontology was defined to provide a common semantic model for describing manufacturing services [4]. However, due to a lack of sound descriptions of manufacturing machines that happen to be accessible, interoperable, and reusable we developed an ontology called *ExtruOnt*[3] for providing detailed descriptions of a real manufacturing machine, in particular, an extruder[4].

3   Overview

The proposal presented in this paper has been developed using data captured from a manufacturing process associated to an extruder machine. Some description of the captured time-series data are described in Table 1.

Table 1. Example of the amount of data collected by the sensors of an average extruder machine in one day under normal conditions.

Sensor type/class	Description	Count	# records[a]	Disk size[b]
ResistorOnOffSensor	Observes whether a resistor is on or off	1	86,400	12.85
FanOnOffSensor	Observes whether a fan is on or off	1	86,400	12.85
TemperatureSensor	Captures the temperature	10	864,000	128.54
MotorConsumptionSensor	Captures the consumption of the motor	1	86,400	12.85
SpeedSensor	Captures the speed of the rotational parts	2	172,800	25.71
PressureSensor	Captures the pressure in the extruder	1	86,400	12.85
MeltingTemperatureSensor	Captures the melting temperature	1	86,400	12.85
BottlesPerShiftSensor	Captures the number of bottles in a shift	4	345,600	51.42
Others	Other sensors in the extruder	23	1,987,200	295.64
	Total	44	3,801,600	565.56

[a]One record per second.
[b]In megabytes, using a Virtuoso quad store due to the performance results shown in [3].

---

[3] http://bdi.si.ehu.es/bdi/ontologies/ExtruOnt/ExtruOnt.
[4] A machine that performs the extrusion process, in which some material is forced through a series of dies in order to create a desired shape.

Even though semantic technologies were not created for Big Data, we have opted to use them in our proposal, as the use of semantic technologies in Big Data challenges has been proved to solve many limitations caused by the use of traditional solutions [2]. The developed *ExtruOnt* ontology contains classes and properties for expressing descriptions about the features of a machine, such as its components and characteristics, their spatial connections and finally the sensors used to capture indicators about the performance of that type of machine. Moreover, we establish mappings between our ontology and SAREF4INMA [7] so that interoperability with standards can be achieved through it.

4   Sensors Modeling

In this paper, we focus only on one of the *ExtruOnt* modules named in the previous section. This contains both specific terms regarding sensors (e.g `Pressure Sensor`) used to capture observations (e.g `DoubleValueObservation`), and terms imported from other well-known ontologies, such as SOSA/SSN [9] and OM [13] in order to favor its interoperability. We extend the classes `Sensor`, `Observation` and `ObservableProperty` of the SOSA/SSN ontology to describe more accurately the nuances of the sensors, observations and properties of our domain, and therefore allowing to provide the most suitable graphical representation.

The main class `Sensor` is a specialization of `sosa:Sensor` where two new properties have been included: `indicatorId` (sensor identifier) and `sensorName` (name of the sensor). In our scenario, sensors capture either true/false data or numerical data. Thus, two subclasses of `Sensor` have been defined to represent this type of information: `BooleanSensor` and `DoubleValueSensor` respectively. Moreover, these subclasses have been further specialized in order to represent the specific sensors needed to monitor an extruder (see Table 1). Classes `ResistorOnOffSensor` and `FanOnOffSensor` are subclasses of `BooleanSensor`, while the remaining classes are subclasses of `DoubleValueSensor`.

For each type of sensor its observable property is indicated by the property `sosa:observes`. For example, the observable property of a `FeedRateSensor` is the `Speed` individual imported from OM. Moreover, for each subclass of `BooleanSensor` the true/false meaning of the observed property can be indicated by properties `meaningState1` and `meaningState0` respectively. For instance, the values of properties `meaningState1` and `meaningState0` in a `ResistorOnOff Sensor` are ``On'' and ``Off'', which indicates that when the sensor registers the value *true* it means that the sensor is on and vice-versa. For each subclass of `DoubleValueSensor`, the expected range of the values captured by these sensors under normal conditions has been specified by properties `minValue` and `maxValue`. This range will help to identify possible outliers in the captured data. Other properties regarding capabilities of the sensors, such as the feasible measurement range captured by the sensor, are defined using properties from SOSA/SSN. The units of measure have been imported from OM. Finally, for each type of sensor an axiom has been added which constrains the type of observations made by the sensor through property `sosa:madeObservation`. For each observation its value and timestamp are indicated by properties `sosa:hasSimpleResult` and `sosa:resultTime`. Two subclasses of `Observation` have been defined, depending on the type of value of the observation: `BooleanObservation` and `DoubleValueObservation`. In Fig. 1 an excerpt of the module can be found. For legibility reasons, only the most important properties and classes, and two specific types of sensors (`ResistorOnOffSensor` and `MotorConsumptionSensor`) are fully pictured.

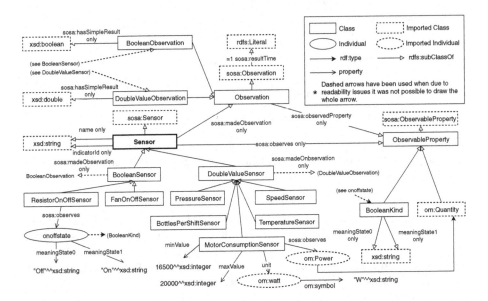

Fig. 1. Excerpt of the ontology showing the main classes and properties.

5   The Semantic-Based Query System

The system provides two functionalities: insertion and querying of data. In order to provide these functionalities, the architecture includes a Virtuoso service[5]. Virtuoso contains a quad store where data are placed after insertion and provides a SPARQL[6] endpoint to access that quad store. Through a series of parsers and an intermediate service, the users' queries are executed against the Virtuoso service, and the results are shown in the user interface in a customized way.

5.1   Insert Data

The original data in CSV format is annotated using the terms in the ontology, converted to a set of RDF triples and stored in the quad store by means of

---

[5] https://virtuoso.openlinksw.com/.
[6] https://www.w3.org/TR/sparql11-query/.

SPARQL insert queries. The original data contains a pair [value, timestamp] for each of the observations and, for each pair, an instance of `Observation` is created, indicating the value and its timestamp, along with the type of data, and the sensor. For example let us assume that sensor `sensor79PWN7` is an instance of class `MotorConsumptionSensor` (Fig. 2a) that according to the CSV has made the observation [18710, 2018-03-22T19:21:33.559Z]. Then, the annotations in Fig. 2b are generated, where `obs1` refers to the newly created observation.

```
(a)   :sensor79PWN7 rdf:type :MotorConsumptionSensor .

(b)   :sensor79PWN7 sosa:madeObservation :obs1 .
      :obs1 sosa:hasSimpleResult "18710"^^xsd:double ;
            sosa:resultTime "2018-03-22T19:21:33.559Z"^^xsd:dateTime .

(c)   :obs1 rdf:type :DoubleValueObservation .
      :sensor79PWN7 sosa:observes om:Power ;
                          :minValue "16500"^^xsd:double ;
                          :maxValue "20000"^^xsd:double ;
                          :unit om:watt .
      om:watt om:symbol "W"^^xsd:string .
```

Fig. 2. (a) Declaration of `sensor79PWN7` as an instance of `MotorConsumptionSensor`. (b) Example of the triples generated when annotating and observation. (c) Some of the triples that can be inferred.

Moreover, due to the knowledge available in the ontology, additional information that does not appear in the CSV file is now related to the observation (Fig. 2c). Since `obs1` was made by `MotorConsumptionSensor sensor79PWN7`, which is a `DoubleValueSensor` that makes `DoubleValueObservations`, `obs1` can be classified as a `DoubleValueObservation`. Moreover, due to the description of the sensor, it is possible to identify that: (1) `obs1` is an observation of `om:Power`, (2) the value of the observation complies with the expected range of values (between 16500 and 20000) for the observations of this type of sensor, (3) the unit of the observation is `om:watt` and (4) the symbol to represent watts is ''W''.

5.2   Query Data

In order to perform the queries, the user is presented with a dynamically generated picture of the extruder, which consists on a background image of the machine and a top layer where its sensors are placed. The background image is selected depending on the number of zones of the extruder (e.g 4-zone-extruder, 5-zone-extruder), which can be obtained from the annotations of the machine in the ontology using a SPARQL query. For creating the top layer, another SPARQL query is asked to obtain information about the sensors that are deployed in the machine, along with their type and deployment data. Both SPARQL queries have been implemented within the system and are transparent to the user. Then, clickable bullets representing the sensors, as well as icons that specify their type, are placed in the aforementioned top layer. By using this approach it is possible to provide customized visualizations of multiple extruders, as stated in the third benefit presented in Sect. 1. For example, in Fig. 3a the representation of a specific 4-zone-extruder is shown. In this case, 15 sensors for different indicators have been placed dynamically: four `TemperatureSensors`, three `ResistorOnOffSensors`, three `FanOnOffSensors`, a `SpeedSensor`, a `MotorConsumptionSensor`, a `PressureSensor`, a `Melting TemperatureSensor` and a `BottlesPerShiftSensor`.

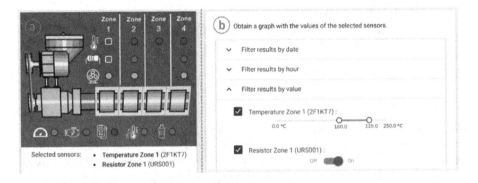

Fig. 3. User interface for querying about the data stored in the quad store.

Information Queries. Information queries are used to ask for information about the observations of specific sensors. The user selects the sensors by clicking on them and inputs the desired constraints (e.g date, hour, limits of values, aggregation functions) in a form that is dynamically generated depending on the characteristics of the sensors that have been selected. For example, if sensor 2F1KT7 is selected, the annotations made about it indicate that it is a `TemperatureSensor`, and by reasoning that is also a `DoubleValueSensor`, meaning that it records numerical values. Thus, a slider is shown which allows to restrict the values of the retrieved information to the user's desired range. Moreover, since properties `minValue` and `maxValue` indicate that the usual range for that type of sensor is [160.0, 220.0] and that the unit is `om:degreeCelsius`, the slider has been customized so that values 160.0 °C and 220.0 °C are highlighted (see Fig. 3b), and its limits have been set to the feasible measurement range of the sensor, which in this case is [0.0, 250.0].

Likewise, if sensor URS001 is selected, the annotations indicate that it is a `ResistorOnOffSensor` (and therefore a `BooleanSensor`) and that the true/false values indicate whether the sensor is activated or not. This information is reflected by using an on/off switch. The simplicity of the used design helps users to formulate queries with a high level of abstraction as stated in the first benefit in Sect. 1. Once the selection has been made, a SPARQL query is generated and executed against the stored data. Figure 4 shows an example of such a query, where the user wants to retrieve information about the observations made by sensor 2F1KT7 between 20th and 22nd March 2018 with value between 170 and 200. The average answer times obtained for this query type were 1.4 and 4.35 s for a time-storage-window of one day and one week respectively.

```
prefix :<http://bdi.si.ehu.es/bdi/ontologies/ExtruOnt/Instances#>
prefix sosa: <http://www.w3.org/ns/sosa/>
prefix xsd: <http://www.w3.org/2001/XMLSchema#>
select ?resultValue ?resultTime
where {
   :sensor2F1KT7 sosa:madeObservation ?obs .
   ?obs sosa:hasSimpleResult ?resultValue ;
        sosa:resultTime ?resultTime .
   filter(?resultValue >= "170"^^xsd:double && ?resultValue <= "200"^^xsd:double) .
   filter((xsd:dateTime(?resultTime) >= "2018-03-20T00:00:00.000Z"^^xsd:dateTime) &&
          (xsd:dateTime(?resultTime) <= "2018-03-22T23:59:59.999Z"^^xsd:dateTime))
} order by asc(?resultTime)
```

Fig. 4. SPARQL query example

Relation Queries. Relation queries are used to ask for the observations made by some specific sensors when certain values hold in the observations made at the same timestamp by some other sensors. First, the user selects all the sensors that take part in the relation. Then they specify which are the sensors whose values they want to ask for, meaning that the remaining selected sensors are the ones whose values are fixed. The user indicates the fixed value for these sensors, which can be a numerical or boolean value (depending on the type of sensor), or the minimum, maximum or average value registered by the sensor in the specified time range. Once again, the form to create the queries is generated dynamically, based on the selected sensors and the information available about them in the ontology. Average answer times of 1.37 and 2.81 s were observed for a time-storage-window of one day and one week respectively.

5.3   Visualization of Results

In order to select the most suitable representation depending on the nature of the query and the sensors involved, a visualization module has been developed in the ontology, where several recommendations for visualization have been described. As an alternative, In [8] can be seen an alternative approach to automate data visualization in Big Data analytics but following a model-driven approach.

In Fig. 5 an excerpt of the module can be found with one example of recommendation. More precisely, recommendation riq07 indicates that when the query is an informationQuery and the selected sensor is a BottlesPerShift Sensor, then the preferred chart is a pie chart, but bar charts and time-series plots are also allowed. In Fig. 6a a time-series visualization is used for an information query about temperature sensor 2F1KT7. Top and bottom outlier lines indicate the expected maximum and minimum values for that sensor. The annotations made in the data and the descriptions in the ontology have been used to generate a semantically enriched customization of the chart, as noted in the second benefit explained in Sect. 1. Since sensor 2F1KT7 is a TemperatureSensor

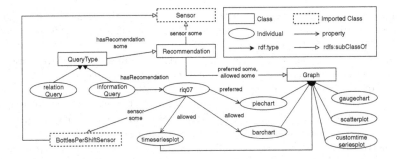

Fig. 5. Excerpt of the visualization module of the ontology.

that captures values in Celsius degrees, symbol °C is indicated. Figure 6b shows the aforementioned pie chart for a sensor of type `BottlesPerShiftSensor`, indicating the number of bottles and percentage of the total made each day.

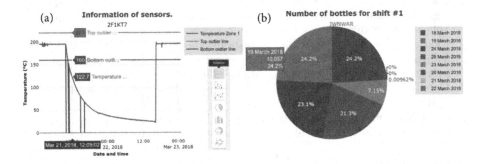

Fig. 6. Examples of visualizations of results.

6   Conclusion

The interest of facilitating data exploration in Industry 4.0 scenarios has been widely acknowledged. Visualization of captured time-series data provides increasing knowledge about the indicators used in the monitoring of machines. In this paper we have presented a semantic-based visual query system that enables domain experts to formulate queries over a customized representation of the machine, and that provides a tailor-made visualization of the results depending on their nature. The whole process is supported by an underlying ontology where the main components of the machine and its sensors have been described.

References

1. Aboulian, A., et al.: Nilm dashboard: a power system monitor for electromechanical equipment diagnostics. IEEE Trans. Ind. Inform. **15**(3), 1405–1414 (2019)

2. Addlesee, A.: Tackling big data challenges with linked data (2018). https://medium.com/wallscope/tackling-big-data-challenges-with-linked-data-278b0761a6de

3. Addlesee, A.: Comparison of linked data triplestores: Developing the methodology (2019). https://medium.com/wallscope/comparison-of-linked-data-triplestores-developing-the-methodology-e87771cb3011

4. Ameri, F., Dutta, D.: An upper ontology for manufacturing service description. In: International Design Engineering Technical Conferences and Computers and Information in Engineering Conference, vol. 3, pp. 651–661 (2006)

5. Brunetti, J.M., García, R., Auer, S.: From overview to facets and pivoting for interactive exploration of semantic web data. Int. J. Semant. Web Inf. Syst. 9(1), 1–20 (2013)

6. Catarci, T., Costabile, M.F., Levialdi, S., Batini, C.: Visual query systems for databases. J. Vis. Lang. Comput. 8(2), 215–260 (1997)

7. ETSI: SmartM2M; SAREF extension investigation; requirements for industry and manufacturing domains. Technical specification TS 103 507 V1.1.1, ETSI (2018)

8. Golfarelli, M., Rizzi, S.: A model-driven approach to automate data visualization in big data analytics. Inf. Vis. (2019). https://doi.org/10.1177/1473871619858933

9. Haller, A., et al.: The modular ssn ontology: a joint W3C and ogc standard specifying the semantics of sensors, observations, sampling, and actuation. Semant. Web 10(1), 9–32 (2019)

10. Kharlamov, E., et al.: Capturing industrial information models with ontologies and constraints. In: International Semantic Web Conference (2) 2016, pp. 325–343. https://doi.org/10.1007/978-3-319-46547-0_30

11. Lloret-Gazo, J.: A survey on visual query systems in the web era (extended version). CoRR abs/1708.00192 (2017). http://arxiv.org/abs/1708.00192

12. Negri, E., Fumagalli, L., Garetti, M., Tanca, L.: Requirements and languages for the semantic representation of manufacturing systems. Comput. Ind. 81(C), 55–66 (2016)

13. Rijgersberg, H., van Assem, M., Top, J.: Ontology of units of measure and related concepts. Semant. Web 4(1), 3–13 (2013)

14. Sir, M., Bradac, Z., Fiedler, P.: Ontology versus database. IFACPapersOnLine 48(4), 220–225 (2015)

15. Soylu, A., et al.: OptiqueVQS: a visual query system over ontologies for industry. Semant. Web 9(5), 627–660 (2018)

16. Zhou, F., et al.: A survey of visualization for smart manufacturing. J. Vis. 22(2), 419–435 (2019)

Towards Understanding Aggressive Behavior in Residential Care Facilities Using Process Mining

Jelmer Koorn[1]([⊠]), Xixi Lu[1], Henrik Leopold[2,3], and Hajo A. Reijers[1]

[1] Utrecht University, Utrecht, The Netherlands
{j.j.koorn,x.lu,h.a.reijers}@uu.nl
[2] Kühne Logistics University, Hamburg, Germany
henrik.leopold@the-klu.org
[3] Hasso Plattner Institute, University of Potsdam, Potsdam, Germany

Abstract. People with intellectual disabilities often live in residential care facilities that aim to provide their clients with the best possible quality of life. Aggressive behavior forms a threat to not only the quality of life of the clients, but also the safety of the staff. This study aims to uncover the dynamics underlying the evolution of aggressive behavior in people with intellectual disabilities. We take a process mining approach to analyze patterns of aggressive behavior. More specifically, we analyze data from 1,115 clients from a Dutch residential care facility over a period of three years. Our results show that there are two different groups of cases: those exclusively showing the same type of aggressive behavior and those who show mixed types of aggressive behavior. What stands out is that physical aggression towards other people plays a key role in the patterns of aggressive behavior. The results were validated with a behavioral expert from the care organization.

Keywords: Process mining · Aggressive behavior · Healthcare

1 Introduction

Many people with intellectual disabilities live in residential care facilities, where they can get support for their daily needs. A central goal of these facilities is to make sure that their clients have an appropriate quality of life. While this primarily means the care facilities attend to the needs of their clients, it also requires them to deal with undesired behavior of clients, such as aggression.

Aggression is a complex phenomenon and has many facets. It involves physical aggression towards other people, verbal aggression, physical aggression towards objects, self-injurious behavior, and sexually inappropriate behavior [5]. In general, aggressive behavior is considered a threat to both staff and clients. Studies have shown that staff members who deal with aggressive behavior are more likely to experience stress and even have burnouts [7,8,13]. What is more, aggressors can be met with severe restrictive measures (e.g., seclusion) as well as

© Springer Nature Switzerland AG 2019
G. Guizzardi et al. (Eds.): ER 2019 Workshops, LNCS 11787, pp. 135–145, 2019.
https://doi.org/10.1007/978-3-030-34146-6_12

suffer physical injuries as a consequence of their aggressive behavior [3,14,18]. Hence, there is a desire to minimize the impact of aggression on staff and clients and, ultimately, prevent aggression incidents from happening altogether.

To do so, many researchers have investigated which factors may contribute to aggressive behavior. By mostly focusing on client characteristics, they found links to factors such as: age [4,19], severity of intellectual disability [4,5], and gender [4,5]. However, some researchers argue that focusing on client characteristics is too limited [12]. More recent research has followed up on this and started investigating how characteristics from the aggression incident itself, such as time, location, and trigger, can help to understand aggressive behavior [15]. In that light, observational data describing aggression incidents are increasingly digitally recorded in Information Systems.

Nevertheless, what all these studies have in common is that they take a static perspective. Due to the increasing digitization of behavioral data, new opportunities emerge to analyze this phenomenon from new dynamic perspectives. That is, to consider the changes in behavior of clients over time rather than for a single incident or client. Such a perspective has the potential to uncover, for instance, how aggression evolves over time and whether different aggression incidents are related. Process mining is such an emerging field that provides techniques to support the analyses of data from a causal perspective [20].

Therefore, we use this paper to study aggression incidents using the technology of process mining. We analyze data from 1,115 clients from a Dutch residential care facility over a time period of three years. We find that, on a high level, we can distinguish between cases exclusively showing the same type of aggressive behavior and cases showing a variety of types of aggressive behavior. Moreover, we find that although the division into both groups is useful, the repetition of the same type of aggressive behavior is the most frequently observed behavior. Lastly, physical aggression towards other people plays a key role as it occurs most often and usually follows after any other type of aggressive behavior.

The rest of the paper is organized as follows. First, the current status of process mining in healthcare is discussed in Sect. 2. Then, Sect. 3 provides a detailed description of the methodology of this paper. This is followed by Sect. 4 describing the results of the analyses. In Sect. 5 we discuss these results and the limitations of this study. Finally, in Sect. 6 the conclusions are presented.

2   Process Mining in Healthcare

Process mining is a family of data analysis techniques that aims to discover, monitor, and improve organizational processes by analyzing data from so-called event logs [20]. These event logs are generated by various information systems that are used in organizations and, therefore, capture how organizational processes are actually executed. Process mining has been applied in various healthcare settings [17]. Among others, process mining has been used to analyze patient care processes [6,9], dentistry processes [1,10], and cancer treatment processes [2].

Table 1. A snippet of the raw data as an example

Client ID	Timestamp	Timeslot	Target	Means	Consequences
L002eR	04/09/2015	16:00–17:00	Themselves	Teeth	Visible injuries
L002eR	11/09/2015	17:00–18:00	Themselves	Hands	Visible injuries
LHZ02	03/05/2016	11:00–12:00	Staff member	Hands	Pain 5 min
LHZ02	22/05/2016	10:00–11:00	Objects	Hands	Damage to property
LH88E3	26/12/2016	19:00–20:00	Staff member	Verbal	Felt threatened
H030E	02/02/2017	14:00–15:00	Objects	Feet	Damage to property

Despite the general potential of process mining in healthcare, the application of process mining in this domain is often associated with particular challenges [11]. One of the most common issues in this context is the absence of accurate timestamps. Healthcare information systems often only capture the day of an activity and not the exact point of time. As a result, the exact order of certain activities remains unclear. Another issue is the absence of a clear start and end point of a process. Often, the data entries for a single patient span several years. This, however, does not mean that all this data relates to the same treatment process. It could be that the patient received several treatments at the same time or had a recurrence after a couple of years. We have encountered both issues, and the steps taken to handle these issues are discussed in the following section.

3   Methodology

3.1   Data Extraction and Overview

For our paper, we acquired a data set from a Dutch healthcare organization that operates 54 residential care facilities in the Netherlands. It specializes in providing care for people with mild intellectual disabilities (IQ between 50 and 70), borderline intellectual functioning (IQ between 70 and 85), co-occurring psychiatric disorders, and physical disabilities. The total number of clients this organizations cares for is about 3,000 (the exact numbers varies over the time period we consider). Our data set covers all aggression incidents reported on all wards starting from the 1st of January 2015 until the 31st of December 2017. The total number of incidents in our data set is 21,706.

Table 1 shows an extract of the raw data we obtained. We can see that each entry about an aggression incident includes: a reference to the aggressor (client ID), the day (timestamp), an approximate point of time (timeslot), information about the target (e.g. objects), the means (e.g. hands), and the consequences (e.g. pain 5 min).

In order to apply process mining to our data set, a number of requirements need to be met. The starting point of every process mining analysis is a so-called event log. These event logs must contain at least three specific attributes:

(1) a unique case identifier (case ID), (2) an activity description, and (3) an appropriate timestamp. As illustrated by the extract shown in Table 1, the raw data set does not fulfill these criteria. Among others, a case ID is missing (note that a client ID is not a case ID since a single client might be associated with several cases) and there is no clear notion of an activity. Against this background, our methodology includes several preparatory steps represented in Fig. 1. The first step is described above in the section *Data Extraction and Overview*.

Fig. 1. Methodology

3.2   Event Log Creation

The second step was the creation of an event log that is suitable for a process mining analysis. To obtain such an event log, we had to introduce (1) a suitable activity attribute, (2) an appropriate case ID, and (3) a proper timestamp. Table 2 shows an extract of the final event log.

Activity Design. In order to introduce a suitable activity attribute, we designed a simple algorithm that categorized each incident into one out of four aggression categories: physical aggression towards other people (PP), self-injurious behavior (SIB), physical aggression towards objects (PO), and verbal aggression (VA). Due to privacy reasons we did not include data on sexually inappropriate behavior. We designed the algorithm using a rulebook approach based on [16]. The rules were adjusted based on the input from experts of the healthcare organization we collaborated with. It is important to note that a single incident can be associated with multiple types of aggressive behavior. In such cases only the most severe type of aggressive behavior is considered. This is in accordance with previous literature [16], who proposed a hierarchy of the severity of aggressive behavior. The four categories we consider are mentioned in their order of severity, that is, PP is most severe and VA is the least.

Case ID Design. Choosing the client ID as case ID may result in a process that spans over three years. To illustrate that this may lead to a distorted view on the data, consider the example of two clients. Client 1 has an SIB incident in early January 2015 and another in late December 2017. Client two has an SIB incident in early May 2016 and another in late May 2016. If the client ID is chosen as case ID, both clients would be considered to show the same pattern of aggressive behavior, although in the former case it is obviously hard to argue that the two incidents are related.

Based on a validation with experts, we decided to slice the data for each client in three ways: traces of 24 h, seven days, and one month. To this end, we created a case ID by combining the client ID with the year, month, week, and hour values from the timestamp. Thus, for example, one specific case for the client LHZ02 would be the case LHZ02-2015-01 including all incidents from January 2015. We found similar patterns using all three forms of data slicing. Thus, for consistency purposes we present our results on the basis of the month level.

Table 2. A snippet of the event log

Case ID	Activity	Timestamp
L002eR-2015-09	Auto mutilation (SIB)	04-09-2015 16:00
L002eR-2015-09	Auto mutilation (SIB)	11-09-2015 17:00
LHZ02-2016-05	Physical aggression towards others (PP)	03-05-2016 11:00
LHZ02-2016-05	Physical aggression towards objects (PO)	22-05-2016 10:00
LH88E3-2016-12	Verbal aggression (VA)	26-12-2016 19:00
H030E-2017-02	Physical aggression towards objects (PO)	02-02-2017 14:00

Timestamp Design. In our raw data set, the date (dd-mm-yyyy) of an incident was provided. To make the timestamp more precise we added available data about the timeslot and combined both into a single timestamp.

3.3   Data Cleaning and Filtering

The event log obtained after the preparatory steps outlined above contains a total of 21,706 aggression incidents related to 1,115 clients or 8,557 cases (client-months). To be able to detect relevant patterns using process mining, we applied three specific filters: (1) an event filter, (2) a time filter, and (3) a recurrence filter. After applying all three filters our final sample size used for process mining contained 16,794 incidents (78.2% of the total sample) spread over 822 clients included in 4,149 cases (48% of the total sample).

The *event filter* removed all incidents for which no aggression incident type could be determined (N = 322). The *time filter* was applied to exclude cases for which erroneous data was recorded for the considered time frame from 2015 to 2017 (N = 20). Finally, we applied a *recurrence filter* to exclude all cases that only contained one single activity (N = 4570). While this had a considerable impact, our analysis aimed to discover behavioral patterns. In order to detect a pattern at least two activities need to be included in a case.

3.4 Pattern Discovery

To discover relevant patterns, we used the commercial process mining tool Disco[1]. After we completed the exploratory analysis, it became clear that the data could be split into two large groups: cases that exclusively contain the same type of aggressive behavior (e.g., case L002eR-2015-09 in Table 2), and cases that contain a mix of aggressive behavior types (e.g., case LHZ02-2016-05 in Table 2). Based on this insight, we analyzed the patterns for each of these groups separately.

More specifically, we analyzed the data of each group from three angles: frequency, time, and variation. *Frequency* relates to the visual patterns and captures information about the number of incidents and transitions. *Time* captures details regarding duration between incidents. *Variation* looks at the various traces (i.e., specific orders of incidents) of which the patterns consist. When performing the analyses, we looked at both the grander schemes of all types of aggression combined per group of behavior as well as at each individual type of aggression within each group of behavior.

Finally, to make sure our understanding of the discovered patterns is correct, we validated our results with a behavioral expert from the care organization.

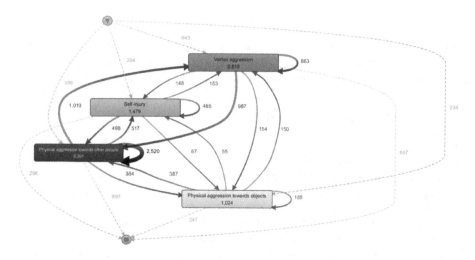

Fig. 2. The directly follows graph for the mixed behavior group, for a detailed account regarding the way this graph should be interpreted please refer to [20, p. 223].

---

[1] https://fluxicon.com/disco/.

4 Results

4.1 Mixed Behavior

The patterns resulting from all cases containing at least two types of aggressive behavior are summarized in Fig. 2. It shows the frequency of occurrence of each type of aggressive behavior as well as the transition frequencies (see respective arc label). In total, Fig. 2 captures 2,170 cases and 10,713 incidents.

Figure 2 illustrates that there are two types of aggressive behavior that are relatively frequent: physical aggression against other people (PP) and verbal aggression (VA). The other two types of aggression (physical aggression towards objects (PO) and self-injurious behavior (SIB)) account for less than 25% of all incidents. Furthermore, we can see that around half the cases start or end with an incident of PP. This indicates that PP serves as both enabler of and amplifier to other types of aggression.

Table 3. Relative transition frequencies

	VA	PP	PO	SIB
VA	**62.0%**	29.7%	4.3%	4.0%
PP	12.0%	**76.4%**	4.8%	6.8%
PO	15.9%	**44.1%**	35.2%	4.9%
SIB	7.2%	26.3%	3.0%	**63.5%**

Table 3 provides further insights into the underlying patterns by showing the relative transition frequencies (i.e. in how many percent of the cases we observe a transition from one type of behavior to another). The bold figures indicate the most frequent transitions and the underlined figures the second most frequent transitions for each type. The data allows for four interesting observations. First, the repetition of the same type of aggressive behavior is the most frequent pattern (see VA-VA, PP-PP, and SIB-SIB). Second, focusing on patterns without repetition, the most frequent transition is to PP (see VA-PP and SIB-PP). Third, PO shows the reverse of both previous points, its most frequent transition is to PP and its second most frequent transition is to itself (PO-PO). Fourth, PO and SIB are rarely followed by other types of aggressive behavior besides a repetition of the same behavior or a transition to PP.

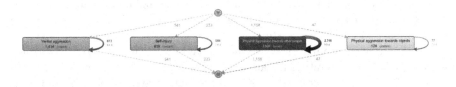

Fig. 3. The directly follows graph for the homogeneous behavior group.

4.2 Homogeneous Behavior

The results for the group with homogeneous behavior is summarized in Fig. 3. It shows the frequency of occurrence of each type of aggressive behavior as well as the transition frequencies (see respective arc label). In total, Fig. 3 captures 1,979 cases and 5,388 incidents.

The numbers in Fig. 3 show that PP is the most frequent type of repetitive behavior (60%) followed by VA (25%). Only about 10% of the incidents relate to SIB and 4% to PO incidents. The same distribution holds when we are looking at the number of cases rather than the number of incidents.

Looking into the average number of incidents per month allows for further insights. Interestingly, this number varies per type of aggression: SIB (3.5 incidents) and PO (3.4 incidents) have a higher average than PP and VA (both 2.6 incidents). In addition, when we consider the aspect of time, we observe that the median duration between two incidents is considerably longer for PO. Here the median between two PO incidents is the longest with 6 days, whereas the median for PP and VA is 4 days and SIB is 3 days. This shows that there is a negative relation between the average number of incidents per month and the median duration between two incidents. In other words, the higher the average number of incidents per month, the shorter the median duration between two incidents. However, PO is an exception to this since the average number of incidents per month is on the high end, but the median number of days between two incidents is high as well.

5   Discussion

Taking a holistic view at the results from our analysis, we identify three findings: (1) repetition of the same type of behavior occurs most frequently, (2) PP plays a central role, and (3) PO exhibits deviating patterns.

First, we see that *repeating* the same type of aggressive behavior is the most frequently observed transition between two incidents. Although the number of cases included in the mixed and in the homogeneous group are roughly equal, we can see that the most observed behavior within the mixed group is still a repetition of the same type of behavior. Through the validation with a behavioral expert we found that this can be explained by the fact that the behavior of clients is usually determined by their habits. As such, it is unexpected for clients to change their behavior. However, most clients also follow behavioral adaptation treatments aimed at changing this behavior. In this light, it is unexpected to see such a high percentage of repeating behavior. It might indicate that the treatments are often not successful.

Second, in both groups of aggressive behavior, PP is the most frequently observed behavior accounting for around 60% of the total number of incidents. Besides being the most frequently observed type of aggressive behavior, in Fig. 2, we see that PP in a mixed behavior environment is the epicenter of the system. There is relatively little interaction among the other forms of aggressive behavior except when accommodated through PP. Through the expert validation we found that one possible explanation is that when an aggressive incident occurs, a nurse usually intervenes, thereby moving the target of aggression towards him/herself.

Third, PO represents an exception to the general patterns observed in both mixed and homogeneous behavior groups. We observed that cases showing this type of aggression follow a different evolution of behavior compared to the other types of aggression. We see for example that the pattern PO-PO is not as frequently observed as with the other types of aggression. In addition, if it is observed, the time in between two incidents is relatively long. This is interesting as it could indicate that PO is a fundamentally different type of aggression compared to the other types of aggression.

It is important to note that our findings are subject to a number of limitations. More specifically, we identify two main limitations to this study. First, our data set is not representative in a statistical sense. While our data set contains a considerable number of patients and incidents, we cannot extrapolate our findings to other care facilities. Second, our data set may contain different kinds of biases due to manual reporting. For example, nurses may report incidents in bulk, meaning multiple incidents are included in a single report at the end of the day or week in order to reduce administrative load. Although we know that this was not used very frequently, the existing bulk reports are counted as a single incident as there is no indication about how many incidents are reported in one bulk report. Another reporting bias relates to VA, SIB, and PO. From the discussion with experts we learned that these incidents are sometimes reported less frequently since they are perceived as less severe by staff.

6   Conclusion

Research looking into the aggressive behavior in clients with intellectual disabilities has exclusively investigated this phenomenon from a static perspective. In this paper we advanced on this by using a process mining approach to look into the evolution of aggressive behavior in clients with intellectual disabilities. This enabled us to obtain insights into the relations among different types of aggression and to infer patterns of aggressive behavior. We found that there are mainly two groups of clients: those with homogeneous and those with mixed aggressive behavior. Among others, we found that repetitive behavior is the most frequently observed behavior. In addition, results show that physical aggression towards other people plays a central role in a majority of the behavioral patterns.

With these insights, this research contributed to a better understanding of aggressive behavior aiding further development in this field. From a practitioner point of view, the discovered patterns can aid the development of prevention and treatment techniques. Despite the interesting findings, we are aware of the limitations of our study. Therefore, we plan to follow up on our work by further developing insights into the discovered patterns. We aim to identify causal relations between the static characteristics of incidents and the behavioral patterns, thereby uncovering more refined patterns of aggression. Furthermore, we plan to include additional care facilities to increase the external validity of our results.

Acknowledgment. This research was supported by the NWO TACTICS project (628.011.004) and Lunet Zorg in the Netherlands. We would also like to thank the experts from the Lunet Zorg for their extremely valuable assistance and feedback in the evaluation.

References

1. Bakhshandeh, M., Schunselaar, D.M., Leopold, H., Reijers, H.A.: Predicting treatment repetitions in the implant denture therapy process. In: 2017 IEEE International Conference on Big Data (Big Data), pp. 1259–1264. IEEE (2017)
2. Binder, M., et al.: On analyzing process compliance in skin cancer treatment: an experience report from the evidence-based medical compliance cluster (EBMC^2). In: Ralyté, J., Franch, X., Brinkkemper, S., Wrycza, S. (eds.) CAiSE 2012. LNCS, vol. 7328, pp. 398–413. Springer, Heidelberg (2012). https://doi.org/10.1007/978-3-642-31095-9_26
3. van den Bogaard, K.J., Nijman, H.L., Palmstierna, T., Embregts, P.J.: Characteristics of aggressive behavior in people with mild to borderline intellectual disability and co-occurring psychopathology. J. Ment. Health Res. Intellect. Disabil. **11**(2), 124–142 (2018)
4. Cooper, S.A., et al.: Adults with intellectual disabilities: prevalence, incidence and remission of aggressive behaviour and related factors. J. Intellect. Disabil. Res. **53**(3), 217–232 (2009)
5. Crocker, A.G., Mercier, C., Lachapelle, Y., Brunet, A., Morin, D., Roy, M.E.: Prevalence and types of aggressive behaviour among adults with intellectual disabilities. J. Intellect. Disabil. Res. **50**(9), 652–661 (2006)
6. Fei, H., Meskens, N., et al.: Discovering patient care process models from event logs. In: Proceedings of the 8th International Conference on Modelling Simulation (MOSIM), pp. 10–12. Citeseer (2010)
7. Hensel, J.M., Lunsky, Y., Dewa, C.S.: Staff perception of aggressive behaviour in community services for adults with intellectual disabilities. Community Ment. Health J. **50**(6), 743–751 (2014)
8. Hensel, J., Lunsky, Y., Dewa, C.S.: Exposure to client aggression and burnout among community staff who support adults with intellectual disabilities in Ontario, Canada. J. Intellect. Disabil. Res. **56**(9), 910–915 (2012)
9. Kim, E., et al.: Discovery of outpatient care process of a tertiary university hospital using process mining. Healthc. Inform. Res. **19**(1), 42–49 (2013)
10. Mans, R., Reijers, H., van Genuchten, M., Wismeijer, D.: Mining processes in dentistry. In: Proceedings of the 2nd ACM SIGHIT International Health Informatics Symposium, pp. 379–388. ACM (2012)
11. Mans, R.S., van der Aalst, W.M.P., Vanwersch, R.J.B., Moleman, A.J.: Process mining in healthcare: data challenges when answering frequently posed questions. In: Lenz, R., Miksch, S., Peleg, M., Reichert, M., Riaño, D., ten Teije, A. (eds.) KR4HC/ProHealth -2012. LNCS (LNAI), vol. 7738, pp. 140–153. Springer, Heidelberg (2013). https://doi.org/10.1007/978-3-642-36438-9_10
12. McClintock, K., Hall, S., Oliver, C.: Risk markers associated with challenging behaviours in people with intellectual disabilities: a meta-analytic study. J. Intellect. Disabil. Res. **47**(6), 405–416 (2003)
13. Mills, S., Rose, J.: The relationship between challenging behaviour, burnout and cognitive variables in staff working with people who have intellectual disabilities. J. Intellect. Disabil. Res. **55**(9), 844–857 (2011)

14. Nieuwenhuis, J.G., Noorthoorn, E.O., Nijman, H.L.I., Naarding, P., Mulder, C.L.: A blind spot? Screening for mild intellectual disability and borderline intellectual functioning in admitted psychiatric patients: prevalence and associations with coercive measures. PLoS ONE **12**(2), e0168847 (2017)
15. Nijman, H., Palmstierna, T.: Measuring aggression with the staff observation aggression scale-revised. Acta Psychiatr. Scand. **106**, 101–102 (2002)
16. Nijman, H.L., et al.: The staff observation aggression scale-revised (SOAS-R). Aggress. Behav. Off. J. Int. Soc. Res. Aggress. **25**(3), 197–209 (1999)
17. Rojas, E., Munoz-Gama, J., Sepúlveda, M., Capurro, D.: Processmining inhealthcare: a literature review. J. Biomed. Inform. **61**, 224–236 (2016). https://doi.org/10.1016/j.jbi.2016.04.007. http://www.sciencedirect.com/science/article/pii/S1532046416300296
18. Tenneij, N., Koot, H.M.: Incidence, types and characteristics of aggressive behaviour in treatment facilities for adults with mild intellectual disability and severe challenging behaviour. J. Intellect. Disabil. Res. **52**(2), 114–124 (2008)
19. Tyrer, F., et al.: Physical aggression towards others in adults with learning disabilities: prevalence and associated factors. J. Intellect. Disabil. Res. **50**(4), 295–304 (2006)
20. van der Aalst, W.: Data science in action. In: van der Aalst, W. (ed.) Process Mining, pp. 3–23. Springer, Heidelberg (2016). https://doi.org/10.1007/978-3-662-49851-4_1

On Complex Value Relations in Hive

Matthieu Pilven[1,2], Stefanie Scherzinger[1(✉)], and Laurent d'Orazio[2]

[1] OTH Regensburg, Regensburg, Germany
stefanie.scherzinger@oth-regensburg.de
[2] Univ Rennes, CNRS, IRISA, Lannion, France
laurent.dorazio@irisa.fr

Abstract. In this paper, we raise the question how data architects model their data for processing in Apache Hive. This well-known SQL-on-Hadoop engine supports complex value relations, where attribute types need not be atomic. In fact, this feature seems to be one of the prominent selling points, e.g., in Hive reference books. In an empirical study, we analyze Hive schemas in open source repositories. We examine to which extent practitioners make use of complex value relations and accordingly, whether they write queries over complex types. Understanding which features are actively used will help make the right decisions in setting up benchmarks for SQL-on-Hadoop engines, as well as in choosing which query operators to optimize for.

Keywords: Hive · Complex value relations · Empirical study

1 Introduction

Originally a Facebook-internal data warehouse [17], the SQL-on-Hadoop engine Hive is now an official Apache project. After only a decade of development, Apache Hive is listed among the top-10 relational database systems on the DB-Engines Ranking website[1], alongside IBM DB2 and Oracle Database. Yet the latter are commercial products with development histories up to four times longer. Part of this success is owed to the fact that working with Hive feels very familiar:

- Hive users conveniently interact with a relational data model, yet the raw data is typically stored in the Hadoop Distributed File System (HDFS).
- While the query language HiveQL closely resembles the SQL dialect of MySQL [18], queries are executed as scalable MapReduce workflows [17].

Moreover, Hive relations need not be in first normal form, where all attribute values are atomic. Rather, the data model allows for (a restricted form of) complex value relations: A tuple constructor **struct** declares tuples. The complex types **map** and **array** declare maps and arrays, concepts familiar from programming languages. These constructors can be applied recursively, to an arbitrary

---

[1] https://db-engines.com/de/ranking/relational+dbms, as of September 2019.

© Springer Nature Switzerland AG 2019
G. Guizzardi et al. (Eds.): ER 2019 Workshops, LNCS 11787, pp. 146–156, 2019.
https://doi.org/10.1007/978-3-030-34146-6_13

```
1   CREATE TABLE employees (
2     name STRING,
3     salary FLOAT,
4     subordinates ARRAY<STRING>,
5     deductions MAP<STRING, FLOAT>,
6     address STRUCT<street:STRING, CITY:STRING, state:STRING, zip:INT>
7   );
8
9   SELECT name, subordinates[0] FROM employees;
10  SELECT explode(subordinates) AS sub FROM employees;
11
12  SELECT name, sub FROM employees
13  LATERAL VIEW explode(subordinates) subView AS sub;
```

Fig. 1. A Hive table declaration and queries, taken from [5].

level of nesting. This allows ingestion of data that already arrives in nested form (e.g., in JSON format). Further, denormalization accelerates query processing in data warehouse settings, where data is updated rarely (if at all). Complex value relations are also supported in related systems, such as Impala [12] and Presto[2].

Example 1 (From [5]). The table declaration shown in Fig. 1 captures employees with their name, salary, and their nested subordinates. It further captures employee-specific tax deductions, as well as their home address. The HiveQL syntax for accessing a field in an array is straightforward, as seen in line 9. HiveQL offers table generating functions: accordingly, the query in line 10 produces one tuple for each element of array subordinates. To list pairs of a manager and a subordinate, we need to declare a LATERAL VIEW, as seen in lines 12 and 13. □

Contributions. The support for complex value relations is one of the major selling points for using Hive, c.f. [5]. Yet it is an open question whether practitioners make use of this feature. We therefore explore complex value relations in Hive by analyzing open source repositories on GitHub. There is a tradition of empirical studies on database schemas in open source projects, typically in the context of schema evolution, e.g. [7,15]. However, we are not aware of any studies on the dissemination of complex value relations in SQL-on-Hadoop processing. In particular,

- we formalize complex value relations in Hive and point out connections to the theory of V-relations [1], dating back to the 80s.
- We identify 133 unique and relevant GitHub repositories with a total of over 900 table declarations. We then identify complex value relations in Hive schemas, as well as the occurrence of matching operators in HiveQL queries.
- We discuss our findings w.r.t. existing benchmarks targeted at Hive.

---

[2] https://prestosql.io/.

Structure. In Sect. 2, we provide formal preliminaries. In Sect. 3, we lay down our methodology. In Sect. 4, we present the detailed study results, which we discuss in Sect. 5. We list threats to the validity of our study in Sect. 6. Section 7 gives an overview over related work. We then conclude with Sect. 8.

2   Preliminaries

We recap the definition of complex value relations and formalize complex types in Hive. We then point out a connection between these concepts.

Complex Value Relations [1]. In complex value relations, attribute values need not be atomic. Intuitively, the data structure makes use of two constructors, which can be applied recursively, (1) a *tuple constructor* to make tuples, and (2) a *set constructor* to make sets of tuples, and thus relations.

Underlying the notion of a schema, there is the notion of *complex types* (or sorts). The abstract syntax for complex types is shown next:

$$\tau = \mathbf{dom} \mid \langle B_1 : \tau, \ldots, B_k : \tau \rangle \mid \{\tau\},$$

where $k \geq 0$, and $B_1, \ldots, B_k$ are distinct attribute names. Intuitively, an element of $\mathbf{dom}$ is a constant, an element of $\langle B_1 : \tau, \ldots, B_k : \tau \rangle$ is a k-tuple with an element of type τ_i in entry B_i for each i. We refer to [1] for the formal definition of $[\![\tau]\!]$, the set of values of type τ, and merely operate on the level of examples. We define a *complex value relation of type τ* to be a finite set of values of type τ.

Example 2. For Fig. 1 (up to line 3), the type (abstracting from **string** and **float**) is $\{\langle \text{name} : \mathbf{dom}, \text{ salary} : \mathbf{dom}\rangle\}$. We state a value of this type: $\{\langle \text{name} : "John Doe", \text{salary} : 100000.0\rangle, \langle \text{name} : "Mary Smith", \text{salary} : 80000.0\rangle\}$.   □

Example 3. Below, we consider a complex type for declaring a non-flat complex value relation (Eq. 1), and a value of this type (Eq. 2):

$$\{\langle \text{name} : \mathbf{dom}, \text{ salary} : \mathbf{dom}, \text{ subordinates} : \{\langle \text{key} : \mathbf{dom}, \text{value} : \mathbf{dom}\rangle\}\rangle\}. \tag{1}$$

$$\{\langle \text{name} : "John Doe", \text{salary} : 80000.0, \tag{2}$$
$$\quad \text{subordinates} : \{\langle \text{key} : 0, \text{value} : "Mary Smith"\rangle, \langle \text{key} : 1, \text{value} : "Tod Jones"\rangle\}\rangle,$$
$$\langle \text{name} : "Mary Smith", \text{salary} : 80000.0, \text{subordinates} : \{\}\rangle,$$
$$\langle \text{name} : "Todd Jones", \text{ salary} : 70000.0, \text{subordinates} : \{\}\rangle\}$$

□

Figure 2 shows a visualization of the complex type from the above example as a finite tree. The tuple constructor is denoted by a node labeled $\times$ and the set constructor is denoted by a node labeled $*$. Outgoing edges from tuple nodes are labeled, while set nodes have a single child.

Based on this tree visualization, it is intuitive to define the *set height* [1] of a complex type as the maximum number of set constructors in any branch. In the tree shown, the set height is 2.

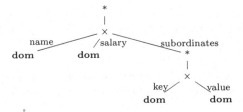

Fig. 2. The complex type from Example 3 as a tree, with a set height of 2.

Hive Types. The Hive data model offers a second tuple constructor via `struct`. While it does not allow to nest with a proper set constructor, we can nest `maps` and `arrays`. We declare the abstract syntax for *Hive type* τ_H as

$$\tau_H = \{\langle B_1 : \tau, \ldots, B_k : \tau\rangle\}$$
$$\tau = \mathbf{dom} \mid \mathbf{map} <\tau, \tau> \mid \mathbf{array} <\tau> \mid \mathbf{struct} <B_1 : \tau, \ldots, B_k : \tau>.$$

Thus, the top-level type is always a set of tuples. Underneath, maps, arrays, and structs may be nested arbitrarily. Given a flat Hive relation over type τ_H, we say the *Hive nesting level* is 1. For any (recursive) declaration of a map, an array, or a struct, the Hive nesting level increases by one.

The set of values of a Hive type τ_H is denoted by $[\![\tau_H]\!]$ and declared next. The values for the tuple and set constructor are defined the same as for complex types. Below, we equate structs with the tuple constructor. Arrays and maps are encoded as sets of key-value pairs:

$$[\![\mathbf{struct} <B_1 : \tau_1, \ldots, B_k : \tau_k>]\!] = [\![\langle B_1 : \tau_1, \ldots, B_k : \tau_k\rangle]\!]$$
$$[\![\mathbf{map} <\tau_k, \tau_v>]\!] = \{\{\langle\text{key} : k_1, \text{value} : v_1\rangle, \ldots, \langle\text{key} : k_j, \text{value} : v_j\rangle\}$$
$$\mid j \geq 0, k_i \in [\![\tau_k]\!], v_i \in [\![\tau_v]\!], i \in [1, j]\}$$
$$[\![\mathbf{array} <\tau>]\!] = \{\{\langle\text{key} : 1, \text{value} : v_1\rangle, \ldots, \langle\text{key} : j, \text{value} : v_j\rangle\}$$
$$\mid j \geq 0, v_i \in [\![\tau]\!], i \in [1, j]\}$$

Then, a *Hive relation of type* τ_H is a value of type τ_H.

Hive Relations as Verso-Relations. The Hive data model does not allow nesting with a proper set constructor, a limitation has also been observed in [16]. Nevertheless, a Hive type may be generalized to a complex value type. For instance, we may generalize a map or an array to a set of key-value tuples:

$$[\![\mathbf{map} <\tau_k, \tau_v>]\!] \subset [\![\{\langle\text{key} : \tau_k, \text{value} : \tau_v\rangle\}]\!]$$
$$[\![\mathbf{array} <\tau>]\!] \subset [\![\{\langle\text{key} : \mathbf{dom}, \text{value} : \tau\rangle\}]\!].$$

Note that the generalized type allows non-consecutive and even repetitive array indexes, so it really defines a superset of values.

Given this generalization, we can relate Hive relations to a data model explored in earlier research: We may safely assume that all recursive nestings of structs with structs have been flattened to a single struct. This can be done without loss of information. Then, the above generalization of Hive types to complex value types actually produces Verso-relations [1]. These data structures have the appealing property that the information contained can be equivalently represented using (several) flat relations. This imposes a polynomial bound on the cardinality of a set in a Verso-relation, which is a nice property for the practical evaluation of tuple constructors (such as `explode`).

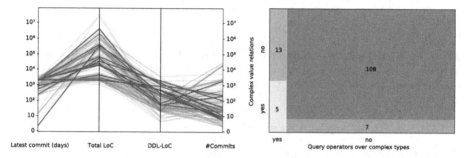

Fig. 3. Overview of the analyzed repositories (axes with log scales).

Fig. 4. Repositories with complex value relations vs. queries over complex types.

3   Methodology

3.1   Context Description

We used Google BigQuery[3] to identify relevant open source repositories on GitHub, as of July 16th, 2019. This cloud service allows for querying the GitHub open data collection, mostly non-forked projects with an open source license. We consider a repository relevant if it contains at least one file with ending `.hql`, which commonly denotes a file with HiveQL statements. This revealed 417 repositories. We discarded any projects that were registered as forks of other repositories, which leaves 158 (the GitHub open data collection is not free of forks). We further eliminated 25 repositories that had no table declarations in `hql`-files.

Figure 3 characterizes the 133 analyzed repositories: We report the days passed since the latest commit, the total lines of code (LoC), and *DDL-LoC*, the lines of code for table declarations (c.f. Sect. 3.3). We further report the number of commits. The lines of code and the number of commits are indicators of project maturity. The lines of code of schema declarations are generally considered a *proxy metric* for schema complexity [10].

3.2   Research Questions

RQ1: How common are complex value relations in Hive schemas?
RQ2: What is the usage of query operators over complex types?

---
[3] https://cloud.google.com/bigquery/.

3.3   Analysis Process

Parsing Hive Schemas. We wrote a Python-based parser for processing `hql`-files. One `hql`-file was missing a semicolon as a delimiter. We fixed this manually to include this file in our analysis. We extract all `CREATE TABLE` statements and pretty-print them such that one attribute is declared per line, like in Fig. 1. This is the pre-processing step in measuring DDL-LoC. Note that we ignore all declarations of the form `CREATE TABLE LIKE` $<T>$ and `CREATE TABLE AS` $<Q>$, of which there are 17 and 117 respectively. We justify this as follows: With the first, we merely create copies of tables that we already analyze, so there is little added value. The second construct is commonly used for storing intermediate results, like one would declare a materialized view. We argue that these are not the base tables holding the original data, and therefore choose to ignore them in our analysis. Along the same line of arguments, we do not analyze `CREATE VIEW` statements, where complex types may be introduced over flat base relations.

Table 1. The subset of repositories with (non-flat) complex value relations.

	Repository	#CVRs	HNL	SH	#Cont
1	`sixeyed/hive-succinctly`	3 out of 16	3	2	1
2	`jbrambleDC/predict_restaurant_success`	2 out of 3	3	2	1
3	`flaminem/flamy`	21 out of 51	2	2	1
4	`yhemanth/hive-samples`	1 out of 22	2	2	1
5	`Benjguin/UnlockLuxury`	1 out of 15	2	2	2
6	`DXFrance/data-hackathon`	1 out of 15	2	2	1
7	`mellowonpsx/ESCA`	2 out of 7	2	1	1
8	`Sicmatr1x/Sicmatr1x.github.io`	1 out of 7	2	2	1
9	`PolymathicCoder/Avempace`	4 out of 5	2	2	1
10	`airbnb/aerosolve`	1 out of 4	2	2	21
11	`gliptak/hadoop-course`	1 out of 4	2	2	1
12	`EXEM-OSS/Flamingo2`	1 out of 3	2	2	1

Analyzing HiveQL Queries. The Hive query language offers several constructs to deal with complex types[4], such as **(1)** collection functions (e.g., the operation `array_contains(A,v)` checks whether array `A` contains value `v`), **(2)** complex type constructors (e.g. for creating a map), and **(3)** built-in table-generating functions (e.g., `json_tuple` for generating a relational tuple from a JSON string). **(4)** Further, there are built-in functions for XPath-style queries.[5]

---

[4] https://cwiki.apache.org/confluence/display/Hive/LanguageManual+UDF.

[5] https://cwiki.apache.org/confluence/display/Hive/LanguageManual+XPathUDF.

We grep for SELECT-statements with these constructs in hql-files. Thus, we cover a wide range of operators and only exclude access to single fields, such as A[i] to access the ith field of array A, or S.c to access component c of struct S.[6]

4   Detailed Study Results

4.1   RQ: How Common Are Complex Value Relations in Hive Schemas?

In the following, whenever we mention complex value relations, we assume *non-flat* relations, and explicitly refer to *flat* relations otherwise. Only 9% of all analyzed repositories contain complex value relations, and are listed in Table 1: next to the repository, we state how many of the relations analyzed are non-flat (column #CVRs). For the first repository, this means 3 out of 16 relations. We state the maximum Hive nesting level (HNL), set height (SH), and the number of contributors (#Cont). The entries are sorted hierarchically, by HNL and the total number of tables analyzed. While Hive does not restrict the nesting level, the maximum HNL observed is only 3. The set height is at most 2, so there is not a single recursive nesting of maps or arrays. Repository 2 is one of the few repositories that is actually a data analytics project, it predicts restaurant success. Further, Repository 8 analyzes server logs. Repository 10 is a machine learning library where complex value relations hold training data. The other repositories seem experimental, as suggested by names like hadoop-course and hive-samples, some even contain the tutorial table declared in Fig. 1. Most are for personal development, aerosolve stands out with 21 contributors.

In Fig. 3, we show these 12 repositories in context. The dark bold lines the repositories from Table 1. What is common to these repositories is that (1) the latest commit dates back half a year or more. Thus, projects undergoing active development have flat relations only. (2) Further, all repositories from Table 1 have schema declarations spanning at least 57 DDL-LoC, which is more than in 40% of all repositories.

Results. We find little evidence of complex value relations being used. Mostly, the developers merely experiment with complex types. Moreover, even though Hive does not restrict the nesting level, the maximum observed is 3. Of course, complex types may also be introduced in views, as discussed next.

4.2   RQ: What Is the Usage of Query Operators over Complex Types?

In total, we have analyzed 2,771 HiveQL queries in hql-files. The mosaic plot in Fig. 4 reads as follows: Along the vertical, we distinguish the repositories that use complex value relations from those that declare only flat relations. Along the horizontal, we distinguish repositories with queries over complex types. The

---

[6] These operators are difficult to match reliably by keyword search alone.

largest area with 108 repositories represents the repositories that have neither complex value relations, nor queries over complex types. Among the repositories with complex value relations, only about half contain matching queries (repositories 5–9). Interestingly, 13 repositories have no complex value relations, but queries over complex types: some evaluate XPath over string-valued attributes, or views introduce complex types and the queries operate over these views.

Next, we list all observed query operators over complex types, ordered by the number of occurrence: `explode`: 27, `lateral_view`: 26, `xpath_string`: 6, `json_tuple`: 5, `size`: 5, `xpath_int`: 4, `stack`:1. Some words on operators that we have not introduced yet. `stack` breaks down tuples into several, smaller-sized tuples. `size` returns the number of elements in a `map` or an `array`. While we have searched for 20 different syntactic constructs, we have only found evidence of 7.

Results. We found query operators over complex types to be rare. There are even repositories with complex value relations but no matching queries. Moreover, despite the richness of the HiveQL query language, authors of queries seem to restrict themselves to a chosen few operators over complex types.

Table 2. Database benchmarks used to also benchmark Hive.

Benchmark	(Non-flat) CVRs	Queries over complex types
TPC-H[c], TPC-DS[c], Hive-600 [14]	◯	◯
HiBench [9], SmartBench[a]	◯	◯
Pavlo et al. [13]	◯	◯
Hive-testbench[b]	◯	◯
BigBench [8], TPC-xbb[c]	✓	✓
UniBench [19]	✓	✓

[a]https://github.com/bomeng/smartbench
[b]https://github.com/hortonworks/hive-testbench
[c]http://www.tpc.org/

5   Discussion

In the repositories analyzed, the majority of schemas is actually in first normal form. This matches our impression from discussions with practitioners. We have several conjectures: **(1)** One reason may be that when data is ingested into Hive from a relational data warehouse, the data is "flat" to start with. **(2)** A further conjecture is that different tools might share access to the data in HDFS, but not all tools can handle complex types. Thus, data architects may be less inclined to declare complex value relations. **(3)** Queries over complex types tend to become complex. In fact, repository 2 in Table 1 contains a "flat" view over a complex value relation, probably to facilitate query formulation.

In Table 2, we list benchmarks commonly used for Hive. Interestingly, few include (non-flat) complex value relations and matching queries. BigBench specifies a log processing scenario, with an `explode` statement in a query over semi-structured data. This matches the results of our study, as we found `explode` to occur most frequently (c.f. Sect. 4.2). UniBench, in contrast, contains multi-model data and is not restricted to complex value relations, e.g., it also includes queries over graph and key-value data. However, there are several benchmarks targeted at Hive that do not include complex value relations or queries over complex types. This mismatch between our findings and the schemas in these benchmarks motivates future and larger-scale studies.

6   Threats to Validity

Construct Validity. (1) In identifying relevant repositories, we rely on the convention that `CREATE TABLE` statements are contained in `hql-files`. However, (1a) `CREATE TABLE` statements can be embedded in the application code. While this is certainly a limitation of our methodology, ignoring SQL statements in application code is common in virtually all earlier empirical studies on relational schemas, e.g. [7, 15]. (1b) Some `CREATE TABLE` statements for Hive are contained in `sql-files`, rather than `hql-files`: if we also were to analyze `sql-files`, then repository 7 in Table 1 would have maximum HNL 3. We carefully assessed the risk of ignoring `sql-files`: Across all analyzed repositories, we count 1,006 `hql-files` and even 5,870 `sql-files`. At first, this seems promising: In Table 1, we could add two further, personal-development projects with HNL 2 and SH 2. Yet while the table would grow by two entries, the maximum Hive nesting level and set height would remain unchanged. Thus, there is little information gain regarding research question 1. Regarding research question 2, analyzing the query constructs in `sql-files` increases the absolute numbers, but not the relative ranking of occurrences (e.g., `explode` being the most frequent). In particular, no new constructs are found. Again, there is little information gain.

At the same time, there is considerable risk in including `sql-files`: For instance, `cloudera/hue` is a SQL workbench that supports several database systems. Analyzing the contents of `sql-files` files would introduce considerable bias into our analysis. Considering this risk, we restrict ourselves to `hql-files`.

(2) Similarly, if an Impala-based repository contains `hql-files`, we falsely include this in our analysis. However, we consider this a minor threat, as we have carefully inspected the repositories from Table 1 for signs that they might not be Hive projects. (3) We currently do not analyze ALTER TABLE statements. We have verified that while ALTER TABLE statements occur 489 times, none of them introduce complex types. Thus, this threat can be safely ignored.

External Validity. It is a fundamental question how representative studies on open source projects are [4, 11]. Actually, we have encountered Stack Overflow questions about declaring tables with deep nesting levels, so some developers go beyond HNL 3, yet we do not see evidence of this in our data.

7   Related Work

There is a long tradition of research on normal forms and also complex value databases, dating back to the 80s [1]. Recent experiments have shown (for Spark) that denormalization into complex value relations can indeed speed up query processing in Big Data scenarios [2].

In software engineering research, analyzing open source applications is an established practice [4]. It is only natural that the availability of public code repositories has enabled empirical studies on database schemas. For instance, there is a line of studies on schema evolution, e.g. [7,15]. There is also a history of empirical studies on real-world data in nested data models, such as DTDs [6] and XML Schema [3]. These studies are very similar to ours in their methodology.

8   Conclusion and Future Work

By analyzing real-world Hive schemas, we are able to show that complex value relations occur to only a small extent and that nesting is shallow.

In future work, we plan to conduct a larger-scale study that involves more data, and further SQL-on-Hadoop engines, to obtain a wider perspective.

Acknowledgements. This work was supported by the *Franco-German Youth Office* (FGYO), which funded Matthieu Pilven's internship at OTH Regensburg. This project was further supported by the *Deutsche Forschungsgemeinschaft* (DFG, German Research Foundation), grant #385808805, as well as a Google Cloud Platform Research Credit award. We thank Uta Störl for her feedback on an earlier version of this paper.

References

1. Abiteboul, S., Hull, R., Vianu, V. (eds.): Foundations of Databases: The Logical Level, 1st edn. Addison-Wesley Longman Publishing Co., Inc, Boston (1995)
2. Arrascue Ayala, V.A., Koleva, P., Alzogbi, A., Cossu, M., et al.: Relational schemata for distributed SPARQL query processing. In: Proceedings of the SBD 2019 (2019)
3. Bex, G.J., Neven, F., Van den Bussche, J.: DTDs versus XML schema: a practical study. In: Proceedings of the WebDB 2004 (2004)
4. Bird, C., Menzies, T., Zimmermann, T.: The Art and Science of Analyzing Software Data, 1st edn. Morgan Kaufmann Publishers Inc., San Francisco (2015)
5. Capriolo, E., Wampler, D., Rutherglen, J.: Programming Hive, 1st edn. O'Reilly Media Inc, California (2012)
6. Choi, B.: What are real DTDs like? In: Proceedings of the WebDB 2002 (2002)
7. Curino, C.A., Tanca, L., Moon, H.J., Zaniolo, C.: Schema evolution in Wikipedia: toward a web information system benchmark. In: Proceedings of the ICEIS 2008 (2008)
8. Ghazal, A., Rabl, T., Hu, M., Raab, F., et al.: BigBench: towards an industry standard benchmark for big data analytics. In: Proceedings of the SIGMOD 2013 (2013)
9. Huang, S., Huang, J., Dai, J., Xie, T., et al.: The HiBench benchmark suite: characterization of the MapReduce-based data analysis. In: Proceedings of the ICDEW 2010 (2010)

10. Jain, S., Moritz, D., Howe, B.: High variety cloud databases. In: Proceedings of the ICDE Workshops 2016 (2016)
11. Kalliamvakou, E., Gousios, G., Blincoe, K., Singer, L., et al.: The promises and perils of mining GitHub. In: Proceedings of the MSR 2014 (2014)
12. Kornacker, M., Behm, A., Bittorf, V., Bobrovytsky, T., et al.: Impala: a modern, open-source SQL engine for Hadoop. In: Proceedings of the CIDR 2015 (2015)
13. Pavlo, A., Paulson, E., Rasin, A., Abadi, D.J., et al.: A comparison of approaches to large-scale data analysis. In: Proceedings of the SIGMOD 2009 (2009)
14. Poess, M., Rabl, T., Jacobsen, H.: Analysis of TPC-DS: the first standard benchmark for SQL-based big data systems. In: Proceedings of the SoCC 2017 (2017)
15. Qiu, D., Li, B., Su, Z.: An empirical analysis of the co-evolution of schema and code in database applications. In: Proceedings of the ESEC/FSE 2013 (2013)
16. Sauer, C., Härder, T.: Compilation of query languages into MapReduce. Datenbank-Spektrum **13**(1), 5–15 (2013)
17. Thusoo, A., Sarma, J.S., Jain, N., Shao, Z., et al.: Hive: a warehousing solution over a Map-Reduce framework. Proc. VLDB Endow. **2**(2), 1626–1629 (2009)
18. White, T.: Hadoop: The Definitive Guide, 3rd edn. O'Reilly Media Inc., Sebastopol (2009)
19. Zhang, C., Lu, J., Xu, P., Chen, Y.: UniBench: a benchmark for multi-model database management systems. In: Proceedings of the TPCTC 2018 (2018)

Data Capture and Analyses
from Conversational Devices in the Homes
of the Elderly

Sandeep Purao[✉] and Chenhang Meng

Bentley University, Waltham, MA, USA
spurao@bentley.edu

Abstract. Conversational devices such as Amazon Echo and Google Home represent more than a way to tap into the behavioral surplus of consumers. They provide an opportunity to address societal problems by examining data streams produced by these devices. In this paper, we describe usage patterns and problems related to the use of Amazon Echo devices at home by one specific demographic: the elderly. We rely on a pilot project to collect usage data over multiple months based on deployment of these devices in the homes of eight elderly individuals who either live alone or with a spouse. The paper describes methods used to ensure confidentiality, data collection and analysis procedures, and our findings. We find that the use of conversational devices remains restricted to single commands instead of conversations, making yourself understood remains a problem, sustained use remains a challenge, and the interaction rarely goes beyond simple commands. We interpret the results, and point to the potential for such devices in the lives of the elderly, specifically for health-related problems. The paper also describes lessons learned for capture and analysis of data from such conversational devices.

Keywords: Conversational devices · Elderly · Use patterns

1 Introduction

Conversational devices have mushroomed. Although exact numbers are difficult to pin down (Lopatovska et al. 2018), it is estimated that more than 25 million people today use devices such as Amazon Echo™, Google Home™ and others[1] (Reis et al. 2017). In spite of their almost ubiquitous presence of these devices, much of what we know about the adoption and use of these devices comes from industry reports. For Amazon and Google, these devices represent the possibility of "colonizing" everyday space such as home and office (Atlantic 2018), by connecting to an ecosystem of other devices and services. Amazon Echo already works with more than 20,000 smart-home devices representing more than 3,500 brands (Atlantic 2018). It has been reasoned that this shift is likely to be wide and profound with the possibility of anthropomorphizing,

---

[1] The home-based conversational devices (the focus of this paper) are different from those embedded in mobile devices (e.g. Cortana™, and Siri™).

© Springer Nature Switzerland AG 2019
G. Guizzardi et al. (Eds.): ER 2019 Workshops, LNCS 11787, pp. 157–166, 2019.
https://doi.org/10.1007/978-3-030-34146-6_14

bringing these devices closer to our own level. According to some accounts, "we [would] communicate with them, not through them" (Atlantic 2018). Their roles today, as devices that deliver news, calendar, weather, recipes, reminders and others are harbingers of what is to come. It is, therefore, important for us to better understand our interactions with these devices. Most of what we know about the use of these devices comes from industry reports (Ong and Suplizio 2016). Few studies have examined the use of such devices (e.g. Sciuto et al. 2018).

In this study, our intent is to focus on the use of a dominant example of conversational devices, Amazon Echo, by a specific segment of the population, the elderly. This is an important population segment for multiple reasons. First, the elderly are a growing segment (Giacardi et al. 2016) that present unique challenges for technology design and use. It is, therefore, important to understand how the elderly use these conversational devices. Second, aging can lead to limited mobility, visual and hearing impairments, and high illness susceptibility (Khoury et al. 2018). These characteristics define the values that these older citizens hold dear, often different from their younger counterparts as seen elsewhere in the design of service platforms (Skouby et al. 2014; Gil and Amaro 2010). The conversational devices represent a timely example that we can investigate to better understand how the promise of technology use by the elderly may be realized.

The primary goal of this work is, therefore, to take first steps towards understanding how the elderly use such conversational devices, and the problems they face. A second goal for this work is to demonstrate how the large streams of data from these conversational devices may be captured and analyzed. We respond to these goals by carrying out a research project that captures and analyzes data from home-based conversational devices deployed in the homes of the elderly, while maintaining important privacy and confidentiality. Key contributions of our work include: findings related to how the elderly use conversational devices, and lessons related to capture and analysis of data from such conversational devices while maintaining privacy and confidentiality. The reminder of the paper is organized as follows. Section 2 reviews prior work. Section 3 describes the research setting and the research approach. Section 4 discusses the findings. In Sect. 5, we wrap up with some concluding remarks.

2   Background and Prior Work

The population on the planet is aging – growth rates for the elderly are twice that of the overall population (Beard et al. 2016). The skyrocketing costs of healthcare and services for the elderly are indications of these trends (Iwasaki 2013). The design of appropriate information technologies is one key response to these trends.

2.1   The Design and Use of Technology for and by the Elderly

The phrase 'elderly' or 'aging' describes individuals who are 65 and over. However, with advances in healthcare, better diet and exercise, the stereotype of the elderly as 'frail, vulnerable, immobile and passive' is being questioned (Harvey and Thurnwald 2009, Kendig and Browning 2011). Instead, there is a much larger group of healthy, active, independent "young old" who possess a very different image of themselves (Giacardi et al. 2016). Today's elderly may have spent a better part of their working lives learning new technologies. Therefore, some of the traditional lessons about "gerontechnology" (Kwon et al. 2016) are being challenged. There is a greater recognition that there is great variety in the everyday lives, needs and motivations of the elderly; and technology design is moving away from making things that are "foolproof" (Hyysalo 2006) to making technology that leads to 'more resourceful aging' (Giacardi et al. 2016). This move to a more enlightened view describes technology design for the elderly in a manner that is ethical and responds to the concerns and values of the elderly (Giacardi et al. 2016; Purao et al. 2015). It is in this context that we study the conversational agents at home for the elderly. They are not necessarily foolproof devices. Rather, they represent a set of capabilities that would allow the elderly to participate in resourceful aging, while still acknowledging that the elderly may not be fully prepared to use all new technological tools.

2.2 Conversational Agents at Home

As pointed out earlier, these conversational agents come in many forms, embedded in our mobile devices as well as location-locked devices such as Google Home and Amazon Echo. They respond to commands that follow what is referred to as a wakeword, e.g. 'Alexa' in case of Amazon Echo. A typical interaction with such a device starts with a command such as "Alexa, What's the weather today?" that results in a response such as "In Boston, it is 80° with a 20% chance of rain." The devices contain software that captures the voice commands, converts these to text, develops a response, which may require accessing resources on the internet and speaks the response. Specialized capabilities can be developed for these devices (e.g. Skills for the Amazon Echo), which allow the device to respond to more specialized commands. According to some analyses, these devices represent an entry into the private homes of individuals with the possibility of tapping into so-called behavioral surplus (Zuboff 2019). Others point to the potential of such devices to become a normal, persistent and important part of many households (Sciuto et al. 2018). Studies that have examined the use of these devices have provided description of use such as the placement of devices at home, types of commands used and other similar statistics (Sciuto et al. 2018). Such studies have remained rare. In this study, we hope to add to this nascent stream.

3 Research Approach

3.1 Research Setting

Driven by our research goal, we collaborated with the Council on Aging in one of the cities surrounding greater Boston. The city has a nominal population of ~60,000, with as one sixth of the population, 10,000+ are elderly. The city is home to large multiple corporate headquarters as well as universities. As a result, people who work in or travel to the city, are known to more than quadruple during the day. The Council on Aging is responsible coordinating activities and support services for the elderly with programs such as meals on wheels, classes for the elderly, trips to different local facilities, visits to groceries and hospitals, and others. It occupies a separate facility in downtown. The Director of the Council participates in city administration along with the Mayor, District Councilors, and appointed members of the city government.

3.2 Subjects and Procedure

Working with this Council on Aging, we recruited individuals who expressed willingness to participate in the study. The research team specified these qualifications for participation: (a) have Wi-Fi available at home to use the Amazon Echo device, and (b) not presently have Amazon Echo or other conversational device at home. Following appropriate research protections, a sign-up sheet was made available at the Council. Individuals who expressed willingness were contacted by the research team. To deploy the devices, the research team visited the homes and activated the devices.

This process did not use any of the personal information of the individuals. Instead, the research team generated Amazon accounts and corresponding Gmail accounts as dummy identifiers. The dummy identifiers ensured privacy, but also limited use of the Amazon Echo devices for purposes such as shopping, ordering transportation and others, controlling other devices at home or making personal phone calls. By removing these, we were then able to focus on the use of Amazon Echo as a truly conversational device, instead of using it as, for example, 'a shopping assistant,' or 'a home hub' or other such modes. Minimal training was provided. A one-page document allayed fears about how to use the device (e.g. you can say 'Alexa, stop' any time), and showed some possibilities such as Alexa, what's the weather today; Alexa, should I carry an umbrella; Alexa, is the pharmacy open today; and so on. The research team retained access to the credentials, which allowed scraping of data about how each individual used the device. A mapping to codes with different individuals responsible for (a) deploying the devices, and (b) scraping the data ensured privacy during this process.

3.3 Data Scraping and Analyses

To access the history of Amazon Echo use, we scraped data for each user by using the normal login process. Figure 1 shows an example from one of the participants.

8	7/18/19	5:34 PM	alexa	117	16 Thursday
9	7/18/19	5:26 PM	how much ti	117	16 Thursday
10	7/18/19	5:11 PM	set a timer f	117	16 Thursday

Fig. 1. Data scraped for a specific user from Amazon Alexa: an example

A Python script read through the front-end and dealt with problems of differential display (text, time), and partial display (screen size, week). Privacy safeguards remained. To facilitate analysis, additional data was inferred such as days the device has been active, day of week, time, an indicator to capture whether the command was understood, and time elapsed since the previous interaction. The data consisted of

7,829 commands from 8 users over 6 months. Following the exploratory nature of the study, we allowed the data to guide our analyses. We describe the findings next.

4   Findings

We begin with a simple conceptual model of the data recorded and generated by the Amazon Echo device (see Fig. 2). To ensure confidentiality, not all the data elements (e.g. recorded user voice commands) were captured.

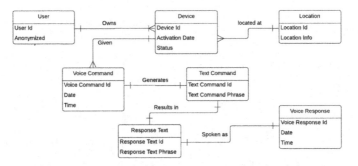

Fig. 2. Conceptual model of data scraped from Alexa

Depending upon the scale, the conceptual model may be translated to a star-schema with the facts of interest as the core, to make the analyses more efficient. The model was populated with the data captured. The analysis results follow next.

4.1   Sustained Use and Intensity of Use

A prerequisite to conceptualizing these devices as intelligent personal assistants (Reis et al. 2017) is frequent and sustained use. The first set of analyses, therefore, examines analyzes how often and how regularly the elderly individuals use these devices: number of days the device was used vs. not used; and the longest contiguous number of days the device was used vs. the longest gap between uses. Figure 3 shows these results. The X-axis indicates the users.

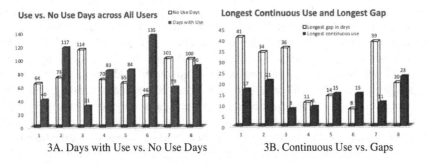

3A. Days with Use vs. No Use Days   3B. Continuous Use vs. Gaps

Fig. 3. Sustained use across all users

The data shows that most users were active at least for some of the days. Figure 3A shows that the number of days with use was higher than the number of non-use days for users 2, 4, 5 and 6. Figure 3B shows that users 5, 6, and 8 had more contiguous days of use compared to the gaps with user 6 showing the most consistent usage with the largest gap between uses as 8 days, compared to users 1, 2, 3 and 7 who had gaps of 30 days or more. Together, the two graphs show that users 3 and 7 were not enthusiastic users of the device. The remaining users suggest possible sustained use. The next set of analyses examined use intensity: average number of commands (per day vs. per day of use); and median vs. maximum commands per day of use (see Fig. 4).

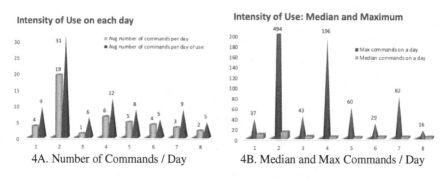

4A. Number of Commands / Day   4B. Median and Max Commands / Day

Fig. 4. Intensity of use across all users

The results continue to show users 2 and 4 as the most intense users of the devices. For example, user 2 used more than 30 commands on average on days that s/he was using the device with one of the days showing 494 commands (a clear outlier). User 4 used more than 12 commands on average on days that s/he was using the device with one of the days showing 196 commands (another outlier). Interestingly, user 7 showed a spike on one day with 82 commands (see Fig. 4B), and the his/her average number of commands on the days of use was 9 (only a little behind users 2 and 4). Based on the data in Fig. 4A, users 1 and 7 were next to users 2 and 4 in terms of average number of commands per day of use in spite of long gaps in usage (see Fig. 3B).

4.2   Commands: Some Understood, Others Not So

To understand whether this use actually resulted in responses, we examined whether the commands of the elderly individuals were actually understood by the conversational devices. This is indicated by the classification 'text not understood' in the data scraped. Such a response from the device meant that when the elderly individuals attempted to use the devices, their command was not understood. While this may not be as significant a concern for other sets of users, it can be significant for the elderly (e.g. see Kwon et al. 2016). When this occurred, in some cases, the individuals appeared to repeat the command (either with the same words or different). Figure 5 shows the results of our analysis. The x-axis shows the users, and the y-axis shows the fraction of commands not understood, followed by a second attempt (Figs. 5A and B).

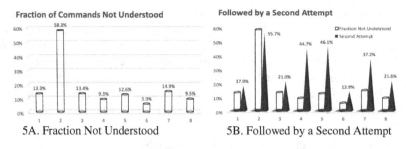

5A. Fraction Not Understood   5B. Followed by a Second Attempt

Fig. 5. Commands (Not) understood as intended, across all users

The data shows that user 2 was a clear outlier with as many as 58% of commands resulting in 'text not understood,' with 55.7% also unsuccessful as second attempts. With this new information, the characterization of user 2 as a frequent user (see Figs. 4A and B) now became suspect. Although this user attempted to use the device a lot, more than half of his/her commands were not understood. All the other users did reasonably well with less than 15% of the commands not understood (although these numbers may still be frustrating for some individuals). Other users that stood out in this analysis included users 4, 5 and 7 (see Fig. 5B). These users used a second attempt to clarify their commands and were still unsuccessful 37 to 46% of the times. Together, these results show that using these devices still remains problematic for the elderly.

4.3   Commands, *Not* Interactions (or Conversations)

Next, we explored the central idea that these are 'conversational' devices (Atlantic 2018), i.e., more than a single command-response pair. We were, therefore, interested in examining the nature of conversations that the elderly individuals were having with these devices. Our simple conceptualization of a conversation was any interaction that was longer than a single command-response pair. To explore this, we separated commands that were part of a larger "interaction (or conversation) episode," against commands that were part of a single "command-response pair" (with a parameter value of 3 min to separate one episode from the next). We also compared the number of "interaction (or conversation) episodes" against the number of days (see Fig. 6).

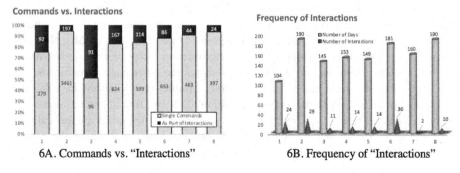

6A. Commands vs. "Interactions"   6B. Frequency of "Interactions"

Fig. 6. Commands, *Not* interactions or conversations, across all users

The results show that only user 3 managed to have such interactions on a somewhat regular basis (see Fig. 6A) with 91 of the commands part of such "interaction (or conversation) episodes" compared to 96 commands that were part of a simple command-response pair. Even with such a high fraction, user 3 managed only 11 such "episodes" over the entire duration of 145 days. User 1, in fact, had more such "episodes" (24) over a fewer days (104) with 92 commands as part of these "episodes" (see Figs. 6A and B). User 2 managed only 2 interactions over the entire period of 160 days.

4.4   Characterizing Conversations and Commands

Finally, even with the problems with sustained use (see Figs. 3 and 4), making yourself understood (see Fig. 5), and engaging in simple command-response pairs instead of longer episodes (see Fig. 6) – the elderly individuals still managed use these devices. To explore these, we considered the length of the interaction (or conversation) episodes, as the number of commands within each episode (Fig. 7A), and examined the types of commands they used with categories similar to prior work (Sciuto et al. 2018) (Fig. 7B). Figure 7 shows these results.

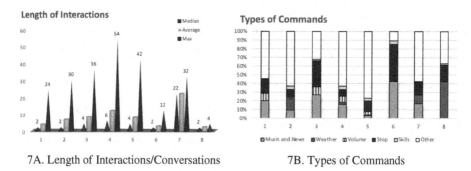

7A. Length of Interactions/Conversations   7B. Types of Commands

Fig. 7. Characterizing conversations and commands, across all users

The data showed that the average length of "interaction/conversation episodes" was fairly low for all users (see Fig. 7A). The outlier (user 7) was an anomaly with an average interaction episode length of 22. However, this was misleading because it represented two episodes (one of length 12 and the other of length 32, with what appeared to be a set of unrelated commands). The results for user 4, on the other hand, had a median of 6 commands (see Fig. 7A) across 14 episodes (see Fig. 6B). Next, we examined the types of commands by examining different categories: music and news, weather, volume, stop, and skills. Figure 7B shows the percentage of commands in each. The users in our set had different emphases, further cementing the idea that the elderly cannot all be treated the same (Giacardi et al. 2016). It is important to use one caveat with these results. No personal uses such as making family phone calls or shopping were part of our study because of our emphasis on keeping the results anonymized. Including these categories may change the outcomes.

5 Discussion and Concluding Remarks

In this paper, we have explored data streams from conversational devices (Amazon Echo) deployed in the homes of the elderly. It is important to note that our intent is to report exploratory analyses of usage patterns for these devices, not explore the strengths or weaknesses of specific devices. The paper described our approach to scraping, and analyzing the data with the use of automated scripts. The approach is scalable. In fact, during this research, we continued to work with the data stream as the data accumulated each week. The key contributions of our work include findings related to the use of conversational devices by the elderly, which include: intensity and sustained use of the devices, examining commands understood and not understood, characterizing interactions and conversations, and exploring different types of commands. The conceptual model we have created can also provide pointers for collecting and analyzing these data streams. The picture that emerged from the analyses shows that the elderly can have different profiles, and these differences are important to consider when designing voice skills for the elderly. It is important to consider the findings to better position the conversational devices as supports for resourceful aging. More specifically, our analyses also show that leveraging conversational devices will require overcoming basic obstacles such as more precise understanding of the commands, and representing and using context to support longer conversations.

Acknowledgements. We acknowledge participation from the elderly, and the Waltham Council on Aging. We also appreciate comments from the review team that have shaped the final version. The work reported has been funded by the National Science Foundation under award number 1641148. Any opinions, findings and conclusions or recommendations expressed in this material are those of the author(s) and do not necessarily reflect the views of the National Science Foundation (NSF).

References

Atlantic, The. 2018. Is Alexa Dangerous? Oct 24. Online. The Atlantic. Accessed 30 July 2018. https://www.theatlantic.com/magazine/archive/2018/11/alexa-how-will-you-change-us/570844/

Beard, J.R., Officer, A.M., Cassels, A.K.: The world report on ageing and health. United Nations (2016)

Bickmore, T.W., et al.: Patient and consumer safety risks when using conversational assistants for medical information: an observational study of Siri, Alexa, and Google Assistant. J. Med. Internet Res. **20**(9), e11510 (2018)

Bjering, H., Curry, J., Maeder, A.J.: Gerontechnology: the importance of user participation in ICT development for older adults. In: HIC, pp. 7–12 (2014)

Bouma, H.: Foundations and goals of gerontechnology. Gerontechnology **11**, 1–4 (2012)

Coyne, M., Thomas, C., Collimore, A., Franzese, C., Hwang, C.: Early user centered insights on voice integrated technologies through retrospective analysis. Iproceedings **3**(1), e49 (2017)

Dall, T.M., Gallo, P.D., Chakrabarti, R., West, T., Semilla, A.P., Storm, M.V.: An aging population and growing disease burden will require alarge and specialized health care workforce by 2025. Health Aff. **32**(11), 2013–2020 (2013)

Giaccardi, E., Kuijer, L., Neven, L.: Design for resourceful ageing: intervening in the ethics of gerontechnology. In: Lloyd, P., Bohemia, E. (eds.) Proceedings of DRS 2016, Design + Research + Society Future-Future-Focused Thinking: 50th Anniversary International Conference, Brighton, UK, 27–30 June 2016, vol. 1 (2016)

Gil, H., Amaro, F.: Active ageing and the role of ICT and assistive technologies: reflections and discussion for their use in Portugal. e-case & e-tech 2010, pp. 2750–2760 (2010)

Gutman, G., Kearns, W., Normie, L., Kort, H.S.M., van den Berg, P.E.W.: Addressing the needs of older adults through technology: the unique focus of the International Society for Gerontechnology (2018)

Harvey, P.W., Thurnwald, I.: Ageing well, ageing productively: the essential contribution of Australia's ageing population to the social and economic prosperity of the nation. Health Soc. Rev. **18**(4), 379–386 (2009)

Karapanos, E., et al.: User experience over time: an initial framework. In: Proceedings of the SIGCHI Conference on Human Factors in Computing Systems, pp. 729–738 (2009). http://doi.org/10.1145/1518701.1518814

Kendig, H., Browning, C.: Directions for ageing well in a Healthy Australia. Acad. Soc. Sci. **31**(2), 23–30 (2011)

Khoury, Y., Purao, S., Duffy, M.: The Influence of Values on the Use of Citizen Services: The Elderly Perspective. ICIS TREO (2018)

Kwon, S., (ed.): Gerontechnology: Research, practice, and principles in the field of technology and aging. Springer Publishing Company (2016)

Laranjo, L., et al.: Conversational agents in healthcare: a systematic review. J. Am. Med. Inf. Assoc. **25**(9), 1248–1258 (2018)

Lopatovska, I., et al.: Talk to me: exploring user interactions with the Amazon Alexa. J. Librarianship Inf. Sci. 0961000618759414 (2018)

Ram, A., et al.: Conversational AI: the science behind the alexa prize. arXiv preprint arXiv:1801.03604 (2018)

Reis, A., Paulino, D., Paredes, H., Barroso, J.: Using intelligent personal assistants to strengthen the elderlies' social bonds. In: Antona, M., Stephanidis, C. (eds.) UAHCI 2017. LNCS, vol. 10279, pp. 593–602. Springer, Cham (2017). https://doi.org/10.1007/978-3-319-58700-4_48

Sciuto, A., Saini, A., Forlizzi, J., Hong, J.I.: Hey Alexa, What's Up?: a mixed-methods studies of in-home conversational agent usage. In: Proceedings of the 2018 Designing Interactive Systems Conference, pp. 857–868. ACM (2018)

Shulevitz, J.: Alexa, should we trust you. The Atlantic (2018)

Skouby, K.E., Kivimäki, A., Haukiputo, L., Lynggaard, P., Windekilde, I.M.: Smart cities and the ageing population. In: The 32nd Meeting of WWRF (2014)

Zuboff, S.: The age of surveillance capitalism: the fight for a human future at the new frontier of power. Profile Books (2019)

Ontologies and Conceptual Modelling (OntoCom) 2019

GORO 2.0: Evolving an Ontology for Goal-Oriented Requirements Engineering

César Henrique Bernabé[1](✉), Vítor E. Silva Souza[1],
Ricardo de Almeida Falbo[1], Renata S. S. Guizzardi[1], and Carla Silva[2]

[1] Ontology and Conceptual Modeling Research Group (NEMO),
Department of Computer Science, Federal University of Espírito Santo (UFES),
Vitoria, Brazil
{chbernabe,vitorsouza,falbo,rguizzardi}@inf.ufes.br
[2] Centro de Informática, Universidade Federal de Pernambuco (UFPE), Recife, Brazil
ctlls@cin.ufpe.br

Abstract. Goal-Oriented Requirements Engineering (GORE) gained prominence by covering some of the limitations of traditional Requirements Engineering (RE). As a result, many GORE modeling languages have been proposed since this field emerged. Aiming at providing formal semantics to the concepts of GORE, the Goal-Oriented Requirements Ontology (GORO) was proposed as a common vocabulary for this domain. However, the first version of GORO lacks important concepts and its applicability was not demonstrated in practice. In this paper, we present GORO 2.0, an evolution of the first version of GORO that overcomes several limitations of its first version, presenting new concepts such as obstacles, conflicts and contributions.

Keywords: Goal-oriented requirements engineering · Goal modeling · Ontology

1 Introduction

Goal-Oriented Requirements Engineering (GORE) emerged in the mid-1990s and became popular for overcoming some of the limitations of traditional Requirements Engineering (RE). For example, goals provide precise criteria for requirements completeness and adequate rationale and justification for a requirement's existence [15]. They are also an efficient tool for identification and negotiation of conflicts [16]. As a result, many GORE modeling languages have been proposed since this field emerged [12].

The multitude of languages and their constructs motivated the creation of the Goal-Oriented Requirements Ontology (GORO), which was proposed with the aim of providing formal semantics to the concepts of GORE [20]. As a consequence, GORO can be used to enable interoperability between models from different GORE languages as it provides a common vocabulary about the GORE domain (and, therefore, improves the communication between stakeholders).

© Springer Nature Switzerland AG 2019
G. Guizzardi et al. (Eds.): ER 2019 Workshops, LNCS 11787, pp. 169–179, 2019.
https://doi.org/10.1007/978-3-030-34146-6_15

Moreover, GORO allows previous and new modeling languages to clearly specify their semantics by grounding their concepts in a formal reference ontology. By providing a common vocabulary, the ontology can also support modelers to create ontologically correct models.

The first version of GORO, however, suffers from some limitations, namely: (i) the ontology was captured from and had its concepts mapped to only three GORE languages (i^* [24], KAOS [7] and Techne [3]) and considered only a subset of concepts of these languages; (ii) it lacks integration with other ontologies on the Software Engineering (SE) domain to strengthen its semantic foundations; and (iii) its applicability was not properly demonstrated as, for example, using a model conversion tool. Hence, we evolved GORO into a new version, hereafter *GORO 2.0*, in order to overcome the aforementioned limitations.

This paper presents GORO 2.0 and is organized as follows: Sect. 2 briefly summarizes the GORE domain; Sect. 3 presents the method used to build GORO 2.0; Sect. 4 presents GORO 2.0; Sect. 5 compares our ontology with related work; and Sect. 6 concludes the paper.

2   GORE Modeling Languages

NFR [19] was the first GORE language proposed (1992) and brought the concept of goals as desirable qualities in a system. It introduced the concept of contribution between Softgoals (goals without clear criteria of satisfaction). In 1993, KAOS was proposed and redefined goals as states of affairs desired by stakeholders, categorizing them as Goal (not sufficiently refined to be assigned to a stakeholder), Expectation (under the responsibility of a human agent) and Requirement (under the responsibility of a software agent). It also introduced the concepts of Operation (a task/plan that can be performed to achieve a goal), Domain Property (a presupposition about the system context considered to be true in certain situations) and Obstacle (an undesired behavior in the context).

In 1995, Yu formalized the specification of i^*, which focuses on the representation of stakeholders' interests within the organizational context. The i^* core concept is the Actor, which depends on others to accomplish goals and perform tasks. The language also highlighted the differentiation between Goal and Softgoal: the former would have a clear satisfaction criteria, while the latter did not. In the following year, GBRAM [2] emerged and defined a method for goal analysis in which the concept of Scenarios, a description of a system and its environment, is used to identify Goals and Obstacles.

In 2004, GSN [14] was proposed with focus on security systems, such as information security, air traffic control and safety systems. In the same year, Tropos [4], a variation of i^*, emerged and brought the concept of Capability as the "ability of an actor of defining, choosing and executing a plan for the fulfillment of a goal". In 2009, the first version of Techne was presented. Based on an ontology, Techne made a more precise differentiation between Hard and Softgoals, as the latter can be restricted through Quality Constraints.

In 2010, GRL [1], a variation of i^*, introduced a differentiation of the OR-Decomposition relation (exclusive and inclusive) and the concept of Correlation (a relation of side effects rather than desired impacts as in the contribution relation). Finally, in 2016, $i*$ was revised and its second version, now spelled iStar, had some elements and relationships removed, and new elements that were popularly used by the community were added. For instance, Softgoal was renamed as Quality; and the means-end and task-decomposition links were grouped in the Refinement Link.

3   Method

GORO 2.0 was built using the Systematic Approach to Building Ontologies (SABiO) [8], an Ontology Engineering method, successful in the development of domain ontologies, particularly in SE. To provide a solid semantic foundation, GORO 2.0 is based on the Unified Foundational Ontology (UFO) [10], and reuses existing ontologies, such as the Common Ontology for Value and Risk (COVR) [23] and the Reference Software Requirements Ontology (RSRO), which is part of the Software Engineering Ontology Network (SEON) [22].

In order to improve domain coverage, GORO 2.0 was created based on the modeling languages mentioned in Sect. 2, which were studied and analyzed to extract concepts that, in fact, belong to the GORE domain. GBRAM, GRL, i*, KAOS, Techne and Tropos were first selected based on a literature review [12]. NFR was added to the list as it is cited in Van Lamsweerde's guided tour on GORE [15]. Finally, when searching for related works (cf. Sect. 5), we also identified GSN. The selected languages were validated with domain experts who advised us to consider $i*$ and $iStar$ as different languages, given the perceptible differences between them. GORO, as its name states, is focused on Requirements. Hence, we do not consider other languages that use goal related constructs but are not specifically GORE modeling languages.

Regarding scope, we have applied two criteria for the inclusion of a construct: it must I_1: appear in more than two GORE modeling languages; and I_2: be considered a GORE concept by domain experts—a group of five academic professionals with more than ten years of experience. We applied I_1 in order to exclude constructs that were not GORE, but actually extra features of specific languages. In order to verify if different languages' elements shared the same meaning, we also consulted the group of experts. It is worth to highlight that GORO 2.0 is concerned with the part of the GORE domain that is covered by the languages selected according to the described heuristics. This decision has been made because one of the purposes of this work is to provide interoperability among the selected GORE languages. As a consequence, other concepts pertaining to GORE domain, but not covered in the selected languages, were not considered to be part of GORO 2.0.

To evaluate GORO, we conducted three activities: verification, validation and an application-based evaluation. To check whether GORO satisfies its own requirements, we verified if its conceptual model can answer all of the proposed Competency Questions (CQs). To validate GORO's domain coverage, we mapped concepts of the GORE modeling languages listed in Sect. 2 to the concepts of the ontology. Finally, to assess the feasibility of GORO in enabling

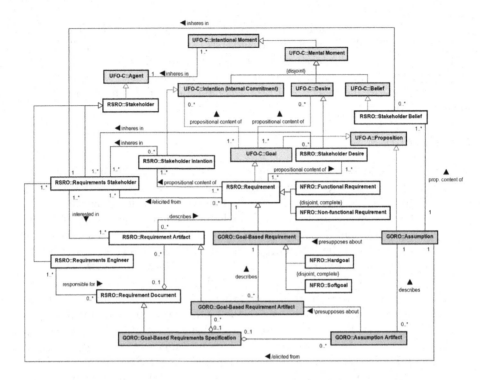

Fig. 1. GORO 2.0's first module: mental moments, goals and assumptions.

interoperability between GORE languages, we implemented a model conversion tool that uses the ontology as an interlanguage. The CQs, the concepts mapping and the conversion tool source code (and conversion examples) are available at https://nemo.inf.ufes.br/projects/rose/.

4   GORO 2.0

Figure 1 presents the module of GORO 2.0 that defines concepts related to mental moments existentially dependent on a single individual, which can be classified as Beliefs, Desires and Intentions. Agent's beliefs are assumed to be true in a given set of situations. Given that desires and intentions are both related to agents' goals, the difference between them is actually related to the fact that the former is only a will of an agent towards a state of affairs (situation) in reality, whereas the latter is an intended state of affair (situation) for which the agent commits to pursuing, causing the agent to perform actions [10].

GORO 2.0 inherits the Stakeholder definition from RSRO: a Stakeholder can be a Requirements Stakeholder, when in the role of the person that provides needs and expectations for the product, or a Requirements Engineer, when in the role of conducting the requirements development activities.

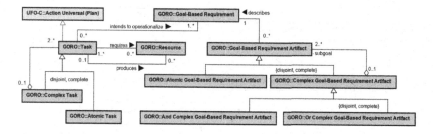

Fig. 2. GORO 2.0's second module: tasks, goals and relations.

A Goal is the *propositional content of* an Intention/Desire, which inheres in an Agent, *supertype* of Stakeholder. Therefore, a Requirement is a goal *elicited from* a stakeholder's intention/desire. A Requirement can be a Non-functional Requirement or a Functional Requirement. When applying a GORE approach to a Requirements Engineering process, a traditional Requirement becomes a Goal-Based Requirement, which can be a Hardgoal or a Softgoal. Both definitions are extracted from [17] and represented in GORO 2.0 with the NFRO prefix.

By combining two perspectives, we end up with four different classifications for a goal-based requirement [17]: Functional Requirement & Hardgoal, Functional Requirement & Softgoal, Non-functional Requirement & Hardgoal and Non-functional Requirement & Softgoal, implicitly represented in Fig. 1. Hence, GORO 2.0 is compatible with NFRO, making adaptations where necessary. We highlight that such adaptations are now incorporated in NFRO. A Goal-Based Requirement Artifact *describes* a Goal-Based Requirement in the same way that a Requirement Artifact *describes* a Requirement, differentiating a documented requirement from a requirement that exists only in the stakeholder's mind. It is important to note that, in GORO 2.0, an Assumption still has the same classifications proposed in GORO 1.0 [20], not shown here due to space limitations and for not being a contribution of this paper.

Figure 2 shows GORO 2.0 second module. A Task *intends to operationalize* a Goal-Based Requirement. Tasks can be Complex Tasks, when composed of two or more Tasks, or Atomic Tasks otherwise. A Task can *require* or *produce* a Resource. As with Tasks, a Goal-Based Requirement Artifact can also be complex or atomic. Complex Goal-Based Requirement Artifact (or Complex GBRA) is further refined into Or/And-Complex GBRA, which are satisfied when at least one/all of their components are satisfied. GORO does not allow tasks to be refined into goals. Yu [24] argues that the refinement between goals and tasks is a way to capture the transition between the problem domain (goal) and the solution domain (task). In addition, according to him, refining a task into a goal would be natural in the analysis and modeling cycle, which generally iterates between these two domains. However, by ontologically analyzing these concepts, the relationship between a task and a goal is not a "refinement". Rather, the task analysis shows that new goals should be considered in the model. In other words, task analysis may motivate the "emergence" of new goals, possibly better characterized if

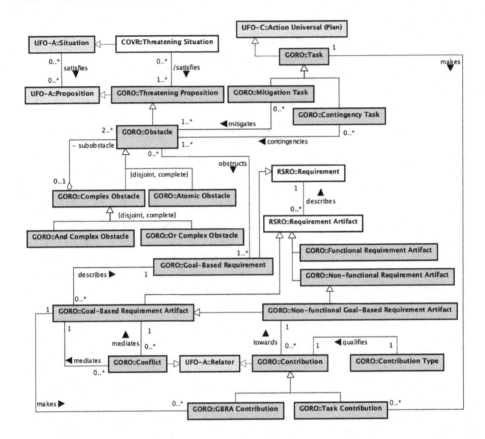

Fig. 3. GORO 2.0's third module: obstacles, conflicts and contribution.

different models are created for the different analysis' cycles. This is an example of how the ontological analysis performed with GORO may have methodological impact.

Figure 3 introduces concepts not previously considered in GORO 1.0, namely: obstacle, conflict and contribution. Van Lamsweerde [16] defines obstacle as a dual notion of goals: "while goals capture desired conditions, obstacles capture undesirable (but nevertheless possible) ones". We argue that obstacles can be equated, here, to the definition used by the Common Ontology for Value and Risk (COVR) [23], i.e., a condition that may be satisfied in certain situations in which something of human value has been put at stake and the outcome is uncertain. Thus, an Obstacle is seen as a Threatening Proposition, which *satisfies* a Threatening Situation and *obstructs* a Goal-Based Requirement satisfaction.

An Obstacle, according to Van Lamsweerde [16], can be *mitigated* by an agent's goal. We consider that what mitigates or contingencies a risk is an action (task) and not a goal. Although KAOS uses goals to mitigate obstacles, the task that intends to operationalize this goal is indirectly mitigating the obstacle.

We also argue that this task definition is overloaded and, thus, propose two distinct types of actions (tasks): contingency (action taken after a Threatening Situation to decrease damage) and mitigation (can reduce or prevent the risk rate of an event to happen). A Threatening Proposition *satisfies* a Threatening Situation in the same way as a Proposition *satisfies* a Situation, hence, the former relation is derived from the latter (denoted by a/symbol). Like goals, an Obstacle can be decomposed in complex/atomic ones, and Complex Obstacles are further refined in Or/And Complex Obstacles, with analogous satisfaction rules.

A conflict happens when two or more goals cannot be achieved in the same solution set of a domain problem [16]. In other words, given goals G_1 and G_2 and a model M, there is no solution set S of M that contains both G_1 and G_2. In GORO, Conflicts are modeled as a *relator* between Goal-based Requirement Artifacts, which potentially *conflicts* with another. It is important to emphasize the difference between conflict and obstacle: the former describes situations in which two goals cannot be achieved in the same solution, although both are desired by stakeholders, whereas the latter describes an undesired state of affairs.

In GORO 2.0, contributions are represented by a Contribution relator that stands between a Goal-Based Requirement Artifact or a Task and a Non-functional Goal-Based Requirement Artifact, which is a non-functional requirement used in a GORE approach. We argue that contributions should only have non-functional requirements as targets because: (i) in the case of total contributions, a negative contribution to a functional requirement would be semantically similar to a Conflict, while a positive contribution would have the same meaning of Complex GBRA or operationalization (*intends to operationalize*); (ii) in the case of partial contributions, it does not make sense to partially satisfy/deny a GBRA which, in turn, has a precise satisfaction criteria. Several GORE languages have certain types of *contribution* relations: *i**, iStar and the NFR Framework, for instance, have some types of contributions, e.g. *make, help, hurt* and *break* [6,19,24]. *Make* and *Break* are positive and negative contributions that sufficiently satisfy a non-functional requirement, respectively, whereas *Help* and *Hurt* are partial positive and negative contributions.

5   Related Works

The initial set of related work was raised based on relevant references of the area, such as Horkoff *et al.* [12] and Guizzardi *et al.* [11]. We consider as related works: (i) the ones that use ontologies as basis for analysis or construction of GORE languages, (ii) the ones that proposed metamodels with the purpose of unifying concepts of goal modeling languages.

Regarding the use of ontologies: the Core Ontology for Requirements Engineering (CORE) [13] has as main objective to review the conceptualization of several RE elements and is the foundation of Techne. However, it is based on a foundational ontology in which essential aspects of conceptual modeling (e.g., material relations and relational properties) have not received sufficiently detailed attention [20]. Guizzardi *et al.* [11], in turn, use UFO as a reference model to analyze *i** and its many variants, therefore aiming to promote interoperability between them, but the work is constrained to the *i** family of languages.

Regarding the use of metamodels: in the work of Fayoumi *et al.* [9], the concepts of eight modeling languages are raised and organized in a metamodel, in which the main objective is the interoperability between GORE models. The work of Lucena *et al.* [18] presents a metamodel created to unify two variants of *i** (its original version and Tropos), considering similarities and differences between them. The work of Cares & Franch [5] defines a *supermetamodel* created on the basis of different variations of *i** (GRL and Tropos), which is validated through a translation algorithm that uses the XML-based iStarML format to depict the relation between tools. Patricio *et al.* [21] propose a unified GORE language called Unified Goal-oriented Language (UGL), which incorporates concepts of *i**, GRL and KAOS and whose metamodel is based on existing metamodels of *i** and KAOS. We argue that, unlike ontologies, metamodels do not provide sufficient semantic foundation to explain complex domain concepts. Metamodels are not efficient enough to promote interoperability between languages because, although they are powerful structures for defining the syntax of a language, they suffer for several limitations in relation to semantic clarifications [11].

6   Conclusions

In this paper, we defined GORO 2.0, a domain reference ontology about Goal-Oriented Requirement Engineering, built based on GORO 1.0, by including concepts related to GORE that had not yet been covered in its previous version. Nine goal modeling languages were chosen based on both literature review and experts' opinion. Their concepts were analyzed and those considered GORE concepts were included. Then, these same concepts were mapped to GORO 2.0 in order to verify and validate the new ontology. Further, a GORO-based tool that converts between two GORE languages (*iStar* and KAOS), was developed as a proof-of-concept. Evaluation results were not presented here due to space constraints, but are available at https://nemo.inf.ufes.br/projects/rose/. GORO 2.0 was built with a strong foundation as it was based on both relevant literature on GORE and on UFO [10]. It also reuses concepts from other ontologies, namely COVR [23] and RSRO. As the latter is part of SEON [22], GORO 2.0 becomes part of this ontology network as well.

By performing validation on GORO, in addition to verifying domain coverage, we were able to notice a few issues in the design of the analyzed languages. Regarding the relations between elements defined in each language, for instance, we could identify that some of them are overloaded. GORO defines decomposition of Goal-Based Requirement Artifacts (GBRA) (Fig. 2), Tasks (Fig. 2) and Obstacles (Fig. 3); the *Conflict* relator between GBRA (Fig. 3); Contribution relation between a GBRA and a Non-functional GBRA (Fig. 3); and finally, an Operationalization relation between a Task and a GBRA (Fig. 2). It was identified that some elements were, at the same time, both an And-Complex GBRA aggregation (when a GBRA is AND decomposed into other GBRAs) and an operational-ization relation (when a GBRA is operationalized into Tasks) or both an Or-Complex GBRA aggregation and an operationalization relation. This is the case, for instance, of Techne's Inference relation.

In terms of interoperability, it is important to mention that, in some cases, elements of a given language cannot be directly converted into elements of another. In this case, we plan to propose conversion patterns as future work. Currently, the tool proposed in this paper creates a log with the elements that were not converted, leaving the user to make the best decision regarding the new model.

In future works, we also intend to: (a) extend the model conversion tool, adding support for more GORE languages and improving its user interface; (b) use GORO 2.0 to make a systematic ontological analysis of GORE languages, verifying possible inconsistencies, construct overload, and other opportunities of improvement in such languages; (c) through the activities performed in (b), propose ontology-based modeling patterns to ensure consistency in the creation of GORE models; (d) use the ontology to identify and incorporate other GORE concepts that the current modeling languages do not cover; (e) use GORO as base for the abstract syntax of a more complete GORE language; and (f) improve the validity of GORE language constructs definition (which was interpreted by our domain experts group), by analysing models on the same subject with the help of GORO.

Acknowledgments. This study was financed in part by the Coordenação de Aperfeiçoamento de Pessoal de Nível Superior - Brasil (CAPES) - Finance Code 001. NEMO (.inf.ufes.br) is currently supported by CNPq (processes 407235/2017-5, 433844/2018-3), CAPES (process 23038.028816/2016-41), and FAPES (process 69382549/2015).

References

1. Amyot, D., Ghanavati, S., Horkoff, J., Mussbacher, G., Peyton, L., Yu, E.: Evaluating goal models within the goal-oriented requirement language. Int. J. Intell. Syst. **25**(8), 841–877 (2010)
2. Anton, A.: Goal-based requirements analysis. In: Proceedings of the 2nd International Conference on Requirements Engineering (RE). pp. 136–144. IEEE Comput. Soc. Press (1996)
3. Borgida, A., et al.: A(nother) Requirements Modeling Language. Technical report, Department Computer Science University of Toronto (2010). ftp://www.cs.toronto.edu/dist/reports/csri/593/techne-techrep-v1.pdf
4. Bresciani, P., Perini, A., Giorgini, P., Giunchiglia, F., Mylopoulos, J.: Tropos: an agent-oriented software development methodology. Auton. Agents Multi-Agent Syst. **8**(3), 203–236 (2004)
5. Cares, C., Franch, X.: A metamodelling approach for i^* model translations. In: Mouratidis, H., Rolland, C. (eds.) CAiSE 2011. LNCS, vol. 6741, pp. 337–351. Springer, Heidelberg (2011). https://doi.org/10.1007/978-3-642-21640-4_26
6. Dalpiaz, F., Franch, X., Horkoff, J.: iStar 2.0 Language Guide. CoRR abs/1605.07767 (2016)

7. Dardenne, A., van Lamsweerde, A., Fickas, S.: Goal-directed requirements acquisition. Sci. Comput. Program. **20**(1–2), 3–50 (1993)
8. Falbo, R.A.: SABiO: systematic approach for building ontologies. In: Proceedings of the 1st Joint Workshop on Ontologies in Conceptual Modeling and Information Systems Engineering, vol. 1201. CEUR (2014)
9. Fayoumi, A., Kavakli, E., Loucopoulos, P.: Towards a unified meta-model for goal oriented modelling. In: Proceedings of the 12th European, Mediterranean & Middle Eastern Conference on Information Systems (EMCIS), pp. 1–10 (2015)
10. Guizzardi, G., Falbo, R., Guizzardi, R.S.S.: Grounding software domain ontologies in the Unified Foundational Ontology (UFO): the case of the ODE software process ontology. In: Proceedings of the 11th Ibero American Conference on Software Engineering (CIbSE) (2008)
11. Guizzardi, R., Franch, X., Guizzardi, G., Wieringa, R.: Using a foundational ontology to investigate the semantics behind the concepts of the i* language. In: Proceedings of the 6th International i* Workshop (iStar), vol. 978, pp. 13–18. CEUR (2013)
12. Horkoff, J., et al.: Goal-oriented requirements engineering: an extended systematic mapping study. Requirements Eng. **24**, 133–160 (2017)
13. Jureta, I.J., Mylopoulos, J., Faulkner, S.: A core ontology for requirements. Appl. Ontol. **4**(3–4), 169–244 (2009)
14. Kelly, T., Weaver, R.: The goal structuring notation–a safety argument notation. In: Proceedings of Dependable Systems and Networks 2004 Ws on Assurance Cases (2004)
15. van Lamsweerde, A.: Goal-oriented requirements engineering: a guided tour. In: Proceedings of the 5th IEEE International Symposium on Requirements Engineering, pp. 249–262. IEEE Comput. Soc (2001)
16. van Lamsweerde, A., Letier, E.: Handling obstacles in goal-oriented requirements engineering. IEEE Trans. Software Eng. **26**(10), 978–1005 (2000)
17. Li, F.L., et al.: Non-functional requirements as qualities, with a spice of ontology. In: 2014 IEEE 22nd International Requirements Engineering Conference (RE), pp. 293–302. IEEE (2014)
18. Lucena, M., Santos, E., Silva, C., Alencar, F., Silva, M.J., Castro, J.: Towards a unified metamodel for i (2008)
19. Mylopoulos, J., Chung, L., Nixon, B.: Representing and using nonfunctional requirements: a process-oriented approach. IEEE Trans. Software Eng. **18**(6), 483–497 (1992)
20. Negri, P., Souza, V., Leal, A., Falbo, R., Guizzardi, G.: Towards an ontology of goal-oriented requirements. In: Proceedings of the 20th Ibero-American Conference on Software Engineering (CIbSE) (2017)
21. Patricio, P., Amaral, V., Araujo, J., Monteiro, R.: Towards a unified goal-oriented language. In: Proceedings of the 35th Annual Computer Software and Applications Conference, pp. 596–601. IEEE (2011)
22. Borges Ruy, F., de Almeida Falbo, R., Perini Barcellos, M., Dornelas Costa, S., Guizzardi, G.: SEON: a software engineering ontology network. In: Blomqvist, E., Ciancarini, P., Poggi, F., Vitali, F. (eds.) EKAW 2016. LNCS (LNAI), vol. 10024, pp. 527–542. Springer, Cham (2016). https://doi.org/10.1007/978-3-319-49004-5_34

23. Sales, T.P., Baião, F., Guizzardi, G., Almeida, J.P.A., Guarino, N., Mylopoulos, J.: The common ontology of value and risk. In: Trujillo, J.C., et al. (eds.) ER 2018. LNCS, vol. 11157, pp. 121–135. Springer, Cham (2018). https://doi.org/10.1007/978-3-030-00847-5_11

24. Yu, E.S.K.: Modelling strategic relationships for process reengineering. Ph.D. thesis, PhD thesis, University of Toronto (1996)

Using Ontologies for Comparing Modeling Techniques: Experience Report

Ilia Bider[(✉)], Erik Perjons, and Paul Johanneson

DSV, Stockholm University, Stockholm, Sweden
{ilia,perjons,pajo}@dsv.su.se

Abstract. The paper presents a comparison of two modelling techniques that can be used to describe an organization as an interconnected set of business processes. The first technique is called Fractal Enterprise Model, which is an invention of the authors of this paper. The second technique is a well-established technique, IDEF0, normally used to present a functional decomposition of an enterprise. The comparison is done based on building a simplified ontology for each technique using UML class diagrams, after which a mapping is established between the concepts of the two ontologies. The discussion that follows analyzes how much of a model designed using one technique can be represented using the other, which is illustrated by an example.

Keywords: Ontology · Fractal enterprise model · IDEF0 · Business process · Enterprise model

1 Motivation

In any modeling field, like business process modeling (BPM), enterprise modeling or conceptual modeling, there are several, sometimes competing, techniques and notations that can be used for modeling in the field. For example, in BPM one can use BPMN [1], UML activity diagrams, IDEF0 [2], IDEF3, and a number of other, less spread techniques, such as state-oriented modeling [3]. Understanding similarities and differences between modeling techniques used in the same field has both theoretical and, which is more important, practical value.

From the practical perspective, understanding the similarities and differences of various modeling techniques can be used for two purposes:

1. Making an informed choice of a technique when building a model for a particular purpose. Given this purpose, the focus is on differences.
2. Using a model designed with one technique as a source of information for designing a model using the other technique. Given this purpose, the focus is on similarities.

To clearly present differences and similarities is of importance when a new modeling technique is introduced in the field where there already exist a number of well-established and less established techniques. As the originators of a new enterprise modeling technique called Fractal Enterprise Model (FEM) [4], we find it essential to compare it with other, possibly competing, techniques to give modelers a clear

© Springer Nature Switzerland AG 2019
G. Guizzardi et al. (Eds.): ER 2019 Workshops, LNCS 11787, pp. 180–190, 2019.
https://doi.org/10.1007/978-3-030-34146-6_16

understanding of FEM's area of applicability (see purpose 1 above), and provide them with a method of translating a FEM to a model in another modeling technique or vice versa (see purpose 2 above).

FEM is aimed to represent an organization as an interconnected set of business processes. FEM has a form of a directed graph with two types of nodes *Processes* and *Assets*, where the arrows (edges) from assets to processes show which assets are utilized by which processes and arrows from processes to assets show which processes help to keep specific assets in "healthy" and working order. The arrows are labeled with meta-tags that show in what way a given asset is utilized, e.g. as *workforce, attraction, infrastructure*, etc., or in what way a given process helps to keep the given assets "in order", i.e. *acquire, maintain* or *retire*.

A FEM is built recursively by using a so-called unfolding procedure and two types of archetypes: *process-assets archetypes* that show which kind of assets might be needed for running a process, and an *asset-processes* archetype that shows which processes are needed to maintain an asset in order. Unfolding starts with a primary process - a process that delivers value to a customer/beneficiary - by applying process-assets archetypes and alternating them with the asset-processes archetype.

This work is the first in a series where we offer a relatively formal comparison of the FEM technique with other techniques that (a) can be used for representing an organization as an interconnected set of processes, or (b) the models built with these techniques could be used as a source of information for building a FEM for a particular business case, as in [5]. More specifically, this work is devoted to comparing FEM with IDEF0 [2], which on a high level can be used for representing interconnections between various business processes in an organization.

IDEF0 is a modeling technique that allows to present a multilevel functional decomposition of an organization. If we stay on the high level of the decomposition where each function represents a business process, IDEF0 can be used for representing interconnections between the processes in an organization. In this capacity, IDEF0 constitutes an alternative technique to FEM, which justifies our goal to compare these two modeling techniques.

To compare the chosen modeling techniques in a more formal way, we use the idea of comparing ontologies that underpin the techniques. The latter can be done by depicting the ontologies formally, e.g. as UML class diagrams, and then mapping the concepts from one ontology into the concepts of the other, similar to what is proposed in [6]. For our task, we do not use any foundational ontologies, like BWW or Chisholm, but create two separate simplified ontologies. The latter have enough concepts to make a comparison, while not covering the details that are not essential for our task. Though we accept that foundational ontologies might be useful for comparing languages, for languages that are closely related, using the foundational ontologies might be an overkill.

The rest of the paper is structured in the following way. In Sect. 2 we present the knowledge base used in our comparison of modeling techniques. In Sect. 3, we present simplified ontologies for FEM and IDEF0 using UML class diagrams. In Sect. 4, we compare FEM with IDEF0 based on their ontologies. In Sect. 5, we discuss the lessons learned during the trial.

2 Knowledge Base

2.1 Fractal Enterprise Model

A Fractal Enterprise Model (FEM) includes three types of elements: business processes (more exactly, business process types), assets, and relationships between them, see Fig. 1 in which a fragment of a model is presented. The fragment is related to a hypothetic management consulting company. Graphically, a process is represented by an oval, an asset is represented by a rectangle (box), while a relationship between a process and an asset is represented by an arrow. We differentiate two types of relationships in the fractal model. One type represents a relationship of a process "using" an asset; in this case, the arrow points from the asset to the process and has a solid line. The other type represents a relationship of a process changing the asset; in this case, the arrow points from the process to the asset and has a dashed line. These two types of relationships allow tying up processes and assets in a directed graph.

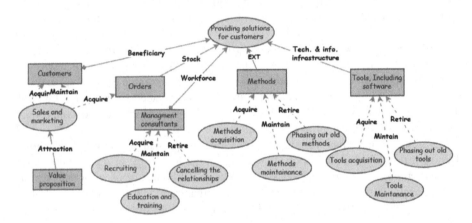

Fig. 1. A fragment of a FEM for a management consulting company

In FEM, a label inside an oval names the given process, and a label inside a rectangle names the given asset. Arrows are also labeled to show the type of relationships between the processes and assets. A label on an arrow pointing from an asset to a process identifies the role the given asset plays in the process, for example, *workforce* and *infrastructure*. A label on an arrow pointing from a process to an asset identifies the way in which the process affects (i.e. changes) the asset. In FEM, an asset is considered as a pool of entities capable of playing a given role in a given process. Labels leading into assets from supporting processes reflect the way the pool is affected, for example, the label *acquire* identifies that the process can/should increase the pool size.

Note that the same asset can be used in two different processes playing the same or different roles in them, which is reflected by labels on the corresponding arrows. It is also possible that the same asset can be used for more than one role in the same process. In this case there can be more than one arrow between the asset and the process, but with different labels. Similarly, the same process could affect different assets, each in the same or in different ways, which is represented by the corresponding labels on the arrows. Moreover, it is possible that the same process affects the same asset in different ways, which is represented by having two or more arrows from the process to the asset, each with its own label.

In FEM, different styles can be used for shapes to group together different kinds of processes, assets, and relationships between them. Such styles can include dashed or double lines, or colored shapes. For example, a diamond start of an arrow from an asset to a process means that the asset is a stakeholder of the process (see "Workforce").

Labels inside ovals (which represent processes) and inside rectangles (which represent assets) are not standardized. They can be set according to the terminology accepted in the given domain, or be specific for a given organization. Labels on arrows (which represent the relationships between processes and assets) can be standardized. This is done by using a set of relatively abstract relationships, such as *workforce* or *acquire*, which are clarified by the domain- and context-specific labels inside ovals and rectangles. Standardization improves the understandability of the models.

While there are a number of types of relationships that show how an asset is used in a process (see example in Fig. 1), there are only three types of relationships that show how an asset is managed by a process – *Acquire*, *Maintain* and *Retire*.

To make the work of building a fractal model more systematic, FEM uses archetypes (or patterns) for fragments from which a particular model can be built. An archetype is a template defined as a fragment of a model where labels inside ovals (processes) and rectangles (assets) are omitted, but arrows are labelled. Instantiating an archetype means putting the fragment inside the model and labelling ovals and rectangles; it is also possible to add elements absent in the archetype, or omit some elements that are present in the archetype.

FEM has two types of archetypes, process-assets archetypes and an asset-processes archetype. A process-assets archetype represents the kinds of assets that can be used in a given category of processes. The asset-processes archetype shows the kinds of processes that are aimed at changing the given category of assets.

2.2   IDEF0

IDEF0 represents the output-input and some other types of relationships between the functional units of an organization. The main block of an IDEF0 diagram is a functional unit which is represented by a rectangle (or box), see Fig. 2. The functional units are connected through the arrows outgoing from one functional box and coming into another box. Outgoing arrows are always coming from the right-hand side of the rectangle. Ingoing arrows can come to three other sides of the rectangle, but the meaning of them depends on the side to which the arrow comes into the rectangle, see Fig. 2.

If an arrow comes from the left-hand side of the rectangle, it represents objects that comes from outside and are consumed by the function to produce an output. If an arrow comes from the top side of the rectangle it represents control objects that guide the work of the functional unit, e.g. instructions, design drawing, laws. If an arrow comes from the bottom side of the rectangle, it represent a mechanism (resource) used in the functional unit to convert inputs to outputs. This can be people, machines, tools, etc., anything that is used but is not totally consumed when the input is converted to the output.

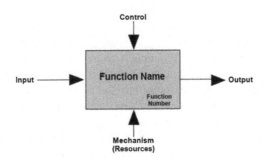

Fig. 2. A building block of IDEF0 diagrams

There can be more than one arrow coming in or out from each side of the rectangle that represents a functional unit. Some outgoing arrows serve as incoming arrows for other functional units in an IDEF0 diagram, thus showing interconnection between the functional units. However, an arrow can come from or point to something outside the diagram to show interconnection between the system being modeled and its environment. In this work, we disregard this feature of IDEF0.

Each functional unit can also be decomposed to sub-units in a separate diagram. However, in this work, we are not considering this possibility, though this is one of the essential features of IDEF0. The meaning of the functional units depends on the purpose of the model. They can represent organizational units of an enterprise, or processes in the set of all enterprise processes, which is how we interpret functional units in this work. They can also represent activities in a process, when IDEF0 is used to depict details of a business process.

2.3   Comparing Ontologies

In this work, we roughly follow the idea of comparing ontologies presented in [6]. The comparison is done in three steps. First, a formal representation of each ontology is built. Then, the concepts from one ontology are mapped into the concepts of the other ontology. In the last step, the mapping is analyzed based on the following rules:

- If between two corresponding elements in two ontologies there is a one-to-one relationship, there is an ontological equivalence regarding these elements.
- In the case when one element in an ontology is further specified by two or more elements in the other ontology, the other ontology has a deeper structure regarding these elements.
- In the case one element in one ontology does not have any correspondence in the other ontology then the first ontology has a more comprehensive scope.

3 Simplified Ontologies for FEM and IDEF0

In this section, we define simplified ontologies for FEM and IDEF0 and present them formally using the UML class diagrams notation.

3.1 Ontology for FEM

An ontology for FEM presented below is based on [4]. A FEM differentiates two types of things in the organizational world that it represents: processes and assets. A process in FEM represents a work system responsible for initiating and finishing process instances of the given type, e.g. manufacturing or sales. We call this system a Business Process Work System or BPWS for short. BPWS is a socio-technical system that includes people, methods, e.g. manuals that prescribes the process flow, technology and structure, i.e., distribution of responsibilities between the members of the team responsible for the process. The components of BPWS are called assets. An asset is a set of entities of a given type, e.g. people, machines, software systems, etc. A set can also include only one element, e.g. a specific software system.

A Business Process Instance (BPI) is considered as a system that is created to handle a specific situation defined by a condition for creating an instance. This system can be thought of as a respondent system in terms of [7], which is created to handle a specific situation and which is disbanded when the situation is resolved. When creating a BPI, BPWS gives it some of its assets to be engaged in the BPI. It also follows the work of BPI, and if needed, the BPWS can provide more assets to carry out the BPI. After the BPI is finished, all assets are returned back to the BPWS. Note that assets may not be given exclusively to a BPI, but may be shared with other BPIs.

A UML class diagram for the simplified FEM ontology that includes processes and assets and their relations is presented in Fig. 3. There are two types of relations between processes and assets included in a FEM. The first type is connected to an asset being a component of a BPWS system filling a certain role in it. This type of relations is called "Used In As" and it is denoted in Fig. 3 as *UsedInAs*. The second type of relations represents a process managing an asset in a certain way. This type of relations is called "Managed by" and it is denoted as *ManagedBy* in Fig. 3.

Both *UsedInAs* and *ManagedBy* relations are further specialized. The *UsedInAs* relations type is split in the following subclasses:

- Stakeholders, which encompasses three types of relationships:
  - *Beneficiary* – an organization or person that receives some value from the process, for which the beneficiary or somebody else is prepared to pay. A typical beneficiary is a customer who buys goods and/or services and pays for them. There can be more than one beneficiary in a given process.
  - *Workforce* – people trained and qualified for employment in the process. Examples: workers at the conveyor belt, physicians, researchers.
  - *Partner* – an agent, external to the given organization, who participates in the process. This, for example, can be a supplier of parts in a manufacturing process; a lab that completes medical tests on behalf of a hospital. Partners can be other enterprises or individuals.

- *Attraction* – something that helps to acquire a stakeholder. For a customer, for example, it could be a value proposition, i.e. a statement of benefits that a customer will get by acquiring certain products and/or services (see Fig. 1). For recruiting staff it could be salary and other benefits that an employee receives.
- *EXT* – a process execution template. This can, for example, be: a software development methodology accepted in a software vendor company; a product design for a manufacturer; a description of the service delivery procedure, e.g., a process map for a service company. It can also be a policy document.

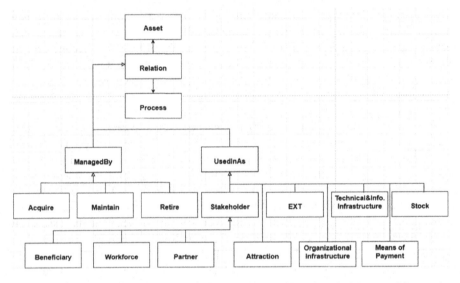

Fig. 3. A simplified FEM ontology as a UML class diagram (associations are of 1:n type)

- *Organizational Infrastructure* – a unit of organization that participates in the process. This, for example, can be: a sales department or a software development team.
- *Technical and Information Infrastructure* – an equipment required for executing the process instances. This, for example, can be: a production line, a computer, a communication line, a building, a software system.
- *Means of Payment* – any kind of monetary fund that is needed to pay participating stakeholders, e.g., suppliers if such payment is considered as part of the process.
- *Stock* – a stock of materials or parts, or other things that are used in the process. This, for example, can be: office products, e.g., paper, pens, printer cartridges, in any office, or spare parts for a car repair shop. It can also be a stock of customer orders, see Fig. 1. A specific feature of the stock asset is that it is depleted by the process for which the asset is attached via the stock relation. It means that this process also function as a *retire* process of the stock (which is omitted in FEM diagrams).

The *ManagedBy* relations type is split into three subclasses:

- *Acquire* – a process that results in the enterprise acquiring new items that fill in an asset of a given type. The essence of this process depends on the type of asset, the type of the process in which the asset is used and the type of the enterprise. For a product-oriented enterprise, *acquiring* new customers (beneficiary) is done through marketing and sales processes. *Acquiring* skilled work force is a task completed by a recruiting process. Acquiring a new EXT for a product-oriented enterprise is a task for a new product and technological process development.
- *Maintain* – a process that helps to keep existing assets in the right shape to be employable in the BPIs of a given type. For customers, it could be Customer Relations Management process. For workforce, it could be training. For EXT, it could be product or process improvement. For technical infrastructure, it could be service.
- *Retire* – a process that phases out assets that no longer can be used in the intended process. For customers, it could be canceling a contract with a customer that is no longer profitable. For the workforce, it could be actual retirement.

3.2   Ontology for IDEF0

The main concept of IDEF0 is a function. A function can be viewed as a system that given certain inputs produces certain outputs using certain mechanisms and guided by certain controls. The second important concept that exists in IDEF0 is an object that is produced by a function or sent as an input to it. The objects are represented by arrows in IDEF0 diagrams. The object in IDEF0 world can be an individual entity or a set of entities. Note that in this work, we do not consider the decomposition of a function in sub-functions, which is an essential feature of IDEF0.

A simplified ontology for IDEF0 depicted as a UML class diagram is represented in Fig. 4. This model includes three classes – *Function*, *Object* and *Relation* between the two. The *Relation* is split into two groups (subclasses) - *Outgoing* and *Incoming*. The outgoing group has only one subclass – *Output*, while the incoming group has three subclasses: *Input, Control* and *Mechanism*.

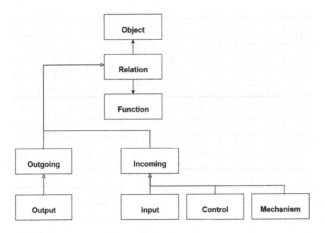

Fig. 4. A simplified IDEF0 ontology as a UML class diagram (associations are of 1:n type)

4   Comparing FEM and IDEF0

On the high-level of ontologies for FEM and IDEF0, we can map *Process* to *Function*, *Asset* to *Object* and *Relation* to *Relation*. On this level of hierarchy, we can say that the two ontologies are equivalent. If we look at sub-classing of the relation concepts, we can map *ManagedBy* to *Outgoing* and *UsedInAs* to *Incoming*. Thus, even on this level we can consider the ontologies as equivalent. The difference starts on the next level of sub-classing and it is represented in Table 1. Note that in this comparison table, we skip the concept of stakeholders, and go directly to the level underneath it, that is, workforce, partner and beneficiary.

Table 1. Mapping from FEM ontology to IDEF0 ontology

Subclass of	FEM	IDEF0
ManagedBy/Outgoing	Acquire	Output
	Maintain	No correspondence
	Retire	No correspondence
UsedIn/Incoming	Beneficiary	No correspondence
	Workforce	Mechanism
	Partner	Mechanism
	Attraction	Mechanism
	EXT	Control
	Organizational infrastructure	No correspondence
	Technical & Information Infrastructure	Mechanism
	Means of payment	Mechanism
	Stock	Input

As follows from Table 1 and the approach for ontology comparison from [6], see Sect. 2.3, the FEM ontology has both a deeper structure and more comprehensive scope. The first is because several concepts of FEM are mapped to the same concept of IDEF0, i.e. *workforce, partner, attraction, technical & info infrastructure and means of payment* are mapped into *mechanism*. The second is because a number of concepts in FEM do not have corresponding concepts in IDEF0. Note that we do not take into consideration the decomposition concept of IDEF0 which has no correspondence in FEM. In regards to this concept, IDEF0 has a more comprehensive scope.

FEM having a more comprehensive scope than IDEF0 is demonstrated in Fig. 5 that shows an IDEF0 diagram that is a translation of the FEM fragment in Fig. 1. As we can see, some concepts from Fig. 1 could not be represented in Fig. 5.

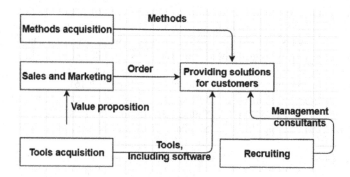

Fig. 5. IDEF0 representation of the diagram on Fig. 1

5   Lessons Learned and Plans for the Future

This paper presents a trial of using ontologies for comparing modeling techniques that can be used for the same purpose. In our particular case, we have compared FEM and IDEF0 that can be used for representing interrelationships between various business processes in an organization. The comparison has been done by building ontologies that underpin each of the modeling technique in a formal way[1], and then compare them based on the principles suggested in [6], see Sect. 2.3. Based on the ontologies comparison, we were able to determine that FEM has both a deeper structure and more comprehensive scope as far as modeling interconnections between business processes is the purpose of modeling.

We believe that the results of our trial has value both from a general and specific point of view. From a general point of view, it shows that a method of comparing

---

[1] Note that our formal FEM ontology might look like a metamodel of FEM language (syntax). This is due to FEM elements have fixed (unambiguous) semantics. The same is (partially) true for IDEF0. For a language with more ambiguous semantics, there can be several ontologies dependent on modeling practices, i.e. how the language elements are interpreted. In this case, a metamodel of the language will differ from any of formal ontologies that can be attached to it.

modeling techniques based on comparing their ontologies works in practice. From our specific point of view, we have succeeded to show the similarities and differences between our relatively new FEM technique and a technique that is well established in the modeling community. The results of the trial seem encouraging, and we will continue the work started with this paper by using the ontological approach for comparing FEM with other modeling techniques. The next planned step is comparing FEM with BPMN.

References

1. Chinosi, M.: Trombetta: BPMN: an introduction to the standard. Comput. Stand. Interfaces **34** (1), 124–134 (2012)
2. NIST: Integration definition for function modeling (IDEF0), Draft Federal Information Processing Standards, Publication 183 (1993). www.idef.com/downloads/pdf/idef0.pdf
3. Andersson, T., Andersson-Ceder, A., Bider, I.: State flow as a way of analyzing business processes - case studies. Logist. Inf. Manag. **15**(1), 34–45 (2002)
4. Bider, I., Perjons, E., Elias, M., Johannesson, P.: A fractal enterprise model and its application for business development. Softw. Syst. Model. **16**, 663–689 (2016)
5. Saarsen, T., Bider, I., Perjons, E.: Testing the fractal enterprise model in practice. In: Reinhartz-Berger, I., Zdravkovic, J., Gulden, J., Schmidt, R. (eds.) BPMDS/EMMSAD - 2019. LNBIP, vol. 352, pp. 103–111. Springer, Cham (2019). https://doi.org/10.1007/978-3-030-20618-5_7
6. Davies, I., Green, P., Milton, S., Rosemann, M.: Using meta models for the comparison of ontologies. In: EMMSAD 2003. Proceedings of Evaluation of Modeling Methods in Systems Analysis and Design Workshop, Klagenfut (2003)
7. Lawson, H.: A Journey Through the Systems Landscape. College Publications, London (2010)

Domain Ontology for Digital Marketplaces

Thomas Derave[1]([⊠]) , Tiago Prince Sales[2] ,
Michaël Verdonck[1] , Frederik Gailly[1] , and Geert Poels[1]

[1] Department of Business Informatics and Operations Management,
Ghent University, Tweekerkenstraat 2, 9000 Ghent, Belgium
{thomas.derave,michael.verdock,frederik.gailly,
geert.poels}@UGent.be
[2] Faculty of Computer Science, Free University of Bozen-Bolzano,
Bolzano, Italy
tiago.princesales@unibz.it

Abstract. Recently the sharing economy has emerged as a viable alternative to fulfilling a variety of consumer needs. As there is no consensus on the definition of 'sharing economy' we use the term 'marketplace' to refer more specifically to Internet/software-based sharing economy platforms connecting two different market segments. In the field of sharing economy and marketplaces we found a research gap concerning the (socio)technological aspects and the development of marketplaces. A marketplace ontology can help to have a clear account of marketplace concepts which will facilitate communication, consensus and alignment. In this paper we design this marketplace ontology in four steps. First the selection of UFO as foundation and UFO-S as core ontology. Second the search for a set of minimal conditions and properties common for marketplaces and the derivation into competency questions. Third, use the competency questions to identify fragmented sub-ontology pieces called Domain-Related Ontology Patterns (DROPs) and apply them informally by extending UFO-S concepts to design a marketplace domain ontology. This marketplace domain ontology is represented in OntoUML. The last step is the validation of the OntoUML model using expert knowledge.

Keywords: Digital marketplace · Sharing economy · Marketplace ontology · UFO-S · OntoUML

1 Introduction

The use of sharing economy platforms like Airbnb and Uber is on the rise. The sharing economy has emerged as a viable alternative to fulfilling a variety of consumer needs, ranging from prepared meals to cars to overnight accommodations, that were previously provided by firms. As the size of the sharing economy has grown, so has the magnitude of its economic and societal impacts [1]. The sharing economy is also an emerging and fast-growing academic field. Based on the current state of the art overview by Trabucchi et al. [2], studies of the sharing economy have focused on three themes: (1) the customers motivation of using these platforms [3]; (2) the impact on society, market and policy [4, 5]; and (3) classifications of sharing economy business

© Springer Nature Switzerland AG 2019
G. Guizzardi et al. (Eds.): ER 2019 Workshops, LNCS 11787, pp. 191–200, 2019.
https://doi.org/10.1007/978-3-030-34146-6_17

models with a dominant focus on the revenue model and pricing mechanism [4, 6, 7]. Problematic for academic studies is that 'sharing economy' is an umbrella concept and there is no consensus on what definition, activities and core building blocks it comprises [8]. In this paper we will follow Laudien and Täuscher [9] and base our research on the better-defined term 'marketplace' to refer more specifically to Internet/software-based sharing economy platforms. This might provide a useful lens to overcome the challenges in defining the boundaries of the sharing economy as currently experienced by the related literature [9]. The most adopted definition of marketplace is the following: "Marketplaces employ a special type of business model known as a multi-sided platform that connects two different market segments which value each other's presence whereas the actual transactions with customers are processed by the marketplace" [10, 11]. Previous marketplace research focused mainly on the business-to-business market [12–14].

The literature of both the sharing economy and marketplaces only offers a very partial view, and just started with research on consumer-to-consumer markets and business models from the perspective of the marketplace itself [9]. There is a lack of research concerning the (socio)technological aspects, the development and the innovations patterns diffusion of marketplaces and sharing economy platforms [2, 15]. This paper contributes to filling this gap by creating a domain ontology for all marketplaces.

A marketplace ontology can help to have a clear account of marketplace concepts which will facilitate communication, consensus and alignment [16]. For example, the terminology and interconnections of concepts such as 'listing', 'transaction' 'marketplace' and 'review' can be better defined and visualized for better communication between the developer and other stakeholders of a marketplace. A common terminology and understanding will help future discussions, marketplace developments and research. Nowadays most people know the sharing economy only through huge companies like Airbnb and Uber paying low wages, avoiding taxes and using their winner takes all model to become a monopolist [17]. Increasing the knowledge of marketplace related concepts can, for instance, be vital for the development of smaller, more alternative and socially responsible marketplaces and can thus contribute to the creation of a more socially responsible sharing economy.

In the next section we explain the methodology used to design the marketplace domain ontology. In Sect. 3 we provide background information on marketplaces. In Sect. 4 we develop the marketplace domain ontology and in Sect. 5 we summarize the paper, give a conclusion and outline our future research.

2 Methodology

To design a marketplace domain ontology we will use the method of [18] consisting of four steps.

First, we searched for an appropriate foundation and core ontology and if needed divide it into sub-ontologies. As foundation ontology we use the Unified Foundational Ontology (UFO) [19] and as core ontology we decided to use UFO-S [16], a commitment-based service ontology concerning the establishment and fulfillment of commitments and claims between service participants. UFO-S is already modularized into three sub-ontologies called service offering, service negotiation and service delivery.

Second, we search for conditions in the literature to classify an organization as a marketplace. We call these conditions Minimal Marketplace Requirements (MMRs). We also add a set of properties that are common for most, but not all marketplace types. We base these Common Marketplace Properties (CMPs) on [9]. We further group and rephrase these MMRs and CMPs to competency questions (CQs), which are needed for performing the next step of the method of [18].

Third, we use the CQs to identify fragmented sub-ontology pieces called Domain-Related Ontology Patterns (DROPs) and Foundational Ontology Patterns (FOPs). DROPs and FOPs are reusable fragments extracted from reference domain/core ontologies and foundational ontologies respectively, packaging the knowledge related to the marketplace domain [20]. We apply them informally by extending UFO-S concepts to design a marketplace domain ontology and represent our marketplace domain ontology in OntoUML [16].

The last step is the validation of the ontology done by UFO and UFO-S experts answering the CQ's using the OntoUML model. If the response differed from the intended outcome, changes to the model were made and the process was repeated until no more changes were needed. We also fitted the example of Airbnb into our model as a second validation of the ontology.

3   Background

To give the reader a better understanding of the basic functioning of marketplaces, we give an overview in Fig. 1.

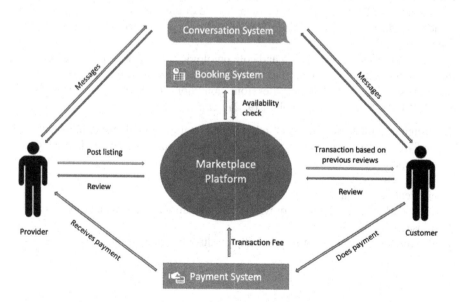

Fig. 1. Marketplace overview

Providers and customers can subscribe on the marketplace platform that can be reached via a site or mobile application. A provider can freely offer a service on the marketplace platform which is called a listing (e.g., an apartment on Airbnb or a concert ticket on Ticketswap). A customer can search through the listings on the marketplace platform for the service he wants. After the customer located the desired service, he or she can make a transaction by acquiring the service via the marketplace platform. After the delivery of the service he or she can leave a review and previous reviews can help customers to find the best service to their needs. A provider and customer can be a person or an organization, and it's possible to be a provider and customer on the same platform. The conversation system is important to create information transparency. This way a customer can receive more information about a listing or transaction. The booking system is dependent on the type of marketplace. For Uber, the system will check the closest available car dependent on the preferences of the customer. In case of Airbnb, the system checks availability and informs the customer whether the accommodation is free or not. The money is transferred through the payment system from the customer to the provider, with a transaction fee for the marketplace itself. It is important to state that this simple overview covers common types of marketplace, but not necessarily all types.

4 Marketplace Domain Ontology

A domain ontology can be a specialization of foundation ontologies (by analogy) and/or core ontologies (by extensions). The reason for using UFO-S as core ontology is that marketplaces are primarily used as digital intermediaries to allow service provisioning. Also, the three sub-ontologies of UFO-S, named service offering, service negotiation and service delivery, are closely related to the process flow of using marketplaces. UFO is the foundation ontology of UFO-S, and therefore ideal to use for specializations of the marketplace domain outside of the service domain. Therefore, we decided to design the marketplace domain ontology as a specialization of the UFO foundation and UFO-S core.

After selecting the foundation and core ontology, we start with the development of the minimum marketplace requirements (MMRs) and common marketplace properties (CMPs). Previous research proposes four conditions or MMRs for classifying an organization as a digital marketplace [9, 21, 22]:

1. A digital marketplace connects independent actors from a demand and supply side (individuals or organizations) via a digital platform. These individual actors can participate on both sides.
2. These actors enter direct interactions with each other (on the platform) to initiate and realize commercial transactions.
3. The marketplace platform provides an institutional and regulatory frame for transactions.
4. The marketplace does not substantially produce or trade products or services itself.

Based on the marketplace properties of Laudien and Tauscher [9] and marketplace functions of Bakos [22], we identified four CMPs:

1. The common definition of the offered service by the provider is called a listing.
2. It is common for a marketplace to have a web-based platform and/or a mobile application to present the listings offered by the providers.
3. After the transaction it is common for a marketplace to manage the payment transfer from customer to provider.
4. After the transaction it is common for a marketplace to allow a review from the customer concerning the transaction.

We translate these MMRs and CMPs into three lists of CQs. Each list is related to a UFO-S sub-ontology. Hence these lists address respectively CQs related to marketplace service offering, marketplace service negotiation and marketplace service delivery. These different lists of CQs are a natural guide for driving the process of creating a domain ontology as a specialization of the UFO-S sub-ontologies. This was not a linear process. After creating a first version the ontology was validated by UFO-S experts answering the CQ's using the OntoUML model. If the response differed from the intended outcome, changes to the model were made and the process was repeated until no more changes were needed.

4.1 Marketplace Offering Sub-ontology

A list of CQs influencing the marketplace offering sub-ontology is given below:

- What is a marketplace? (MMR1, MMR4)
- What is a marketplace platform (MMR1, MMR2)
- What is a listing? (MMR1, CMP1)
- Who is involved in a listing? (MMR1)
- How is a listing described? (CMP1, CMP2)

A marketplace is an organization managing one to multiple digital platforms. A listing is the service offered on the marketplace platform, hence is a subclass of the UFO-S service offering. The listing is the interaction between three actors: the marketplace platform; a marketplace provider who offers the listings and the potential marketplace community as the target of the provider who might be willing to buy the service using the platform. The listing description is a category specialized into the type's as web page and application page. During the validation the marketplace entity was split into a role which is the company or organization and the relator, which is the digital platform where the listings are visualized.

In case of Airbnb, the organization manages two platforms, one offering places to stay and another offering experiences (activities organized by locals). An apartment owner can offer his apartments as listings on the 'places to stay' platform. The potential marketplace community can search through all the apartments on the platform via the descriptions visible on the Airbnb site or app (Fig. 2).

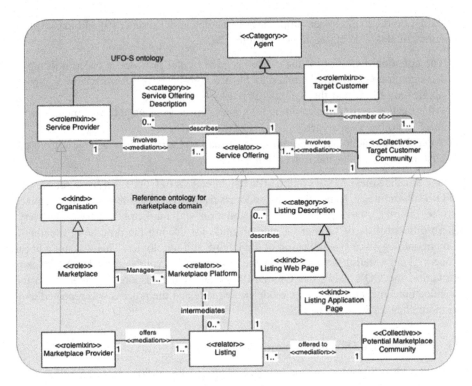

Fig. 2. Offering sub-ontology

4.2 Marketplace Negotiation Sub-ontology

A list of CQs influencing the marketplace negotiation sub-ontology is given below:

- What is a marketplace conversation? (MMR2)
- What is a transaction? (MMR2, MMR3)
- Who is in involved in a transaction? (MMR2, MMR4)

The marketplace conversation between a marketplace provider and a target marketplace customer concerning a certain listing is via a conversation system transferred by the marketplace platform. This conversation can result in a transaction. A transaction is the agreement between the booked marketplace provider and the marketplace customer concerning a listing. In the marketplace domain there is a restriction on the cardinalities allowing only one target marketplace customer to participate in a conversation and only one marketplace customer to be bound to a transaction.

For Airbnb, a conversation is transferred by the platform between the apartment owner and interested customers searching for a holiday rental. Every conversation refers to a certain apartment, and the conversation can result in a booking of the apartment in question (Fig. 3).

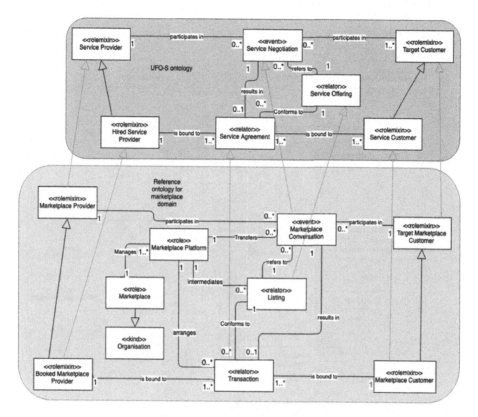

Fig. 3. Negotiation sub-ontology

4.3 Marketplace Delivery Sub-ontology

A list of CQs influencing the marketplace delivery sub-ontology is given below:

- What is a payment? (CMP3)
- Who is involved in a payment (CMP3)
- What is a review? (CMP4)
- Who is involved in a review (CMP4)

In case of a transaction, none (when free) to multiple payments are made by the marketplace customer to the booked marketplace provider. After the marketplace delivery, the customer can create a review. This review is collected by the marketplace platform. For the marketplace domain the cardinalities of the marketplace customer are always restricted to one. During the validation the relators 'Payment' and 'Review' and their relationships where further refined.

For Airbnb, after booking the apartment the customer makes the payment and spends his/her holidays in the apartment. This service can also include fresh towels, free soap, etc. After the delivery the customer can write a review, and these are collected by the marketplace platform to provide more insights for future customers (Fig. 4).

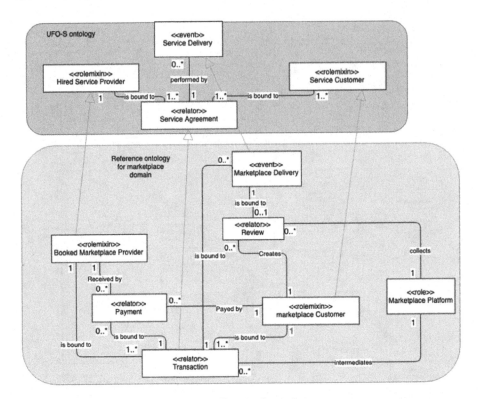

Fig. 4. Delivery sub-ontology

5   Conclusion

In this paper we designed a marketplace domain ontology as an extension of the UFO-S core ontology for services. For the foundation of our marketplace domain ontology we used competence questions (CQs) based on the minimal marketplace requirements (MMRs) and common marketplace properties (CMPs) derived from previous literature. The design of the marketplace was done using the method of [18] and visualized in OntoUML.

A restriction of our research is the lack of literature sources for deriving the MMPs and CMPs, hence CQs. A systematic literature review of marketplaces could result in additional sources, however, in absence of these an empirical validation of our ontology with a sample of existing marketplaces could provide a viable alternative. By using different types of existing marketplaces and validate them with our model we can further expand the ontology. In future research, we will also formalize sub-ontology fragments linked to individual CQs as Domain-Related Ontology patterns (DROPs) and Foundational Ontology Patterns (FOPs) [18]. These DROPs and FOPs can help to design the marketplace domain ontology in a more structured and expanded manner.

In this paper we also restrict the number of providers for a single transaction to one. Some existing marketplaces (e.g. Deliveroo, Uber Eats) have different providers for the same transaction. When ordering a meal via Deliveroo, both the preparation of the meal by the restaurant and the delivery of the mail by a deliverer are linked to a single transaction.

As a marketplace domain ontology can facilitate communication, consensus and alignment in future discussions, marketplace developments and research, we plan to use this ontology as a basis for the development of a conceptual data model for a comprehensive variety of different marketplaces. This conceptual data model can then be compared to software products for marketplace creation (e.g. Sharetribe [23]) and the gaps between them can result in the design a software reference architecture for marketplaces. A marketplace ontology, conceptual data model and software reference architecture can accelerate the development of smaller, more alternative and socially responsible marketplaces and can thus contribute to the creation of a more socially responsible sharing economy.

References

1. Zervas, G., Proserpio, D., Byers, J.W.: The rise of the sharing economy: estimating the impact of airbnb on the hotel industry. J. Mark. Res., 2731799 (2014)
2. Trabucchi, D., Muzellec, L., Ronteau, S., Trabucchi, D.: Sharing economy: seeing through the fog economy (2019)
3. Hamari, J., Ukkonen, A.: The sharing economy: why people participate in collaborative consumption. J. Assoc. Inf. Sci. Technol. **67**, 2047–2059 (2016)
4. Frenken, K., Schor, J.: Putting the sharing economy into perspective. Environ. Innov. Soc. Transit. **23**, 3–10 (2017)
5. Kenney, M., Zysman, J.: The rise of the platform economy. Issues Sci. Technol. **32**, 61–69 (2016)
6. Bardhi, F., Eckhardt, G.M.: Access-based consumption: the case of car sharing. J. Consum. Res. **39**, 881–898 (2012)
7. Botsman, R., Rogers, R.: What's Mine Is Yours: The Rise of Collaborative Consumption (2010)
8. Codagnone, C., Martens, B.: Scoping the Sharing Economy: Origins, Definitions, Impact and Regulatory Issues. Ssrn (2016)
9. Täuscher, K., Laudien, S.M.: Understanding platform business models: a mixed methods study of marketplaces. Eur. Manag. J. **36**, 319–329 (2018)
10. Hagiu, A., Wright, J.: Multi-sided platforms. Int. J. Ind. Organ. **43**, 1–32 (2015)
11. Kestenbaum, R.: What Are Online Marketplaces And What Is Their Future? (2017). https://www.forbes.com/sites/richardkestenbaum/2017/04/26/what-are-online-marketplaces-and-what-is-their-future/#7db183243284
12. Choudhury, V., Hartzel, K.S., Konsynski, B.R.: Uses and consequences of electronic markets: an empirical investigation in the aircraft parts industry. MIS Q. **22**, 471–507 (2019)
13. Dai, Q., Kauffman, R.J.: Business models for internet-based e-procurement systems and B2B electronic markets: an exploratory assessment, vol. 00, pp. 1–10 (2004)
14. Stockdale, R.: A framework for the selection of electronic marketplaces: a content analysis approach. ECU Publ., 221–234 (2004)
15. Sutherland, W., Jarrahi, M.H.: The sharing economy and digital platforms: a review and research agenda. Int. J. Inf. Manag. **43**, 328–341 (2018)

16. Cesar, J., et al.: A commitment-based reference ontology for services. Inf. Syst. **54**, 263–288 (2015)
17. Kenney, M., Zysman, J.: Choosing a future in platform economy: the implications and consequences of digital platforms. J. Chem. Inf. Model. **53**, 1689–1699 (2013)
18. Ruy, F.B., Guizzardi, G., Falbo, R.A., Reginato, C.C., Santos, V.A.: From reference ontologies to ontology patterns and back. Data Knowl. Eng. **109**, 41–69 (2017)
19. Guizzardi, G.: Foundations for Structural Conceptual (2005)
20. Falbo, R.A., Guizzardi, G., Gangemi, A., Presutti, V.: Ontology patterns: clarifying concepts and terminology. In: CEUR Workshop Proceedings, vol. 1188 (2013)
21. Täuscher, K., Berkeley, U.C.: Supporting business model decisions: a scenario-based simulation approach. Int. J. Mark. Bus. Syst. **2**, 45–67 (2016)
22. Bakos, Y.: The Emerging role of electronic marketplaces on the Internet. Commun. ACM **41**, 35–42 (1998)
23. Sharetribe. https://www.sharetribe.com/

Exploring Semantics in Clinical Data Interoperability

Jacqueline Midlej do Espírito Santo[1]($\boxtimes$), Erich Vinicius de Paula[2],
and Claudia Bauzer Medeiros[1]

[1] Institute of Computing, University of Campinas - UNICAMP, Campinas, Brazil
{jacqueline.santo,cmbm}@ic.unicamp.br
[2] Faculty of Medical Sciences, University of Campinas - UNICAMP,
Campinas, Brazil
erich@unicamp.br

Abstract. The increasing amount of digital clinical information has prompted research in interoperating across numerous clinical data sources. Most solutions to this problem follow one of two main directions: (a) adoption of Electronic Health Records (EHR) standards, or (b) structuring medical knowledge via Knowledge Organizations Systems (KOS). Related research sometimes addresses the combination of the two directions but does not explore the knowledge of KOS, which are just used to define and disambiguate concepts. This paper discusses the solution for clinical data interoperability that we designed and implemented. It is a two step process - (a) we provide initial integration via mediators to provide mappings across heterogeneous sources, and (b) KOS to extend navigation possibilities across data sources. This paper is centered in the second part, discussing the challenges of semantic query expansion for clinical data analysis. We illustrate our solution through a real case study from one of Brazil's largest hospital complexes.

Keywords: Interoperability · Medical knowledge organizations systems · Semantic query · Query expansion

1 Introduction

This paper is concerned with interoperability challenges in eHealth[1], in particular those associated with clinical data management. Two directions have been taken to facilitate clinical data interoperability: (a) adoption of Electronic Health Records (EHR) standards or (b) structuring medical knowledge via Knowledge Organizations Systems (KOS). EHR standards are specifications about how medical data should be structured and stored to facilitate interoperability among different health systems. Their adoption often requires extensive recoding. We, instead, adopt the classical mediator strategy to deal with different clinical

---

[1] Here defined as a multidisciplinary research field that requires collaboration of computer scientists with researchers in Health Sciences.

© Springer Nature Switzerland AG 2019
G. Guizzardi et al. (Eds.): ER 2019 Workshops, LNCS 11787, pp. 201–210, 2019.
https://doi.org/10.1007/978-3-030-34146-6_18

information systems regardless of EHR standards. The other prevalent solution to interoperability is based on KOS. The term KOS is intended to encompass all types of schemes for organizing information and promoting knowledge management, such as dictionaries, taxonomies, thesauri, and ontologies [5]; the two latter are the most common KOS used to semantically organize clinical data. There are hundreds of medical KOS; some of them are *de facto* standards (such as the International Classification of Diseases - ICD) but most have no consensual use. Research on clinical data interoperability that involves KOS can be classified in two main directions: the first uses them to disambiguate terms for interoperability, but does not take advantage of the power of ontologies to expand queries; the second constructs (usually small) case-specific ontologies to expand queries, thereby helping find new facts in a specific clinical (sub)domain.

We, instead, use existing generic KOS to expand queries, thereby generalizing the second approach to arbitrary clinical information systems. To the best of our knowledge, ours is the first proposal to combine mediators to KOS to expand queries, thereby helping users query and explore data in clinical information systems. The term *users*, in this text, refers to health professionals that work and perform research in primary or secondary health care (e.g., doctors or nurses). Indeed, our approach addresses the interoperability of arbitrary clinical information systems, regardless of ERH standards, exploring semantic aspects by navigating integrated medical KOS.

We showcase our approach through a real case study that illustrates the challenges of extracting, from a large set of heterogeneous clinical data sources, *ad hoc* patient groups for subsequent analysis. This scenario is typical of the demands of clinical research, but is also found in situations where, e.g., hospital administrators need to analyze costs associated to a given set of pathologies. Our architecture was published previously in [3], where we restricted ourselves to the mediator aspects, but did not discuss semantic query expansion. Thus, our main contributions are: (a) a new approach to support semantic queries over arbitrary clinical information systems; and (b) a discussion of challenges in a real scenario exploring knowledge extracted from KOS to help users in query formulation.

Part of the complexity of our work lies is the complexity of our clinical scenario and associated data, which is typical of many clinical systems in which legacy data have to live with new systems and data collecting devices. Our work is being validated in a real, big data, health environment - one of Brazil's largest medical complexes, located at the University of Campinas (UNICAMP), Brazil. Clinical care in UNICAMP dates back to the 60's. The hospital systems rely on 19 different databases, each of which with tens of tables, with hundreds of attributes, and under distinct DBMS. Besides the hospital itself, the medical complex has 4 large specialized health centers each with its own independent systems and data, and do not interoperate. Our testbed comes from two distinct centers inside this complex: Hospital das Clínicas (HC) and Hemocentro. Hemocentro is a center of hematology and hemotherapy that treats 1500 patients/month and manages 70 thousand blood donations/year. The hospital has 44 medical specialties, performs about 5 thousand laboratory test/day and

15 thousand hospitalizations/year. Our tests are being conducted on a 5 year extract of these data, for approximately 40 thousand patients.

2   Related Work

Our approach to interoperability in clinical systems combines the use of mediators with semantics provided by KOS to expand queries. We discussed our mediator approach in [3]. Thus, this section focus on the semantic query formulation process, including query expansion. Given the specificity of the clinical domain, most of our references relate to the use of ontologies in this field.

Semantic queries can be defined as queries that leverage the semantic information stored in ontologies to filter and retrieve data from relational tables [8]. In the health context, data from clinical centers are mostly stored in relational databases while other medical information can be found in ontology models, spreadsheets or textual documents. Semantic annotations are used to establish the linkage between ontologies and relational data. Similarity functions can be used to find their correspondences. We adopt the definition of [9] of semantic annotations, as follows: "Semantic annotations combine concepts of metadata and ontologies: metadata fields are filled with ontology terms, which are used to describe these fields. A semantic annotation unit is a triple <s, m, o>, where s is the subject being described, m is the label of a metadata field and o is a term from a domain ontology." We use Bioportal [14] to annotate clinical data. Bioportal is a repository with 768 integrated biomedical ontologies and offers a REST API and SPARQL endpoint to access this repository programmatically.

One can organize the query formulation process, from a high point of view, in a sequence of interconnected phases: initial query formulation, query reformulation, and query processing. The initial query formulation can appear under different guises, which can be roughly classified into (a) direct formulation (the user writes the query in some sort of language), and (b) interactive formulation (a query system, e.g. in [8], guides users into expressing the query via record patterns). Query reformulation basically consists in, given a query in some language, rewriting it - in the same, or another language - to achieve some kind of goal (e.g., extending results [2,13,15–17] or semantic interpretation [2,16]). Finally, query processing involves the execution of the reformulated query. These phases can be repeatedly executed until the user is satisfied with the result.

Table 1(a) summarizes related work, identifying in which phase the work has their main contribution, the most common goals to work in some query formulation phase, the role of ontologies in the process and the domain of the research and case study. Table 1(b) shows some related works.

Related work centered on the initial query formulation phase usually provides solutions to facilitate query construction. Most papers propose a query interface to guide the user in the query formulation process, either by navigating through concepts in the ontology (e.g. [1,12]), helping the user to specify search conditions in a graphical way (e.g. [10]), or proposing a query language (e.g. [7]).

Though, of course, an initial formulation is required, we are more interested in the reformulation phase. According to Vilar [13], reformulation can be found

Table 1. Classifications of related work in query formulation process

(a) Query formulation process

Criterion	Approach
Phase	P1. Initial query formulation
	P2. Query reformulation
	P3. Query processing
Goal	G1. Facilitate the use (in P1)
	G2. Data integration (in P2)
	G3. Obtain extended results (in P2)
	G4. Semantics interpretation (in P2)
	G5. Optimization (in P3)
Ontology	O1. Application data model
	O2. Additional domain information
Domain	Generic, Health or Other

(b) The related work

Work	Phase	Goal	Ontology	Domain
Boonprapasri [1]	P1	G1	O1	Other: GIS
Lelong [7]	P1	G1	O2	Health: EHR
Tiede [12]	P1	G4	O2	Other: Geography
Munir [10]	P1 P2	G1	O1 O2	Health
Zheng [17]	P2	G3	O2	Heath: Biomedicine
Yunzhi [15]	P2	G3	O2	Health: Hepatitis
Zhao [16]	P2	G3 G4	O2	Health: Image note
Vilar [13]	P2	G3	O1 O2	Other: Biology
Calvanese [2]	P2	G2 G3 G4	O1	Generic

under different names, each of which denotes some kind of algorithmic rewriting technique - semantic rewriting, syntactic rewriting, expansion. These classifications vary from author to author. For instance, semantic rewriting is often intended to obtain distinct results (either more generic or more specific). Hence, some authors do not consider this a reformulation, given that the results may not be identical to the original formulation.

Research that addresses query reformulation adopts one of the following strategies: (1) define operations over ontologies, applying the results in relational query language declarations or (2) transform the relational schema into an ontology and then address queries only via ontology processing. In the first strategy, the ontology always plays the role of bringing additional domain information into the application. In the second strategy, the ontology always plays the role of the application data model. This means that an ontology model is used to organize the data sets of the application. Both strategies can be applied together using multiple ontologies. For example, we can have one application ontology that corresponds to the specific data itself (e.g., modeling how results of laboratory tests are stored); and we can have multiple ontologies to bring additional knowledge about the tests and possible diagnoses (e.g., the range of reference values of a test, and diseases it can detect).

For example, Zheng, Wang and Lu [17] use the first strategy to define some operations used as an extension for relational query languages (such as getHyponym, getHypernym, getSynonym, and getSibling). The operations expand the query by adding new terms related to the original one, thus enabling to recover more information than the original query.

Vilar [13] and Calvanese [2] adopt the second strategy – that maps all relational schemas into ontologies. Vilar [13] performs two expansion options: the system finds existing domain ontologies that are potentially good for query expansion, or the users choose the expansions they want, using a predefined set of operations to navigate through the ontologies. While Vilar [13] adopts a relational query language extended with a set of operations (similarly to [17]), Calvanese et al. [2] use an ontological query language and address the issue of mapping queries in an ontology model to relational data sources.

Query expansion is also widely used to recover documents lacking relational structure. For instance, Zhao et al. [16] combine query expansion to Natural

Language Processing (NLP) to retrieve reports concerning medical image studies. Yunzhi et al. [15] create a Hepatitis ontology to expand the terms annotated in health publications. Rather than creating an ontology Sonntag and Moller [11] use an existing domain ontology for query expansion.

As will be seen, our approach follows the first strategy - we propose a sequence of steps instead of operations to expand queries, and add new terms to query declarations based on ontology navigation. Unlike the second strategy, we do not transform a relational schema into an ontology.

3   Combining Mediators to Semantic Processing for Clinical Data Interoperability

Figure 1 depicts our architecture for interoperability of clinical systems, catering to both precision medicine and medical research needs. It shows, on the left side, a classical mediator approach to integrating data from several health centers (details in our previous work [3]). In most cases, the information needed in clinical care can be obtained using only the left part of the architecture, since clinical care is strongly dependent on a patient's medical history, which can be recovered following our mediator approach. However, medical research requires more complex analyses, whose specification depends on the researcher's needs and vocabulary, which seldom matches schema definitions, or terms entered in clinical databases.

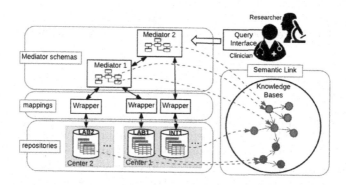

Fig. 1. Integration architecture - figure extracted from our previous work [3]

4   Adding Semantic Linkage

To address this issue, we use knowledge extracted from medical KOS, which we combine with the mediator integration approach. This section details how we explore semantics from the KOS and how they can help complex query processing and writing. This corresponds to the right part of Fig. 1.

Our semantic processing follows two stages: (A) semantic annotation and (B) query (re)formulation. Stage A concerns the creation of semantic annotations via inserting links between data and ontologies. Creation of these annotations requires finding the appropriate semantics for a term, and inserting the appropriate links. Semantics can be found by some similarity function that relates a term to ontology concepts. We use the annotator service in Bioportal REST API to find the appropriate semantics. It returns a set of ontology links for an input term (or a set of terms).

In many situations - such as our case study - creating one annotation per database term wastes storage space. In our sample data, HC performed more than 3 million lab tests, thus a given test name may appear in the HC database a few thousand times. Thus, we decided to store the semantic annotations themselves in a separate data table – our *Semantic Link Table – SLT –* to allow associating the same semantic annotation with many data records. Each entry in *SLT* is of form <database-term, id, url, ontology-name>, where "database-term" is, for instance, "hemogram". Afterwards, when needed, the semantic linkage is obtained via natural join of the data tables with SLT.

Once SLT is created, query reformulation (stage B) combines queries over medical ontologies with queries over our relational clinical data, as follows:

1. Query Bioportal to retrieve all ontological terms associated with a query term Q, given specific criteria (e.g., all descendants), obtaining a set $\{OT\}$. Each OT in $\{OT\}$ is a complex object containing all properties and relationships associated with Q.
2. For each OT, check if its id is in SLT.
3. If yes, add the corresponding SQL WHERE clause.
4. Once all clauses are written, pose the expanded query in the mediator-defined tables.

5   Case Study

We showcase our approach via a case study based on real, anonymized, data from Hemocentro and HC. The interoperability approach unifies datasets with five years (2012 to 2016) of information about laboratory tests, hospitalizations, and drug prescriptions for approximately 40 thousand patients, 13 million lab tests and 8 million drug administrations. We omit the mediator details (the left part of our architecture) and concentrate on how to take advantage of ontologies to process specific queries.

Every hospital in Brazil stores ICD codes associated with procedures, for billing information. However, the ICD hierarchy is exclusionary, not allowing the same disease to be part of several categories. Moreover, experts may consider disease categories not included in ICD classification. In any such case, the solution is to manually complement the ICD codes to create the context of interest. For example, in [6] the US Institute for Health Metrics and Evaluation. Shows the ICDs codes selected to analyze the burden of diseases and causes of death in different categories. Some of them are not included in the ICD classification and, even considering the categories that are in ICD, they may include specific ICD codes outside the category.

Consider the following query *Retrieve all patients diagnosed with some Sexually Transmitted Disease (STD)*. There is no single ICD code for STD, and many such diseases are recognized via combinations of symptoms. Therefore, to process such a query, experts need to manually provide a combination of factors, a tiresome and error-prone task.

We now show how this can be performed via navigation through KOS. The following steps exemplify how to navigate in the Medical Subject Headings (MESH) via the Bioportal service to find the group of patients with STD (this correspond to steps 1 to 4 of Sect. 4).

1. Given a term ("STD"), we create a chain of queries to Bioportal to: (a) recover the matching concept in MESH; (b) recover its descendants and (c) recover, for each descendant, it is mapping to the ICD classification.
2. Check if each ICD code is in SLT.
3. Construct the SQL clause.
4. Pose the query to the mediator-defined tables.

Focusing on ontology navigation, Part A of Fig. 2 shows an extract of the implementation, abstracting some details. Part a, b and c correspond to requests to Bioportal. In b, we obtain all MESH concepts included in the STD category (descendant concepts). However step c is needed because MESH terms are not directly linked to clinical databases, whereas ICD codes are in SLT. In 3, we show the expanded query in WHERE clause. Hiding details about the mediation process, part B shows a small excerpt of the result set: patients diagnosed with some STD.

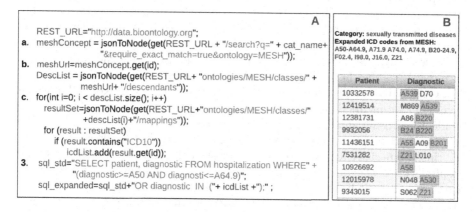

Fig. 2. Extracting MESH knowledge to help identifying patients with STD

In ICD classification, STD covers the code range A50–A64.9. Using MESH, we get more comprehensive results: (A50–A64.9), HIV range (B20–24.9) and 7 additional ICD codes, as shown in Part B of Fig. 2. To expand even more the results, we can follow the same process using additional KOS, such as SNOMED CT and Disease Ontology. The standard query (without MESH expansion) for patients with STD only retrieved 95 patients from HC databases, while the MESH-expanded query retrieved 846 patients. Most of the latter were associated with some ICD code in the HIV range.

6 Discussion

Our full approach combines the use of mediators with semantic expansion. Mediators allow recovering individual patient data from heterogeneous data sources in a unified way, addressing precision medicine needs. Semantic expansion relies on the construction of our Semantic Link Table, SLT, and subsequent ontology navigation to help query formulation. Although KOS are widely adopted in the literature as part of interoperability strategies, they often play a minor role in clinical query reformulation. We highlight two benefits of exploring ontologies: (1) helping users formulate queries: since some information can be extracted from ontologies, they do not need to exhaustively describe the whole context; (2) formulate more complex queries and expand the results. These queries characterize clinical research needs, and are requested less often than those for clinical care needs.

In the case study we simplify the user's task by inferring diseases that belong to the STD category, instead of letting the user specify all such diseases. Although UNICAMP health centers link data using ICD codes, this is insufficient to, e.g., categorize diseases. ICD is a mutually exclusive and exhaustive statistically-based classification that creates arbitrary associations; when a concept should belong to two classes, and one is chosen, the underlying assumption is that it does not belong to another [4]. Also, search for patients within a given disease category is a complex query because it retrieves patients and diagnoses that are not directly annotated with the indicated query term. In the case study, the query term is "STD" and the result set includes patients with diagnoses that have been classified by their doctors as having, for instance, A55-Chlamydial lymphogranuloma or B24-Unspecified HIV disease, all of which were included in the STD category thanks to our approach (but which cannot be identified using an ICD-based approach alone).

Finding appropriate semantic concepts given a term is a challenging task. At HC this is especially aggravated because most of the data are entered using the hospital's internal codes – e.g., replacing test names by abbreviations. Automatic search for semantic links may return wrong associations. A semi-automatic approach increases link accuracy, for example letting the database designer validate the semantic links or choosing the main target ontologies. Another challenge in this approach is language translation. Brazilian health centers store data in Portuguese, while most medical KOS have no accredited Portuguese version. Therefore, an expert needs to validate the semantic links of our solution, otherwise we run the risk of creating wrong associations.

Another challenge is ontology navigation. Besides synonyms, narrower and broader terms, we can further explore the links between multiple ontologies and the other kinds of relations of a concept. For example, finding means to characterize a given disease via ontology navigating, such as to know its common symptoms, test results, and drug prescriptions. By doing this, we can infer additional diagnoses even if the name or ICD code is not written on the health centers database.

Last but not least, a combination of NLP and ontology linkage is yet another possibility to help query expansion, using the annotations entered by doctors on their patients. Unfortunately, our preliminary studies show that this created a large amount of false positives. We identified a non negligible number of records in which doctors' annotations identified both the illness, and explained discarded hypotheses. Thus, we would need to invest into more sophisticated NLP techniques to be able to retrieve meaningful records.

7 Conclusions and Ongoing Work

This paper discussed the challenges of exploring knowledge from ontologies for clinical data interoperability. In spite of extensive research in this field, solutions still tend to concentrate in a given trend – namely, use of standards and mediators, or adoption of semantics to enhance data understandability, without exploiting the full possibilities of ontological processing. To the best of our knowledge, ours is the first proposal that combines both trends in a generic, extensible architecture in which ontologies are used in query expansion. We exemplify how it can be used via real life, big data, test case from one of Brazil's largest medical compounds. The discussion of this case shows some of the many challenges faced in handling clinical data – from its intrinsic heterogeneity, even within a single dataset, to the dependence on non-consensual vocabularies and ontologies, and need for NLP. While some of these challenges are specific to our test environment (e.g., the particular characteristics of the systems and data we had to deal with), others are generic. Our case study helps to exemplify generic challenges, such as having to cope with legacy data and systems and different query requirement patterns, such as finding clusters to support research and decision making.

Our ongoing work involves both research and development activities. On the latter side, we are continuing our development efforts to include additional ontologies and vocabularies, and to check more complex situations. In this, we are being helped by medical experts to express requirements and validate (and question) results. On the research side, more needs to be done towards NLP. In our test context, some of the medical systems within our complex are being remodelled to support automated electronic health record handling, and support patient care "workflows". This, in turn, requires considering the evolution of data and versioning of database schemas, while at the same time supporting the legacy systems.

Acknowledgements. Work partially supported by FAPESP/CEPID CCES under grant 2013/08293-7, CNPq grants 142243/2017-5, 309317/2016, 428459/2018-8 and 305110/2016-0, and FAPESP grant 2016/14172-6.

References

1. Boonprapasri, T., Sriharee, G.: An applied ontology: a semantic query builder for health GIS system. In: ICSEC, pp. 1–6. IEEE (2015)
2. Calvanese, D., et al.: Ontop: answering SPARQL queries over relational databases. Semant. Web **8**(3), 471–487 (2017)
3. do Espírito Santo, J.M., Medeiros, C.B.: Semantic interoperability of clinical data. In: Da Silveira, M., Pruski, C., Schneider, R. (eds.) DILS 2017. LNCS, vol. 10649, pp. 29–37. Springer, Cham (2017). https://doi.org/10.1007/978-3-319-69751-2_4
4. Haendel, M.A., Chute, C.G., Robinson, P.N.: Classification, ontology, and precision medicine. N. Engl. J. Med. **379**(15), 1452–1462 (2018). https://doi.org/10.1056/NEJMra1615014. pMID: 30304648
5. Hodge, G.: Systems of knowledge organization for digital libraries: beyond traditional authority files. Digital Library Federation, Washington, D.C. (2000)
6. IHME: Global burden of disease study 2016 (GBD 2016) causes of death and nonfatal causes mapped to ICD codes. http://ghdx.healthdata.org/record/ihme-data/gbd-2016-cause-icd-code-mappings. Accessed 1 Apr 2019
7. Lelong, R., Cabot, C., Soualmia, L.F., Darmoni, S.: Semantic search engine to query into electronic health records with a multiple-layer query language. In: Proceedings of ACM SIGIR Workshop on MedIR (2016)
8. Lim, L., Wang, H., Wang, M.: Semantic queries by example. In: Proceedings of the ACM International Conference on Extending Database Technology - EDBT, pp. 347–358. ACM, New York (2013). https://doi.org/10.1145/2452376.2452417
9. Macário, C.G., Sousa, S.R., Medeiros, C.B.: Annotating geospatial data based on its semantics. In: 17th ACM SIGSPATIAL Conference (2009)
10. Munir, K., Odeh, M., McClatchey, R.: Ontology assisted query reformulation using the semantic and assertion capabilities of OWL-DL ontologies. In: Proceedings of the ACM International Symposium on Database Engineering and Applications, pp. 81–90. ACM (2008)
11. Sonntag, D., Möller, M.: Unifying semantic annotation and querying in biomedical image repositories. In: Proceedings of KMIS, pp. 89–94 (2009)
12. Tiede, D., Baraldi, A., Sudmanns, M., Belgiu, M., Lang, S.: Architecture and prototypical implementation of a semantic querying system for big earth observation image bases. Eur. J. Remote Sens. **50**(1), 452–463 (2017)
13. Vilar, B.S.C.M.: Processamento de Consultas Baseado em Ontologias para Sistemas de Biodiversidade. Master's thesis, Instituto de Computação - Unicamp (2009)
14. Whetzel, P.L., et al.: BioPortal: enhanced functionality via new web services from the national center for biomedical ontology to access and use ontologies in software applications. Nucleic Acids Res. **39**(Suppl. 2), W541–W545 (2011)
15. Yunzhi, C., Huijuan, L., Shapiro, L., Travillian, R.S., Lanjuan, L.: An approach to semantic query expansion system based on hepatitis ontology. J. Biol. Res. Thessal. **23**(1), 11 (2016)
16. Zhao, Y., Fesharaki, N.J., Li, X., Patrick, T.B., Luo, J.: Semantic-enhanced query expansion system for retrieving medical image notes. J. Med. Syst. **42**, 1–11 (2018)
17. Zheng, S., Wang, F., Lu, J.: Enabling ontology based semantic queries in biomedical database systems. Int. J. Semant. Comput. **8**(01), 67–83 (2014)

ER 2019 Doctoral Symposium

Framework for Construction and Incremental Maintenance of High-Quality Linked Data Mashup

Narciso Arruda[✉]

Departamento de Computação, Federal University of Ceará,
Fortaleza, Ceará, Brazil
narciso@lia.ufc.br

Abstract. Due to the Linked Data initiative, previously isolated datasets are published as linked data. This enables the creation of applications that consume data from multiple Linked Data sources. Applications are confronted with the challenge of obtaining a homogenized view of this global data space, called a Linked Data Mashup view. This work proposes a framework to perform the fusion of Linked Data and quality assessment of Linked Data Mashup. Quality assessment of Linked Data mashup is computed based on the result of the data fusion. We also propose the implementation of a platform for creation and incremental maintenance of mashup views.

Keywords: Linked Data Mashup · Incremental maintenance · Quality assessment · Data fusion · Fuzzy logic

1 Introduction

The adoption of the Linked Data initiative [2] for publishing data on the Web has triggered a global-scale growth of interlinked data space, denoted Web of Data. The key idea behind the concept of Web of Data is to provide a common data space where data from heterogeneous sources may be published. One can "view" the web of data as a huge agglomerate of heterogeneous data. In such a scenario, data integration is a critical requirement for many applications, which need to consume data in the Web of Data in an integrated manner.

In this sense, a special kind of web application, called Linked Data Mashup (LDM), is responsible for combining, aggregating, and transforming data available on the Web of Data [11]. Hence, Linked Data Mashup applications are confronted with the challenge of building an integrated view of different Linked Data sources. That view is denoted Linked Data Mashup view (LDM view). The creation of an LDM view is a complex task which involves four major challenges: (1) selection of the Linked Data sources that are relevant for the application; (2) extraction and translation of data from different, possibly heterogeneous Linked Data sources to a common vocabulary; (3) identification of links between

© Springer Nature Switzerland AG 2019
G. Guizzardi et al. (Eds.): ER 2019 Workshops, LNCS 11787, pp. 213–221, 2019.
https://doi.org/10.1007/978-3-030-34146-6_19

resources in different Linked Data sources; (4) combination and fusion of multiple representations of the same real-world object into a single representation and resolution of data inconsistencies to improve the quality of the data.

In [13], the authors propose an ontology-based framework for formally specifying LDM views. In the framework, an LDM view is specified with the help of exported views, sameAs linkset views, and data fusion rules. The LDM view specification is used to materialize the mashup view automatically.

Linked data sources continue to change over time. Thus, mashup views become obsolete and need to be maintained from time to time. For a materialized view to reflect updates to data sources, there are two strategies. Re-materialization recalculates all data in the view, while incremental maintenance modifies part of the data in view to reflect updates of the data sources. Incremental maintenance is typically more efficient than the full re-materialization approach because reprocessing of unchanged parts of the data can often be avoided.

However, to be useful, a view of mashup should have good quality. Quality assessment of the mashup view is not a simple process since it involves other complex factors, such as quality of data sources, quality of mappings, and quality of sameAs links. Consequently, a key challenge is to determine the quality of LDM view.

In this work, we consider the following research questions: (1) How to compute the quality of mashup? (2) How to perform the data fusion so that the quality of the mashup meets the user's quality requirements with the best possible score. (3) How to do mashup incremental maintenance?

In this work, we investigate the problem of incremental maintenance of mashup views based on the formal specification of the mashup view [13]. We propose a framework for data fusion and quality assessment to LDM view based on the fuzzy logic, and finally the implementation of a platform for the creation and incremental maintenance of LDM views. In this platform, data fusion is implemented based on fuzzy quality metadata. The use of fuzzy logic is a way to overcome imprecision and subjectivity data quality. Allowing users to express data quality requirements by means of a set of linguistic expressions on quality indicators.

The remainder of this paper is structured as follows. Section 2 presents the specification of Linked Data Mashup. Section 3 presents a brief summary of the quality of mashup view. Section 4 presents our approach for materialization and quality assessment of LDM view. Section 5 presents our approach for incremental maintenance of LDM view. Section 6 discusses related works. Finally, Sect. 7 contains the conclusions.

2   Specification of Linked Data Mashup

We use a three level ontology-based framework [13], as summarized in Fig. 1, to formally specify LDM views. In the Mashup View Layer, the mashup view ontology O_D specifies the concepts of the mashup application, which is the common vocabulary for integrating data exported by the Linked Data sources.

In the Web of Data Layer, each data source Si is described by a source ontology O_{Si}, published on the Web according to the Linked Data principles. These source ontologies are depicted in the Web of Data layer in Fig. 1.

LDM view specification is an n-tuple $\lambda = (D, O_D, \{E_1, ..., E_n\}, \{L_1, ..., L_m\}, Q, F)$, where:

- D is the name of the mashup view;
- O_D is the mashup view ontology;
- $E_1, ..., E_n$ are exported view specifications. Each view E_i has an ontology O_{Ei}, a set of rules M_{Ei} that maps concepts O_{Si} to concepts O_D;
- $L_1, ..., L_m$ are sameAs linkset view specifications between $E_1, ..., E_n$. We consider two types of sameAs links: imported sameAs links, which are exported by a Linked Data source, and mashup sameAs links, which are automatically created based on a sameAs linkset view specification [4] specifically defined for the mashup application; and the provenance of the exported data;
- Q is the set of quality requirements mashup specified by the user;
- F is a set of fusion rules that specify how different representations of the same real-world object are combined into one representation. These rules are defined based on quality requirements of the mashup.

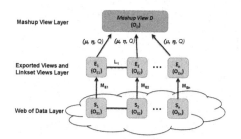

Fig. 1. Three level ontology-based framework.

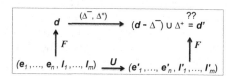

Fig. 2. Problem of view incremental maintenance.

3   Linked Data Mashup Quality Assessment

Data quality is commonly conceived as a multi-dimensional construction with dimensions which are composed of quality metrics, which measure the quality of the data along the dimensions [3]. More specifically, quality metrics are heuristics designed to fit a specific assessment situation [16].

Quality assessment of mashup view is not a simple process, as it involves other factors such as quality of data sources, quality of mappings, and quality of sameAs links. Normally, LDM view quality is calculated along at least three dimensions [6]: completeness, conciseness, and consistency. Consistency expresses how much the data are in the real world, while completeness and conciseness are in a way analogous to recall and precision in information retrieval [7].

Table 1 shows quality metrics of exported view, linkset view and mashup view used to quality assessment of consistency dimension. Figure 4 shows how they relate to factors. The consistency of the mashup view (MV_CONSISTENCY) is computed by the quality metrics MV_M1, MV_M2, and by the consistency of the instances of mashup view (MV_INSTANCE_CONSISTENCY), that is computed by the consistency of its triples (MV_TRIPLE_CONSISTENCY). Which in turn is computed by the metrics MV_M3 and MV_M4, and by the consistency of the exported views (LV_CONSISTENCY) and linkset views (EV_CONSISTENCY). The consistency of the exported views and linkset views are computed by the metrics LV_M1, LV_M2 and metrics EV_M1, EV_M1, respectively. They depend on the consistency of the data source (DS_CONSISTENCY), the consistency of the linkset view also depends on the consistency of the exported views.

Table 1. Quality metrics of the consistency dimension for mashup view.

Factor	Metric	Description
Mashup view	MV_M1	Conformance of the source ontology and mashup ontology (schema consistency) [15]
	MV_M2	Mappings conforms to the semantics of information represented (mapping consistency) [15]
	MV_M3	Difference between value v and other (conflicting) values [7]
	MV_M4	Confirmation values [7]
Exported view	EV_M1	The degree to which exported ontology is free of (logical/formal) contradictions [17]
	EV_M2	Proportion of mappings in the exported view error-free [17]
Linkset view	LV_M1	Measures the similarity of instances linked to sameAs based on functional properties [10]
	LV_M2	Measures the similarity of instances linked to sameAs based on linkage in linkset view

4 Materialization of Linked Data Mashup

In this section, we present an approach to materialization of LDM view. In our approach, data quality assessment and performed with materialization. Figure 3 shows the main steps of the materialization process of LDM view.

As shown in Fig. 3, materialization is performed incrementally, and at each step, the quality of the triples and datasets (materialized views) generated is also computed. The process of computing data quality is called quality assessment, in which process quality metadata is computed to measure data quality. Thus errors can be detected by directing modifications that increase the quality of the data.

The following briefly describes the steps of materialization and quality assessment of the mashup view. As shown in Fig. 3, the input of the process is to view specification, data sources and quality metadata from data sources.

Step 1. Materialization and Quality Assessment of Exported Views.

In this step, each E_i view in V is materialized using the E_i mappings. In this step, the quality of the exported view is also computed based on the quality metadata of the data sources, mapping rules, and the exported view materialization.

Step 2. Materialization and Quality Assessment of Linkset Views.

This step identifies and materializes sameAs links. For each L_i view in L is materialized using the L_i linkage rule. Due to the importance of sameAs links, various approaches have been proposed to compute link quality, for example based on functional properties [10] and using network measurements.

Step 3. Data Fusion and Quality Assessment of Mashup View.

In this step, the fusion of multiple representations representing the same real-world entity into a single representation is performed. Fusion rules in F define how to solve the problem of conflicts that can occur in fusion objects. Resolving data inconsistency improves the quality of mashup view.

As shown in Fig. 3, during the data fusion process, the quality assessment of the generated triples is performed. The quality of export views, and links, are important in determining the quality of the triple, also taking into account the equality and similarity of conflicting values [7].

Quality metadata provides information that helps data consumers understand the quality of data exported by data sources and data published by a mashup view. They are essential in the data fusion step because quality information can be used as criteria in conflict resolution [7,9].

In [1], we propose a fuzzy approach to quality assessment of Linked Data sources. This approach consists of the generation of fuzzy concepts of quality metrics, dimensions of quality metadata. The fuzzy quality metadata can be easily adapted and used as criteria in conflict resolution. The use of fuzzy quality assessment allows a reasonable justification for the evaluation result. Moreover, the fuzzy quality metadata allow users to express data quality requirements by means of a set of linguistic expressions on quality indicators.

5   Incremental Maintenance of Linked Data Mashup

The LDM view specification is critical in the incremental maintenance process, since the incremental maintenance strategy uses the LDM view specification to incrementally maintain the mashup view.

Next, we discuss the problem of maintaining the LDM view, when update operations are applied to the Linked Data sources. The following are:

- $\lambda = (D, O_D, \{E_1, ..., E_n\}, \{L_1, ..., L_m\}, F)$ is a LDM view specification;
- $e_1, ..., e_n$ are states of $E_1, ..., E_n$ and $l_1, ..., l_m$ are states of $L_1, ..., L_m$;
- $s = (e_1, ..., e_n, l_1, ..., l_m)$;

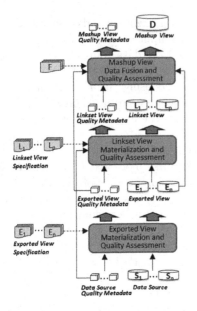

Fig. 3. Process of LDM view materialization.

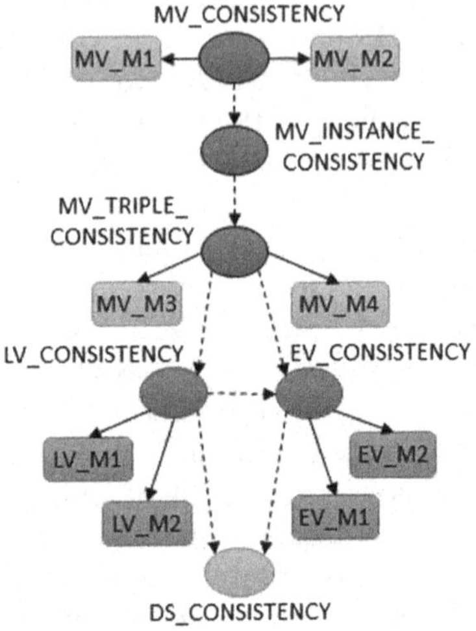

Fig. 4. Quality metrics to compute
mashup consistency.

- d is the state of D induced by s;
- U is a set of updates against data sources.

The incremental view maintenance problem is schematically described by the diagram in Fig. 2. The user specifies an update U against a base data source, which results in new states $e_1, ..., e_n$ of the exported views and new states $l_1, ..., l_m$ of the sameAs views. Let d' be the state of D induced by $(e_1, ..., e_n, l_1, ..., l_m)$. We say that the changesets $< \Delta^-, \Delta^+ >$, where Δ^- is the set of triples removed from d, and Δ^+ is the set of triples added to d, is correctly calculated, if the new state of view $(d - \Delta^-) \cup \Delta^+$, computed with the help Δ^- e Δ^+, and the new view state of mashup d', are identical.

Next, we show the main components of the LDM View D Incremental Maintenance Platform Architecture.

- For each data source S_i that exports an exported view E_i to view D, there is an Exported View Controller (EVC), which is responsible for computing and publishing the changeset required to maintain the exported view E_i, and source quality metadata. In [12] we propose a framework to compute the changesets to maintain an RDF view exported from a relational database.
- For each linkset view L_i, there is a Linked View Controller (LVC), which is responsible for computing and publishing the changeset required to maintain the linkset view L_i. In [14] we propose a framework to compute the changesets to maintain a sameAs view from the changesets of the Linked Data sources.

– The LDM View Controller is responsible for computing and publishing the changeset for the mashup view D. In [13] we present an algorithm that uses the changesets published by the EVCs and LVCs and the new state of the exported visions to compute, the changeset of the mashup view.

6   Related Work

In recent years, many works have been developed to assess the quality of a Linked Data source. In [17] metrics and quality dimensions of the main works in the area were cataloged. The Luzzu tool [5] implements a part of the cataloged quality metrics. Luzzu generates quality metadata from LD sources. This metadata provides information that helps data consumers better understand data quality. However, these works are not sufficient to evaluate the quality of the mashup view.

In the process of creating the LDM view, some approaches have been proposed, for example, LDIF [11] and ODCleanStore [7]. Typically, these approaches use data quality as part of the data fusion process. Sieve [9] is a module included in Linked Data Integration Framework (LDIF) that is dedicated to quality assessment and fusion of Linked Data. Sieve uses metadata about named graphs to assess data quality as defined by users. In ODCleanStore [7], quality metadata (containing data provenance and quality scores) can be used in the data fusion process. It is quality assessment component checks whether the dataset (converted in a named graph) satisfies custom consistency policies and them calculate the quality score of the dataset [7].

In [8], the authors propose an integration methodology incorporating iterative quality assessment. In this methodology, description logic is used as the formal basis for reasoning about user's quality requirements and for validating that an integrated resource satisfies these requirements. However, only quality metrics associated with mappings, schema are defined in the integration, quality metrics associated with the data source and linksets view (sameAs links) are not defined. Another differential to our approach is that we use fuzzy logic to address the imprecision often inherent in the user's quality requirements.

7   Conclusion

In this work, we investigate the problem of the quality assessment and incremental maintenance of the mashup view. We present a framework for Linked Data fusion and quality assessment of the mashup view, and we proposed to use fuzzy logic in quality assessment of the mashup view.

In the proposed platform, we already present a framework for mashup specification that allows automatic data mashup materialization and incremental maintenance [13]. In [12] we present an approach to incremental maintenance of exported views (RDB-to-RDF) and in [14] to incremental maintenance of linkset view. For quality assessment was presented in [1] a fuzzy approach to data quality assessment that can be applied to the generated quality metadata.

At the current stage of the work, we are implementing the quality metrics of mashup view in the data fusion process to compute the quality of mashup view, and implementing incremental maintenance of mashup view maintaining mashup quality.

References

1. Arruda, N., et al.: A fuzzy approach for data quality assessment of linked datasets. In: Proceedings of the 21st International Conference on Enterprise Information Systems (2019)
2. Berners-Lee, T.: Linked data (2006). https://www.w3.org/DesignIssues/LinkedData.html
3. Bizer, C., Cyganiak, R.: Quality-driven information filtering using the WIQA policy framework. Web Semant. **7**(1), 1–10 (2009)
4. Casanova, M.A., Vidal, V.M.P., Lopes, G.R., Leme, L.A.P.P., Ruback, L.: On materialized sameAs linksets. In: Decker, H., Lhotská, L., Link, S., Spies, M., Wagner, R.R. (eds.) DEXA 2014. LNCS, vol. 8644, pp. 377–384. Springer, Cham (2014). https://doi.org/10.1007/978-3-319-10073-9_31
5. Debattista, J., Auer, S., Lange, C.: Luzzu–a methodology and framework for linked data quality assessment. J. Data Inf. Qual. (JDIQ) **8**, 4 (2016)
6. Dong, X.L., Naumann, F.: Data fusion: resolving data conflicts for integration. Proc. VLDB Endow. **2**(2), 1654–1655 (2009)
7. Knap, T., et al.: ODCleanStore: a framework for managing and providing integrated linked data on the web. In: International Conference Web Information Systems Engineering (2012)
8. Martin, N., Poulovassilis, A., Wang, J.: A methodology and architecture embedding quality assessment in data integration. JDIQ **4**, 17 (2014)
9. Mendes, P.N., Mühleisen, H., Bizer, C.: Sieve: linked data quality assessment and fusion. In: Proceedings of 2012 Joint EDBT/ICDT Workshops, EDBT-ICDT 2012, pp. 116–123. ACM, New York (2012)
10. Papaleo, L., Pernelle, N., Saïs, F.: On evaluating the quality of RDF identity links in the LOD. In: The Proceedings of IC 202014 Workshop from Open Sources to Web of Data (SoWeDo 2014) (2014)
11. Schultz, A., Matteini, A., Isele, R., Bizer, C., Becker, C.: LDIF - linked data integration framework. In: Proceedings of Second International Conference on Consuming Linked Data, COLD 2011, Aachen, Germany. CEUR-WS.org (2011)
12. Vidal, V.M.P., Arruda Jr, N.M., Cruz, M., Casanova, M.A., Brito, C.E., Pequeno, V.M.: Computing changesets for RDF views of relational data. In: MEP-DaW/LDQ@ ESWC, pp. 43–58 (2017)
13. Vidal, V.M.P., et al.: Specification and incremental maintenance of linked data mashup views. In: Zdravkovic, J., Kirikova, M., Johannesson, P. (eds.) CAiSE 2015. LNCS, vol. 9097, pp. 214–229. Springer, Cham (2015). https://doi.org/10.1007/978-3-319-19069-3_14
14. Vidal, V.M.P., Casanova, M.A., Menendez, E.S., Arruda, N., Pequeno, V.M., Paes Leme, L.A.: Using changesets for incremental maintenance of linkset views. In: Cellary, W., Mokbel, M.F., Wang, J., Wang, H., Zhou, R., Zhang, Y. (eds.) WISE 2016. LNCS, vol. 10042, pp. 196–204. Springer, Cham (2016). https://doi.org/10.1007/978-3-319-48743-4_16

15. Wang, J.: A framework and architecture for quality assessment in data integration. Ph.D. thesis, University of London (2012)
16. Wang, R.Y.: Information Quality (Advances in Management Information Systems). M. E. Sharpe, Inc., Armonk (2005)
17. Zaveri, A., Rula, A., Maurino, A., Pietrobon, R., Lehmann, J., Auer, S.: Quality assessment for linked data: a survey. Semant. Web **7**(1), 63–93 (2016)

A Reference Architecture
for Customizable Marketplaces

Thomas Derave$^{(\boxtimes)}$ (iD)

Department of Business Informatics and Operations Management,
Ghent University, Tweekerkenstraat 2, 9000 Ghent, Belgium
`thomas.derave@UGent.be`

Abstract. A broader term used for a platform in the sharing economy is
'marketplace'. This is a type of e-commerce site or app where transactions
for services of-fered by multiple providers are processed by the marketplace operator (e.g. Uber, Airbnb, eBay). Lately the number and popularity of marketplaces has exploded, with more variety and focus on niche
markets. Software products like Sharetribe make it possible to create a
customized marketplace quick and with few resources. It is, however, not
known whether such products cater for the needs of all possible varieties
of marketplace, nor how such products can be selected and/or customized
to provide the best fit with a particular marketplace. The goal of this PhD
project is to design a Software Reference Architecture (SRA) for marketplaces which can be used to select or create the most suitable software
product. Our first step in the project is to design a conceptual data model
for this SRA based on a marketplace do-main ontology.

Keywords: Sharing economy · Marketplace · Domain ontology ·
UFO-S · Conceptual data modeling · Software Reference Architecture ·
Sharetribe

1 Motivation and Research Question

The topic of my PhD research is online marketplaces (e.g. Airbnb, eBay), which
are web applications that support initiatives in the sharing economy. My goal
is to investigate the current limitation of marketplace software regarding customization and to come up with a solution that addresses this limitation. I got
the idea thanks to my brother, who is starting a travel agency in Rwanda and
offers pre-made packaged tours to tourists. As the number of local guides is
high, and the transparency of prices and tours is low the idea popped-up to
start a marketplace for packaged tours. Just like Airbnb my brother wanted an
online platform where guides can easily register and offer trips, and a customer
can register, login, select the packaged trip and specify the (starting) date. The
price and other information is given, and the customer can book (and pay) right
away. Automatically the guide is notified, and with a chatting system they can
arrange further details. After the trip, feedback and a rating can be given by the
customer.

© Springer Nature Switzerland AG 2019
G. Guizzardi et al. (Eds.): ER 2019 Workshops, LNCS 11787, pp. 222–229, 2019.
https://doi.org/10.1007/978-3-030-34146-6_20

After searching for a good way to create the envisioned marketplace for packaged trips, I came across an open-source software named Sharetribe Go [1] with the catch phrase 'create your Airbnb in 2 days'. According to this phrase, it is possible to make a customizable marketplace in a fraction of the time it would normally take. This started me thinking, does this software work for all kinds of marketplaces, and if not, what is missing? Also, are there alternatives to Sharetribe on the market? Finally, how should the 'ideal' software product having advanced customizability and being able to create complex marketplaces look like?

We believe that a Software Reference Architecture (SRA) for marketplaces can provide an answer to these questions. Therefore, I did some search for previous scientific work related to marketplaces. Based on the current state of the art overview by Trabucchi et al. [2] and our own research, the sharing economy literature has focused on three themes: the customers' motivation of using marketplaces [3]; the impact on society, market and policy [4]; and the classification of business models for marketplace operators, in particular with respect to the revenue model and the pricing mechanism [3–7]. The reviewed studies were primarily about the business-to-business market [8–10] and the classification of business models [11]. In future re-search we plan to conduct a systematic literature review on the whole digital platform domain, but based on our first search we observe that the literature only offers a very partial view. There is a lack of research concerning the technological aspects of marketplaces and their development [2,12]. This is why I defined the goal of my PhD research as follows: *To design a SRA for marketplaces which can be used to create a new or extend an existing software product with advanced customizability that facilitates the design of all types of marketplaces.*

This doctoral consortium paper proceeds as follows. Section 2 defines the concepts "sharing economy" and 'marketplace' and gives a general overview of marketplaces. Section 3 then presents the research methodology. Section 4 describes the method that we plan to use to design a marketplace domain ontology and a first selection of variations between marketplaces defined as marketplace properties and their values. In Sect. 5 we propose a basis of a conceptual data model for customizable marketplaces. In Sect. 6 we describe the method that we plan to use to analyze current software products for marketplaces and a short description of the SRA. In Sect. 7 we summarize the paper and give a conclusion.

2   Definitions of the Sharing Economy and Marketplaces

For Dalberg, the sharing economy involves "sharing assets – physical, financial and/or human capital, between many without transferring ownership, via a digital platform to create value for at least two parties" [13]. Of course, the sharing economy is not a new phenomenon—it existed for thousands of years—but Internet and Web/Mobile applications have strongly decreased transaction costs, which has popularized the concept again [4]. By using a testimonial system with ratings, providers on the platform can also increase their reputation, giving

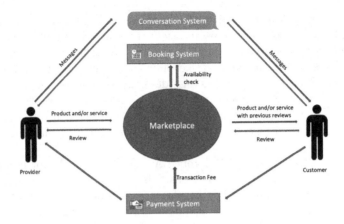

Fig. 1. Marketplace overview.

a solution to the lemon problem [14]. Frenken [4] defines the sharing economy as: "Customers granting each other temporary access to under-utilized physical assets, possibly for money".

In our research we will use a more practical definition of the concept 'sharing economy' with the term 'marketplace'. An online marketplace is a type of e-commerce site or application where products or services are offered by third parties (persons or companies) and where the actual transactions with customers are processed by the market-place itself [15].

A possible overview of a marketplace is given in Fig. 1. A provider can freely offer a (used) product and/or service on the marketplace platform (which can be accessed via a site or an app) and a customer can freely search on the marketplace for the product and/or service he wants. The customer can buy, receive or swap products/services easily on the marketplace and upload reviews. This helps future customers to find the preferred and best product and/or service to their needs. The provider and customer can be a person, but also a group, organization or business. The conversation system is important to create information transparency. This way a customer can receive more information about the offered product/service. The booking system is dependent on the type of marketplace. For Uber, the system will check the closest available car dependent on the preferences of the customer. In case of Airbnb, the system checks the availability and sends back if the accommodation is free or not. For eBay, the booking system checks if the requested quantity isn't higher than the availability of the product offered by the provider. The money is transferred through the payment system from the customer to the provider, with a transaction fee for the marketplace itself. It is important to state that this simple overview covers some marketplaces, but not all of them. Hence, a starting point of our research will be the further conceptualization of marketplaces.

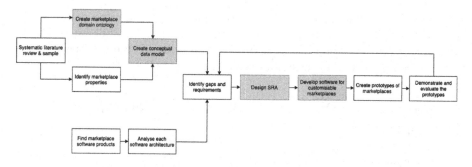

Fig. 2. PhD research process.

3 Research Methodology

In the domain of Information Systems, Design Science Research (DSR) is considered an appropriate research methodology for developing new artifacts [16,17]. In Fig. 2 we give an overview of our envisioned research process with in total 4 DSR artifacts represented in green. As explained in Sect. 1, our research was triggered by a specific problem from practice (i.e., what would be a suitable marketplace for packages trips?), which we broadened to a research question (how to support different types of marketplaces?) and research objective (design of a SRA for customizable marketplaces).

A first step is a systematic literature review for the sharing economy, marketplaces and the field of digital platforms in general. This systematic literature review (following the general guidelines of Kitchenham [18]) will be complemented with an empirical study based on a sample of existing marketplaces to create a domain ontology for marketplaces and identify variations between marketplaces defined as marketplace properties and their values. The marketplace domain ontology offers a conceptual model of what a marketplace is, and it will act as a foundation for a conceptual data model for customizable marketplaces. The identification of specific marketplace properties, partly derived from our sample of existing marketplaces, will help to design a generic conceptual data model for marketplaces starting from the ontological foundation.

A second step is to find existing customizable marketplace software products and analyze their architecture. After, we can identify gaps by comparing the generic conceptual data model with the architecture of each existing software product. By doing so we identify requirements for a customizable marketplace SRA that should cover the whole marketplace domain applicable for multiple projects, applications, contexts and stakeholders and is broader, more abstract and less defined as a specific software architecture for one type of marketplace [19]. This SRA will function as a mapping between what exists (the marketplace software products) and what a marketplace can be (the conceptual data model).

The next step is the implementation of the SRA by developing a software package that is able to create customizable marketplaces (this can be an extension of an already existing open-source marketplace software product). The final step is to create market-place prototypes out of our software to demonstrate that the tool proves useful for creating marketplaces in the full range of our predefined scope. Based on this demonstration we will evaluate whether we have met the requirements for a customizable marketplace SRA.

4   Marketplace Domain Ontology and Marketplace Properties

Our plan is to base the marketplace domain ontology on the commitment-based reference ontology for services named UFO-S [20]. The reason for using UFO-S as core ontology is that marketplaces are primarily used as digital intermediaries to allow service provisioning. Also, the three sub-ontologies of UFO-S, named service offering, service negotiation and service delivery, are closely related to the process flow of using marketplaces. Our goal is to incorporate the concept of a third-party service provider who can propose his/her service offering to the target customer community on a digital platform and extend the marketplace ontology with domain-specific entities and relationships based on other foundational and core ontologies related to marketplaces (e.g. [21]). We will try to classify existing marketplaces concepts like listing (=service offering) and transaction (=service agreement) as UFO-S concepts and represent the marketplace domain ontology in OntoUML.

After, we define the scope of our research by setting requirements based on our systematic literature review and check if certain online platforms can be classified as marketplaces or not. Within this scope, variations between market-places that influence the conceptual data model are subdivided into marketplace property values. A first version of marketplace properties is given in Table 1 and is based on the framework of Laudien and Täuscher [11]. We define a unique combination of property values as a marketplace type.

Table 1. Marketplace properties.

Properties	Property values			
Listing content	Product		Service	
Listing type	Digital		Offline	
Marketplace participants	C2C		B2C	
Key revenue stream	Commission	Subscription	Advertising	Service sales
Price calculation	Free	Fixed	Quantity	Market
Security mechanism	User verification		Security deposit	
Price discovery	Set by provider	Set by customer	Set by marketplace	Auction / Quote
Review system	Customer review	Mutual review	Review by marketplaces	No reviews

As an example, the marketplace type of Airbnb is shown in green. Airbnb offers offline services and the transactions are C2C. The price is set by the provider and based on the quantity (number of nights). They allow mutual reviews; the revenue stream is a commission of the transaction price and they use user verification for the providers and security deposit for the customers for security. Our plan is to evaluate and modify these properties and property values by conducting a systematic literature review, using expert knowledge and verify using a sample of existing marketplaces. After, the influence of these marketplace properties on the conceptual data model will be demonstrated.

5   Conceptual Data Model

A next step is to design a marketplace conceptual data model based on the market-place domain ontology and the identified marketplace properties. Figure 3 shows a preliminary conceptual data model of marketplaces based on the data model of Sharetribe Go [1]. There are four primary entity types. The Actor entity type is a placeholder for attributes capturing the data of providers and customers. The Listing entity type rep-resents the services or goods offered on the marketplace. The Transaction entity type represents the actual transacting of services or goods. Finally, the 'Marketplace' entity type is used to gather general information and settings about the platform.

Only an actor that is a provider can create a listing. A target customer and a provider can communicate about a listing with each other via messages. All messages from and to the same customer and provider are grouped as a conversation. Every listing has a title, description, possibly some images and a description of its commitments to the customer. In this preliminary model a listing can only have one price, gathered in the listing entity type. The transaction entity type has the attribute 'transaction_transitions' giving the status of the payment process of every transaction (e.g. free, initiated, preauthorized, paid, confirmed).

6   Software Architecture and SRA

Software architecture is like a blueprint, but instead of a building it is for the design and implementation of high-level structures of a software system. It is the result of assembling a certain number of architectural elements in some well-chosen forms to satisfy the major requirements of the system [22]. After identifying the gaps between the marketplace types and the software architecture of marketplace products, we can work on the architecture of an ideal, customizable marketplace software product where marketplaces of all different types can be created. This can be done using a SRA, but also other methods such as product line engineering will be considered. Product line engineering is the process of reusing domain knowledge for the production of new software. SRA is a reference model, a required system functionality divided in elements with data flows

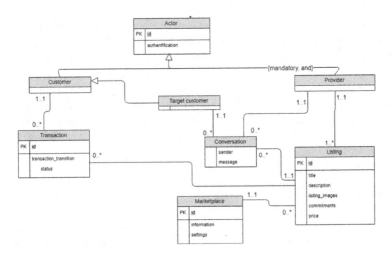

Fig. 3. Preliminary conceptual data model of marketplaces.

between them, mapped on software elements within a specific context with concrete stakeholder goals [19]. After, we plan to evaluate our SRA using the ATAM method [23] and with experts of the marketplace developer's community. Using this SRA, we hope to develop a software that is capable to compose all types of marketplaces. During the creation of marketplace prototypes we can evaluate both the SRA and the software design as a summative assessment.

7   Conclusion

First, we defined 'marketplace' as a broader term used for online platforms in the sharing economy. Software products like "Sharetribe Go" [1] make it possible to create a customized marketplace quick and with few resources. It is, however, not known whether such products cater for the needs of all possible varieties of market-place, nor how such products can be selected and/or customized to provide the best fit with a particular marketplace one has in mind. The goal of my PhD project is to de-sign a SRA for marketplaces which can be used to select the most suitable software product or, if no such product is available, create a new software product or extend an existing software product that facilitates the design the desired type of marketplace. Our methodology to design such reference architecture involves a systematic literature review into digital platforms and an empirical study aiming to discover a marketplace domain ontology and different marketplace properties. A conceptual data model based on the domain ontology will be designed and mapped on existing marketplace soft-ware products, and a gap analysis can give insights for the design of a SRA for mar-ketplaces. The last step is the design of a software product based on the SRA which we plan to instantiate for currently underrepresented marketplace types and to demonstrate and verify the software using prototypes and expert knowledge.

References

1. Sharetribe. https://www.sharetribe.com/
2. Trabucchi, D., Muzellec, L., Ronteau, S., Trabucchi, D.: Sharing economy: seeing through the fog economy. Internet Res. **29**(5), 996–1013 (2019)
3. Hamari, J., Ukkonen, A.: The sharing economy: why people participate in collaborative consumption. J. Assoc. Inf. Sci. Technol. **67**, 2047–2059 (2016)
4. Frenken, K., Schor, J.: Putting the sharing economy into perspective. Environ. Innov. Soc. Transitions **23**, 3–10 (2017)
5. Acquier, A., Carbone, V., Massé, D.: How to create value(s) in the sharing economy: business models. Scalability Sustain. **9**, 5–25 (2019)
6. Bardhi, F., Eckhardt, G.M.: Access-based consumption: the case of car sharing. J. Consum. Res. **39**(4), 881–898 (2012)
7. Botsman, R., Rogers, R.: What's Mine Is Yours: The Rise Of Collaborative Consumption. HarperCollins, London (2010)
8. Choudhury, V., Hartzel, K.S., Konsynski, B.R.: Uses and consequences of electronic markets: an empirical investigation in the aircraft parts industry. MIS Q. **22**, 471–507 (2019)
9. Dai, Q., Kauffman, R.J.: Business models for internet-based e-procurement systems and B2B electronic markets: an exploratory assessment. In: Hawaii International Conference on System Sciences, pp. 1–10 (2001)
10. Stockdale, R.: A framework for the selection of electronic marketplaces: a content analysis approach. Internet Res. **12**(3), 221–234 (2004)
11. Täuscher, K., Laudien, S.M.: Understanding platform business models: a mixed methods study of marketplaces. Eur. Manage. J. **36**(3), 319–329 (2018)
12. Sutherland, W., Jarrahi, M.H.: The sharing economy and digital platforms: A review and research agenda. Int. J. Inf. Manage. **43**, 328–341 (2018)
13. Dalberg: Digital Sharing for Global Growth (2016)
14. Akerlof, G.A.: The market for "Lemons": quality uncertainty and the market mechanism. Q. J. Econ. **84**, 488–500 (1970)
15. Kestenbaum, R.: What are online marketplaces and what is their future? (2017). https://www.forbes.com/sites/richardkestenbaum/2017/04/26/what-are-online-marketplaces-and-what-is-their-future/#7db183243284
16. Peffers, K.: A design science research methodology for information systems research. J. Manage. Inf. Syst. **24**, 45–78 (2008)
17. Hevner, R.A., March, S.T., Park, J., Ram, S.: Design science in information system research. MIS Q. **28**, 75–105 (2004)
18. Kitchenham, B.: Procedures for performing systematic literature reviews. Jt. Tech. rep., Keele University TR/SE-0401 NICTA TR-0400011T.1. 33 (2004)
19. Angelov, S., Grefen, P., Greefhorst, D.: A framework for analysis and design of software reference architectures. Inf. Softw. Technol. **54**, 417–431 (2012)
20. Cesar, J.: A commitment-based reference ontology for services. Inf. Syst. **54**, 263–288 (2015)
21. Von Hoffen, M., Matzner, M., Chasin, F.: Designing an ontology-based web directory for the discovery of sharing and collaborative consumption platforms. In: IEEE Conference Business Informatics, CBI 2015, vol. 1, pp. 108–115 (2015)
22. Kruchten, P.: Architectural blueprints – The "4 + 1" view model of software architecture. IEEE Softw. **12**, 42–50 (1995)
23. Kazman, R., Klein, M., Clements, P.: ATAM: Method for Architecture Evaluation (2000)

Keyword Search Algorithm over Large RDF Datasets

Yenier Torres Izquierdo[(✉)] [ID]

Pontifical Catholic University of Rio de Janeiro, Rio de Janeiro, RJ 22451-900, Brazil
yizquierdo@inf.puc-rio.br

Abstract. Keyword search tools have been used to query RDF data. They can be labeled as *schema-based* when the RDF schema is used to compile a keyword-based query into a SPARQL query, or *graph-based* when the RDF dataset is directly traveled or summarized. The approach proposed in the thesis belongs to this latter category. Unlike recent approaches that summarize the RDF graph, the proposed approach explores the similarity between the property domains and ranges and the class instance sets present in the RDF dataset. The approach estimates set similarity using the Jaccard and the set containment measures. To achieve good performance, even for large RDF datasets, the similarity measures are estimated based on **k-M**inimum hash **V**alues (KMV) synopses [3]. This paper presents the research methodology to implement a keyword search algorithm over large RDF graphs, which does not rely on schema information and uses KMV-synopses. However, the use of KMV-synopses introduces new challenges. So, the research includes the implementation of strategies to efficiently compute KMV-synopses for large RDF datasets and to keep them synchronized when the RDF dataset is up-dated, avoiding full re-computation of the synopses. Finally, the paper presents the status of the research, the open issues and the roadmap to address them.

Keywords: Keyword search · RDF · KMV-synopses

1 Introduction

Keyword search applications over relational databases have been studied for quite some time. However, more recently, examples of such applications designed for RDF datasets have emerged. The problem of finding answers for keyword-based queries over RDF datasets, briefly known as *RDF-KwS*, is formalized as *"finding a possibly minimal subgraph of the RDF graph that covers the keywords"*.

There are three main tasks in RDF-KwS: (1) finding pieces of information in the RDF graph; (2) assembling the retrieved pieces of information to compose complete answers; (3) ranking the complete answers. These tasks are challenging due to the complex and heterogeneous structure of RDF graphs, that, unlike relational databases, do not necessarily have a schema. Approaches to address the RDF-KwS problem can be classified as *schema-based*, when they use the

G. Guizzardi et al. (Eds.): ER 2019 Workshops, LNCS 11787, pp. 230–238, 2019.
https://doi.org/10.1007/978-3-030-34146-6_21

RDF schema to compile a keyword-based query into a SPARQL query, or *graph-based* when they directly traverse the RDF dataset or use summaries thereof. The approach proposed in this research falls in this last category.

RDF graph summarization techniques [1,6,13] have been adopted to address the RDF-KwS problem. Contrasting with these approaches, the proposed approach explores the similarity between the property domains and ranges and the class in-stance sets observed in the RDF dataset to synthesize a SPARQL query that returns answers to the keyword query. The strategy estimates set similarity using the Jaccard and the set containment measures. To achieve good performance, even for large RDF datasets, the similarity measures are in turn estimated using KMV-synopses [3], which concisely represent the property domains and ranges and class instance sets. However, the use of KMV-synopses raises new challenges: (1) How to efficiently compute the set of KMV-synopses for large RDF datasets that have millions of property domains, non-literal ranges and class instances; (2) How to keep the KMV-synopses synchronized with the RDF data after updates.

This paper is structured as follows. Section 2 briefly describes related work. Section 3 presents the basic concepts involved in the research. Section 4 presents the research methodology. Finally, Sect. 5 presents the proposed solutions, lists open issues and suggests a roadmap for tackling them.

2   Related Work

As for graph-based tools, SPARK [22] uses techniques, such as synonyms from WordNet and string metrics, to map keywords to knowledge base elements. Minimum spanning trees from which SPARQL queries are generated then connect the matched elements in the knowledge base. A recent paper [16] also explores WordNet and proposes a ranking method to implement keyword search over RDF graphs. Han et al. [10] described an algorithm that uses the keywords to first obtain elementary query graph building blocks, such as entity/class vertices and predicate edges, and then applies a bipartite graph matching-based best-first search method to assemble the final query. Tran et al. [18] combined the idea of generating summary graphs for the RDF graph, using the class hierarchy, to generate and rank candidate SPARQL queries. Le et al. [14] also proposed to process keyword queries using another RDF graph summarization algorithm. Lin et al. [15] summarize all the inter-entity relationships from RDF data to translate keywords to SPARQL queries.

Contrasting with [10,14,15,18], rather than summarizing the RDF graph, the proposal implementation adopts KMV-synopses [3] to concisely represent the property domains and ranges and class instance sets and to estimate set similarity measures, which in turn drive the SPARQL query compilation process. KMV-synopses [3] permit estimating the cardinality of multiset expressions and the set similarity measures used in this paper, including a generalized Jaccard similarity measure for more than two sets. Hadjieleftheriou et al. [9] used set synopses to estimate the size of the result of set similarity queries. Yang et al. [20]

introduced a KMV sketch technique to address the problem of approximating containment similarity search. Venetis et al. [19] proposed a similarity index for set-valued features based on KMV-synopses. The index methods proposed in these last two references could be useful to filter the candidate property domains and ranges and class instance sets to be included in a SPARQL query during the query compilation process.

To the best of our knowledge, no approach efficiently solves the problems of saving, indexing, and updating the KMV synopses, which raises new challenges. However, [5] presents a system called *Aurum*, where authors proposed attractive strategies to create data attribute profiles and keep them up to date. Firstly, they defined a scalable, IO-efficient profiler that summarizes each data attribute into a profile, which maintains information such as content sketches (MinHash), cardinality, data distributions, types, etc. Then, they created a structure, which internally indexes the same profile multiple times, in multiple LSH indexes [2,17,23] configured with different similarity thresholds. Finally, they introduced a method to maintain the profiles up-to-date when data changes without re-reading all data every time and by only using a small sample of the data. Similar approaches applied to KMV-synopses will be adopted to address these challenges.

3   Background

3.1   RDF Keyword-Based Queries

An Internationalized Resource Identifier (IRI) is a global identifier that denotes a *resource*. RDF describes data as *triples* of the form (s, p, o), where s is the subject, p is the predicate and o is the object of the triple. The subject of a triple is an IRI or a blank node, the predicate is an IRI, and the object is an IRI, a blank node or a literal. An *RDF dataset* is a set T of RDF triples; T is equivalent to a labeled graph G_T whose set of nodes is the set of RDF terms that occur as subject or object of the triples in T and there is an edge (s, o) in G_T labeled with p iff $(s, p, o) \in T$.

RDF Schema [4] permits defining classes and properties, and hierarchies thereof, among other constructs. Meanwhile, SPARQL 1.1 [11] is a query language to access RDF datasets.

Let T be an RDF dataset and $\mathcal{L}$ be the set of all literals. A keyword-based query is simply a set of literals, or *keywords*, $K = \{k_1, ..., k_n\}$. Let *match*: $\mathcal{L} \times \mathcal{L} \rightarrow \{True, False\}$ be a Boolean function that returns $True$ iff two literal are considered similar, or they match, and $False$ otherwise.

An *answer* for K over T is a subset A of T such that there is a subset of K, denoted K/A, such that, for each $k_i \in K/A$, there is $(s, p, o) \in A$ such that k_i and o match; we also say that k_i and (s, p, o) *match* and that K/A is the set of keywords *matched* by A. An answer A is *total* iff $K/A = K$, and *partial* otherwise.

Note that a keyword may match the label of a class or property, which alters the interpretation of the keyword-based query. For example, if Actor is declared as a class with label *"actor"*, then the keyword query $K = \{actor, Washington\}$ may be interpreted as requesting instances of the class `Actor` that have properties that match the keyword *"Washington"*.

This notion of an answer is quite liberal since it allows the RDF graph G_A induced by an answer A to be disconnected. However, answers that induce minimal, connected graphs and that match as many keywords as possible should be preferred.

3.2   Set Similarity Measures and KMV-Synopses

A generalized form of the Jaccard similarity index can be found in [21]. Given n sets, $S = \{S_1, ..., S_n\}$, define the *n-way Jaccard similarity index* of $S_1, ..., S_n$ as:

$$J(S_1, ..., S_n) = \frac{|S_1 \cap ... \cap S_n|}{|S_1 \cup ... \cup S_n|} \quad if \quad S_1 \cup ... \cup S_n \neq \emptyset$$

$$J(S_1, ..., S_n) = 1 \qquad\qquad otherwise \tag{1}$$

Note that $J_2(S_1, S_2)$ is the standard Jaccard similarity index, which can be denoted as $J(S_1, S_2)$. Also, as abuse of notation, we may leave n implicit and write $J(S)$, instead of $J_n(S_1, ..., S_n)$, and consider that $J_1(S_1) = 1$.

Likewise, a generalization of the set containment similarity measure is defined as:

$$C_n(S_1, ..., S_n) = \frac{|S_1 \cap ... \cap S_n|}{|S_1|} \quad if \quad S_1 \neq \emptyset$$

$$C_n(S_1, ..., S_n) = 1 \qquad\qquad otherwise \tag{2}$$

For our research, we are especially interested in estimating set containment when S is a conjunction $S_1 \cap ... \cap S_n$. KMV-synopses [3] permit estimating the cardinality of multiset expressions and thereby the above similarity measures.

Let k be a positive integer, h be a hash function from $\mathcal{D}$ to $\{0, ..., M\}$, with $M \sim \mathbf{O}(|\mathcal{D}|^2)$. The *KMV-synopses* of a set $S \subseteq \mathcal{D}$ is the set L of the k smallest values of the set $\{v \in [0, 1] \mid v = h(s)/M \text{ and } s \in S\}$ (note that $h(s)$ is normalized by the maximum hash value M). If h is a perfect hash function, then L induces a random sample $V = \{s \in S \mid h(s) \in L\}$ of S of size k. Let $U_{(k)}$ denote the kth smallest value of L. Then, an estimation for $|S|$ is $\widehat{|S|} = \frac{(k-1)}{U_{(k)}}$ with absolute ratio error given by [3]:

$$E[\frac{abs(\widehat{|S|} - |S|)}{|S|}] \approx \sqrt{\frac{2}{\pi(k-2)}} \tag{3}$$

Let $L_1, ..., L_n$ be the synopses of $A_1, ..., A_n$; $k_1, ..., k_n$ be the sizes of $L_1, ..., L_n$; and $k = \min(k_1, ..., k_n)$. Then, $L = L_1 \oplus ... \oplus L_n$ is the set of the k smallest values in $L_1 \cup ... \cup L_n$. Let $U_{(k)}$ denote the kth smallest value of L. Finally, let $K_\cap = |L_1 \cap ... \cap L_n|$. Then, the following estimations hold [3]:

$$\widehat{|S_1 \cup ... \cup S_n|} = \frac{(k-1)}{U_{(k)}}, \quad \widehat{J(S_1, ..., S_n)} = \frac{K_\cap}{k}, \quad \widehat{|S_1 \cap ... \cap S_n|} = \frac{K_\cap}{k} \cdot \frac{(k-1)}{U_{(k)}}$$

An estimation for $C_n(S_1 \cap ... \cap S_n, S_{n+1})$ can then be obtained from $|S_1 \cap ... \cap S_n \cap S_{n+1}|$ and $|\widehat{S_1 \cap ... \cap S_n}|$ as:

$$C(\widehat{S_1 \cap ... \cap S_n}, S_{n+1}) = \frac{|\widehat{S_1 \cap ... \cap S_n} \cap S_{n+1}|}{|\widehat{S_1 \cap ... \cap S_n}|} \qquad (4)$$

4   Research Methodology

Our work is divided into three stages, each with an objective:

O-1: To implement a keyword search algorithm for large RDF datasets, which does not rely on the RDF Schema and uses KMV-synopses.

O-2: To propose an index for large sets of KMV-synopses.

O-3: To develop an efficient mechanism to keep the KMV-synopses updated when the RDF dataset changes.

In order to address these objectives, we initially formulated the following research questions:

RQ-1: How to automatically translate user-specified keyword-based queries to SPARQL queries by exploring the similarity between the property domains and ranges and the class instance sets observed in the RDF dataset?

RQ-2: What similarity measures will be computed?

RQ-3: To achieve good performance for large RDF datasets, how to efficiently compute or estimate the similarity measures?

RQ-4: How to evaluate the implemented keyword-based query to SPARQL query translation algorithm? What data will be used?

RQ-5: How to efficiently compute KMV-synopses for large RDF datasets?

RQ-6: What data structure should be used to index or save the computed KMV-synopses?

RQ-7: What is an efficient strategy to update KMV-synopses when the RDF graph is updated?

Research Questions **RQ-1** to **RQ-4** refer to Objective **O-1**, Research Questions **RQ-5** and **RQ-6** are associated with **O-2**, and Research Question **RQ-7** with **O-3**.

When answering these research questions, the following contributions are expected:

C-1: A novel strategy to automatically translate user-specified keyword-based queries to SPARQL queries that return correct answers with respect to the keywords. The strategy does not rely on an RDF schema, but it synthesizes SPARQL queries by exploring the similarity between the property domains and ranges and the class instance sets observed in the RDF dataset.

C-2: The strategy uses set similarity using the Jaccard and the set containment measures.

C-3: To efficiently compute the similarity measures, the strategy estimates these measures based on KMV-synopses for the property domains and ranges and the class instance sets, which can be efficiently computed using a hash function and a single pass over the RDF dataset.

C-4: Construction of a benchmark specifically designed to test keyword search approaches for RDF.

C-5: A quick way to scan the RDF dataset to compute the KMV-synopses set.

C-6: Indexed and optimized data structures to save the KMV-synopses.

C-7: An efficient mechanism to update the KMV-synopses when the RDF graph is updated, avoiding the full re-computation of the synopses.

Table 1 summarizes the planning of the proposed research.

Table 1. Summary of research planning

Stage	Objective	Research questions	Contribution
1	O-1	RQ-1, RQ-2, RQ-3, RQ-4	C-1, C-2, C-3, C-4
2	O-2	RQ-5, RQ-6	C-5, C-6
3	O-3	RQ-7	C-7

5   Proposed Solution

5.1   Current Status

From the objectives defined in Sect. 4, we began working over the first objective. A greedy algorithm to translate keyword-based queries to SPARQL was implemented (see Algorithm 1).

Algorithm 1. TRANSLATEKEYWORDQUERY

Input: T- an RDF dataset
          K- a keyword-based query K over T
Output: Q - a query for K over T that outputs answers for K
Step 1: Match the keywords in K with literals in T, creating a set S of property matches (p, k_i, w_i) such that p is a property that occurs in T, $k_i \in K$ and w_i is a score that indicates how well k_i matches literal values of p.
Step 2: Use the set S of property matches found in Step 1 to construct an initial query forest as follows: for each property match (p, k_i, w_i) in S, where D is the domain of p, the query has a join node a, labelled with $\{D\}$, a match node b, labelled with "k_i", and an edge (a, p, b).
Step 3: Reduce the number of trees of the query forest by combining join nodes and by adding new join edges, using the similarity measures estimated by the KMV-synopses.
Step 4: Construct a SPARQL query Q from the query forest and output Q.

In order to evaluate the implementation and answering the research question **RQ-4**, a benchmark specifically designed to test keyword search approaches for RDF was built. Our benchmark was inspired in the Coffman and Weaver benchmark [7], which was created to evaluate keyword search tools over relational databases based on data and relational schemes for IMDb[1], Mondial[2], and Wikipedia. Our benchmark consists of two RDF datasets triplified from the IMDb and Mondial databases, keyword-based queries over these RDF datasets and their expected answers. So, a set of experiments was executed and the proposed algorithm achieved a good performance, outperforming early implementations [8,12], taken as baseline.

Therefore, the first stage of this research is completed and Objective **O-1** is fulfilled. So, the Research Questions **RQ-1** to **RQ-4** were answered and Contributions **C-1** to **C-4** were reached. These contributions were reported in a paper that was submitted to a prestigious conference. The paper is currently under review.

5.2   Open Issues and Roadmap

At present, Objectives **O-2** and **O-3** are pending. So, we decided to first address **O-3** and then **O-2**. To achieve **O-3**, firstly we decided to use RDF datasets that have publicly available change logs, such as DBpedia. However, we do not rule out that, in the future, we could use some existing approach to capture the changes in an RDF dataset. So, we plan to study the structure of the change logs, to evaluate the structure and size of the KMV-synopses, to implement an efficient strategy for updating the KMV-synopses using the information of the change logs, and finally to design an evaluation mechanism of the proposed strategy.

In the last step and to achieve Objective **O-2**, we intend to study clustering and parallelization approaches to scan RDF graphs and to search for optimized data structures that allow indexing large sets of KMV-synopses. From this, we propose to implement an efficient mechanism to compute and save the KMV-synopses and then to apply the developed strategy in different large RDF datasets. Finally, the author of the publication aims at submitting the results obtained in this research stages to prestigious conferences and journals. He is a third year Ph.D. student, who intends to defend his Ph.D. in February 2021.

Acknowledgment. I would like to give a special thank you to my advisor Marco Antonio Casanova for his help and unconditional support. I would also like to thank my colleague and friend Grettel Monteagudo Garcia for her hard work in this research, mainly in the implementation tasks. The Institute Tecgraf/PUC-Rio, CNPq, and FAPERJ support this research.

---

[1] http://www.imdb.com.
[2] http://www.dbis.informatik.uni-goettingen.de/Mondial.

References

1. Ayvaz, S., Aydar, M.: Using RDF summary graph for keyword-based semantic searches. arXiv preprint arXiv:1707.03602 (2017)
2. Bawa, M., Condie, T., Ganesan, P.: LSH forest: self-tuning indexes for similarity search. In: 14th International Conference on WWW, pp. 651–660. ACM (2005)
3. Beyer, K., Haas, P.J., Reinwald, B., Sismanis, Y., Gemulla, R.: On synopses for distinct-value estimation under multiset operations. In: SIGMOD, pp. 199–210. ACM (2007)
4. Brickley, D., Guha, R.V., McBride, B.: RDF Schema 1.1. Technical report (2014)
5. Castro Fernandez, R., Abedjan, Z., Koko, F., Yuan, G., Madden, S., Stonebraker, M.: Aurum: A data discovery system. In: ICDE, pp. 1001–1012. IEEE (2018)
6. Čebirić, Š., Goasdoué, F., Manolescu, I.: Query-oriented summarization of RDF graphs. VLDB **8**(12), 2012–2015 (2015)
7. Coffman, J., Weaver, A.C.: A framework for evaluating database keyword search strategies. In: CIKM, pp. 729–738. ACM (2010)
8. García, G., Izquierdo, Y., Menendez, E., Dartayre, F., Casanova, M.A.: RDF keyword-based query technology meets a real-world dataset. In: EDBT, pp. 656–667 (2017)
9. Hadjieleftheriou, M., Yu, X., Koudas, N., Srivastava, D.: Hashed samples: selectivity estimators for set similarity selection queries. VLDB **1**(1), 201–212 (2008)
10. Han, S., Zou, L., Yu, J.X., Zhao, D.: Keyword search on RDF graphs-a query graph assembly approach. In: CIKM, pp. 227–236 (2017)
11. Harris, S., Seaborne, A., Prud'hommeaux, E.: SPARQL 1.1 query language. W3C Recomm. **21**(10), 778 (2013)
12. Izquierdo, Y.T., García, G.M., Menendez, E.S., Casanova, M.A., Dartayre, F., Levy, C.H.: *QUIOW*: a keyword-based query processing tool for RDF datasets and relational databases. In: Hartmann, S., Ma, H., Hameurlain, A., Pernul, G., Wagner, R.R. (eds.) DEXA 2018. LNCS, vol. 11030, pp. 259–269. Springer, Cham (2018). https://doi.org/10.1007/978-3-319-98812-2_22
13. Kondylakis, H., Kotzinos, D., Manolescu, I.: RDF graph summarization: principles, techniques and applications (tutorial). In: EDBT/ICDT (2019)
14. Le, W., Li, F., Kementsietsidis, A., Duan, S.: Scalable keyword search on large RDF data. TKDE **26**(11), 2774–2788 (2014)
15. Lin, X.Q., Ma, Z.M., Yan, L.: RDF keyword search using a type-based summary. J. Inf. Sci. Eng. **34**(2), 489–504 (2018)
16. Rihany, M., Kedad, Z., Lopes, S.: Keyword search over RDF graphs using WordNet. In: BDCSIntell, pp. 75–82 (2018)
17. Shrivastava, A., Li, P.: Asymmetric minwise hashing for indexing binary inner products and set containment. In: 24th International Conference on WWW, pp. 981–991 (2015)
18. Tran, T., Wang, H., Rudolph, S., Cimiano, P.: Top-k exploration of query candidates for efficient keyword search on graph-shaped (RDF) data. In: ICDE, pp. 405–416 (2009)
19. Venetis, P., Sismanis, Y., Reinwald, B.: CRSI: a compact randomized similarity index for set-valued features. In: ICDT, pp. 384–395. ACM (2012)
20. Yang, Y., Zhang, Y., Zhang, W., Huang, Z.: GB-KMV: an augmented KMV sketch for approximate containment similarity search. In: ICDE, pp. 458–469. IEEE (2019)
21. Zhai, E., Chen, R., Wolinsky, D.I., Ford, B.: Heading off correlated failures through independence-as-a-service. In: OSDI, pp. 317–334 (2014)

22. Zhou, Q., Wang, C., Xiong, M., Wang, H., Yu, Y.: SPARK: adapting keyword query to semantic search. In: Aberer, K., et al. (eds.) ASWC/ISWC -2007. LNCS, vol. 4825, pp. 694–707. Springer, Heidelberg (2007). https://doi.org/10.1007/978-3-540-76298-0_50
23. Zhu, E., Nargesian, F., Pu, K.Q., Miller, R.J.: LSH ensemble: internet-scale domain search. VLDB Endow. 9(12), 1185–1196 (2016)

Representing the Filter Bubble: Towards a Model to Diversification in News

Gabriel Machado Lunardi[✉] [iD]

Institute of Informatics, UFRGS, Porto Alegre, Brazil
gmlunardi@inf.ufrgs.br
http://ppgc.inf.ufrgs.br

Abstract. Filtering techniques like recommender systems are commonly employed to help people selecting items that best fit their conceptual needs. Although many benefits, recommender systems can put the user inside a filter-bubble given their high focus on similarity measures. This effect tends to limit user experiences, discovering new things, and so on. In the news domain, filter-bubbles are quite critical once they are means of changing people opinions. Therefore we propose a diversification approach to pop the bubble through a representation model based on points of view.

Keywords: Filter-bubble · Recommender system · Filtering · Model

1 Introduction

The web environment is full of all kinds of information presented in various media types textual News, music, videos, and figures are some examples. Giant platforms like Google and Facebook play an important role in providing a place where information can be disseminated and searched. However, the increase in the amount of information available to the average web user leads to the cognitive overload problem. This arises when the amount of available information overpass the user capacity to process, this corresponds to a complex model of information [12]. Filtering techniques like recommender systems together personalization are commonly employed to help people selecting items that best fit their conceptual needs, reducing the cognitive overload problem. Other benefits are increasing supplier revenue, customer loyalty, and support for decision-making [7].

Despite all the benefits, recommender systems may put the user inside an invisible bubble. This happens especially because algorithms emphasize similarity measures which can generate obvious though accurate recommendations. This effect is called filter bubble and Eli Pariser [11] coined it as the users' isolation from a diversity of content and experiences, making them less likely to discover and learn new things. We may say that this corresponds to define different conceptual classes where each user cluster belongs to the same class. This effect is quite critical in the News domain where they are a way of changing

© Springer Nature Switzerland AG 2019
G. Guizzardi et al. (Eds.): ER 2019 Workshops, LNCS 11787, pp. 239–246, 2019.
https://doi.org/10.1007/978-3-030-34146-6_22

people opinions [9]. For instance, a user's News feed can show much News about a new popular song and ignore the News about hunger in Africa [11]. In an ideal situation, both News should be in a user's feed. However, this is not the case because the algorithms tend to recommend similar News to those consumed in the past, similar News creates a specific class. As a consequence, filter bubbles create a conducive environment for spreading fake News as well as for creating echo chambers where the community reinforces opinions that may not be entirely true.

In order to pop the bubble, Pariser suggests promoting "the different", especially regarding novel and serendipitous items, i.e. a good surprise to the user. Therefore, diversifying news recommendation lists could be a solution. However, three main challenges, traditional in information retrieval, and opportunities come up: (i) increasing diversity decreases the accuracy of the rating prediction (which corresponds to the probability that the user likes the recommended item) and vice versa [12]; (ii) actual diversification methods are based on pre or post-filtering i.e. the diversification process happens inside recommendation algorithm or after the recommendation items are computed, i.e. in the candidate recommendation list, which may cause a sub-optimal diversification [10]; (iii) News are unstructured data and diversification requires features which need to be extracted from such text; and (iv) enable the user to perceive the bubble and let him decide what to do, i.e. give the user some control over the filtering.

In this paper, we introduce a diversification approach to pop the bubble based on a representation model of points of view in News recommendation. We propose the use of a model constituted of points of view as features, extracted actively, to be used in diversification algorithms. To obtain an optimal News diversifier, i.e. diversity maximization with low impact to accuracy, we propose a novel model that combines diversification during recommendation phase and post-filtering approaches. Our main research question is: Could a diversification approach pop the filter bubble?

The rest of this paper is structured as follows: Sect. 1 presents previous works related to diversification approaches. Section 2 presents the proposed model as well as their components. Section 3 presents the framework for diversification. Section 4 presents the conclusions and future works.

2   Related Work

In the literature, two research lines propose solutions for the diversification of recommendation. The first one focuses on the post-filtering approach. This approach receives as input the result of a traditional recommendation algorithm and selects, from the candidate items, the subset that balances diversity and accuracy. This approach corresponds to reducing an extended model to a subset restrict to the user's preferences. The second line focuses on modifying the existing recommendation algorithms to generate diversified recommendations [6], this is equivalent to the expansion of the retrieval model with additional characteristics.

In the context of post-filtering approach, we highlight the authors [1,16,19]. Ziegler et al. [19] suggest the topic-based diversification method and use them as diversification aspects. This algorithm reclassifies the input list and obtains a diversified (top-N) final list. Besides, they were the first to propose a metric to evaluate diversity, called ILS (Intra-List Similarity) in which higher values indicate lower diversity. However, Vargas [16] explains that the approach of Ziegler et al. [19] have a limitation because users do not necessarily navigate to the end of the list and that the order in which the items are presented may influence the practical utility of the recommendation. Adomavicius and Kwon [1] propose methods of reclassifying items to increase aggregate diversity while maintaining acceptable levels of accuracy for the recommendation results. They have developed five new recommendation ranking methods that can control precision losses. The five ranking methods were evaluated through three collaborative filtering techniques: user-based, item-based, and matrix-factorization. Each ranking was measured in terms of top-N accuracy and top-N diversity (aggregate diversity). The authors conclude that all ranking approaches sacrificed accuracy to gain diversity. The key is to find a boundary that offers a high gain of diversity with loss of tolerable accuracy. Vargas [16] identified an opportunity in adapting the metrics and diversity techniques applied in the area of Information Retrieval (IR) for Recommendation Systems (RS). The author proposes the aspect-space model. Techniques and metrics associated with diversity in IR can be adjusted for RS. To demonstrate the application of the aspect-space model, Vargas [16] adapted the IA-Select algorithm that serves to diversify research results in RI [2], to diversify the results in RS. As a baseline, they used two collaborative filtering algorithms: user-user and matrix-factorization. It was concluded that the diversification algorithm works better than non-diversified baselines.

In the context of research that addresses traditional RS incremental algorithms we highlight the authors [13,15,17,18]. Zhang and Hurley [18] propose a new collaborative filtering recommendation algorithm to raise the likelihood of recommending items that are new and relevant. For this, the authors suggest that it is better to offer recommendations from the individual clusters in the user profile and not the entire user profile. They explore user profile partitioning techniques. After identifying user preference clusters, these are classified according to the average novelty of the items. Similar to this study, Vargas and Castells [15] partition the user profile into sub-profiles using public information about categories in the item domain. To combine the results and obtain a final diversity aware recommendation lists, the authors use an adapted version of the xQuAD diversification algorithm. The original version of this algorithm (for IR) is modified based on the idea of aspect-space presented by Vargas (2012). Zhang [17] and proposes a recommendation algorithm that selects multiple neighbors based on trust. The author has developed a greedy diversification optimization strategy to select a diverse set of neighboring users in a collaborative, trust-based filtering algorithm. The objective function has the same structure as the Maximal Marginal Relevance (MMR), in which the relevance of a neighbor is interpreted as the trust value, and the diversity is measured with traditional user similarity metrics. As a different approach, Said et al. [13] present a newer collaborative neighbors filtering technique to increase serendipity and diversity. The authors find that their method provides greater diversity and a tolerable loss of accuracy compared to the more traditional neighborhood technique.

In the sphere of the diversification of News recommendation, we highlight the authors [5,8,14]. Desarkar and Shinde [5] considered a problem of diversity of News recommendation in which were not collected or stored data of the users, for privacy concerned users. The post-filtering approach was used. The authors identified that some aspects of the News in which diversification can be performed: Topics (LDA) and Named Entities (NE). An approximation algorithm is used to generate diversified recommendations. They concluded that the using NE algorithm resulted in more positive results than the LDA algorithm. However, the proposed algorithm lacks the personalization of the recommendation, since only recency and popularity are used to determine the candidate set. Jenders et al. [8] analyzed the concept of serendipity in News recommendations by proposing a framework that encompasses recommendation techniques based on serendipity and similarity. It modifies the recommended list for the promotion of serendipity using ranking algorithms based on NE and LDA, with the post-filtering approach. Tintarev et al. [14] proposes a way of diversifying the news recommendation using points of view. Uses topics and introduces a new measure of similarity between them. The diversified list is generated using the MMR ranking algorithm that uses the proposed similarity measure. Despite announcing the proposal as diversification of points of view, this does not happen. The authors only seek to diversify based on topics extracted using LDA.

The proposed solutions from both research lines can be used together to create diversification aware RS: the output of the improved diversification recommendation algorithm could serve as input to the post-filtration diversification approach. A combined approach seems to be an ideal approach, because: (i) using a post-filtering approach alone, if the set of candidate items is not sufficiently diversified, can generate a sub-optimal result as pointed out by [17]; and (ii) improvement of a traditional SR algorithm to generate several recommendations, but classifying this by relevance may also produce sub-optimal results, as evidenced by [18]. Therefore, this motivates this research, whose proposal was presented in the following section.

3   The Point of View Diversification Model

In this section, we present the proposed approach. Figure 1 presents a general view of the model's components. From left to right the first component presents two active data crawlers for tweets and multiple News data sources. Then all these data are submitted to a common Natural Language Processing (NLP) workflow to enable text computation. The pre-processing component receives News and tweets recognizing Named Entities on them. DBpedia was chosen as the knowledge base and Alchemy API as Named Entity Extractor to detect Named Entities which are inputs to the Point Of View model. This model is based on [3] which can predict a news point of view based on their discovered Named Entities. Its prediction and training are possible thank to an annotated Named Entity database that tells what is the point of view of any database entry. As the last step, each news is classified into a feature range that varies from left to right (e.g. political News).

The next component comprehends the recommendation and diversification processes. As input, it receives News and their points of view features and users. The recommendation algorithm uses an intra-diversifier to generate a pre-diversified candidate recommendation list. Such list is then the input of a post-filtering diversifier algorithm which will generate the final diversified recommendation list. The main idea is to combine both processes to reach high diversity and minimum accuracy loss.

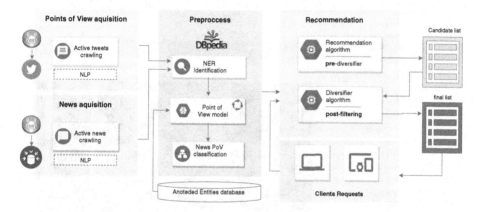

Fig. 1. The proposed framework's architecture

We have adopted Named Entities to determine points of view features as diversification aspects because they are often critical in the News domain, e.g. presenting similar News but with different points of view. Moreover, Desarkar and Shinde [5] have demonstrated that Named Entities overcome other diversification aspects like topics through user satisfaction comparisons.

4   Current Work

Currently, we have developed an exploratory study which comprehends an online News recommender experiment[1] including fake News and a close facebook-like interface. In this experiment, we want to verify what is the role the algorithms play in creating the filter bubbles and what effects such bubbles may have in conducting the user to interact with more of the same content reinforcing a belief that cannot be entirely true. So we ask: Can the exposition to different

---

[1] Available at https://sisrec.inf.ufrgs.br/news-rec/.

topics, outside the bubble, have a positive effect in reducing the user interaction with fake News? What is the isolated influence of the recommenders algorithms in creating filter bubbles?

To that end, we have collected news from the Brazilian presidential elections between July and October of 2018. True News were crawled from known Brazilian portals G1[2] and R7[3]. On the other hand, fake News were crawled from LUPA Agency[4], the first fact-checking agency in Brazil. No other data sources were chosen because they did not keep spreading News on Facebook. In total, we have collected: 905 News from G1; 959 News from R7; and 78 News from LUPA Agency.

Figure 2 shows a News recommendation list of a given user in the online experiment. It is possible to see the interface similarity to Facebook feed. Users can rate news but they do not know if it is true or fake unless they open the news detail. The experiment is now online and will be there until August.

Fig. 2. News-rec: news recommender diversification experiment

We have implemented three collaborative-filtering algorithms: the KNN both user-based and the item-based, as well as the Matrix Factorization (MF) with SVD. Besides such algorithms, two post-filtering diversification approaches are also implemented, the well-known TD (topic diversification) [19], and MMR (Maximal Marginal Relevance) [4]. We choose such strategies because they are

---

[2] https://g1.globo.com/.
[3] https://www.r7.com/.
[4] https://piaui.folha.uol.com.br/lupa/.

between the most popular diversification approaches in recommender systems. As input, these algorithms require diversification aspects and we employed topics which were modeled through Latent Dirichlet Allocation (LDA). As for similarity measure, we have used cosine-similarities.

In total, we have nine algorithms, three non-diversified, three topic diversified and three MMR diversified. Each one of them is attributed to each user during the registration in the system. This strategy tries to ensure an equal distribution of the algorithms creating two groups, test (users who have used diversified algorithms) and control (users who have user non-diversified algorithms). In this way is possible to discover if diversification approaches can in fact pop the filter bubble.

5   Conclusion

In this paper, we introduce the filter-bubble problem especially regarding recommender systems' role in generating it when talking about the News domain. A point-of-view diversification approach is proposed to solve this problem. Compared to existing research our method is the first that propose a working and active News recommender with a point of view diversification. In future we will perform user experiments under the already developed exploratory study considering the proposed framework to answer the main question: Can point-of-view diversification pop the bubble?

References

1. Adomavicius, G., Kwon, Y.: Toward more diverse recommendations: item re-ranking methods for recommender systems. In: Proceedings of the 19th Workshop on Information Technology and Systems. Phoenix, Arizona (2009)
2. Agrawal, R., Gollapudi, S., Halverson, A., Ieong, S.: Diversifying search results. In: Proceedings of the Second ACM International Conference on Web Search and Data Mining - WSDM 2009, p. 5. ACM Press, New York (2009). https://doi.org/10.1145/1498759.1498766
3. Barberá, P., Jost, J.T., Nagler, J., Tucker, J.A., Bonneau, R.: Tweeting from left to right: is online political communication more than an echo chamber? Psychol. Sci. **26**(10), 1531–1542 (2015). https://doi.org/10.1177/0956797615594620
4. Carbonell, J., Goldstein, J.: The use of MMR, diversity-based reranking for reordering documents and producing summaries. In: Proceedings of the 21st Annual International ACM SIGIR Conference on Research and Development in Information Retrieval, SIGIR 1998, pp. 335–336. ACM, New York (1998). https://doi.org/10.1145/290941.291025, http://doi.acm.org/10.1145/290941.291025
5. Desarkar, M.S., Shinde, N.: Diversification in news recommendation for privacy concerned users. In: 2014 International Conference on Data Science and Advanced Analytics (DSAA), pp. 135–141 (2014). https://doi.org/10.1109/DSAA.2014.7058064
6. Galway, N.U.I.: XploDiv: Diversification Approach For Recommender Systems. Technical report (2015). https://doi.org/10.13025/S8PC74

7. Jannach, D., Adomavicius, G.: Recommendations with a purpose. In: Proceedings of the 10th ACM Conference on Recommender Systems - RecSys 2016, pp. 7–10. ACM Press, New York (2016). https://doi.org/10.1145/2959100.2959186

8. Jenders, M., Lindhauer, T., Kasneci, G., Krestel, R., Naumann, F.: A serendipity model for news recommendation. In: Hölldobler, S., Krötzsch, M., Peñaloza, R., Rudolph, S. (eds.) KI 2015. LNCS (LNAI), vol. 9324, pp. 111–123. Springer, Cham (2015). https://doi.org/10.1007/978-3-319-24489-1_9

9. Karimi, M., Jannach, D., Jugovac, M.: News recommender systems - survey and roads ahead. Inf. Process. Manag. **54**(6), 1203–1227 (2018). https://doi.org/10.1016/j.ipm.2018.04.008

10. Kunaver, M., Poržl, T.: Diversity in recommender systems - a survey. Knowl. Based Syst. **123**, 154–162 (2017). https://doi.org/10.1016/j.knosys.2017.02.009

11. Pariser, E.: The Filter Bubble: How the New Personalized Web Is Changing What We Read and How We Think. Penguin Publishing Group (2011)

12. Ricci, F., Rokach, L., Shapira, B.: Recommender Systems Handbook, 2nd edn. Springer, Boston (2015). https://doi.org/10.1007/978-1-4899-7637-6

13. Said, A., Kille, B., Jain, B., Albayrak, S.: Increasing diversity through furthest neighbor-based recommendation. In: Proceedings of the fifth ACM International Conference on Web Search and Data Mining, pp. 1–4 (2012)

14. Tintarev, N., Sullivan, E., Guldin, D., Qiu, S., Odjik, D.: Same but different. Linguist. Philos. **38**(4), 289–314 (2015). https://doi.org/10.1007/s10988-015-9176-x

15. Vargas, S., Castells, P.: Exploiting the diversity of user preferences for recommendation. In: Proceedings of the 10th Conference on Open Research Areas in Information Retrieval, pp. 129–136 (2013)

16. Vargas, S.S.: Novelty and diversity evaluation and enhancement in recommender systems. Ph.D. thesis, Universidad Autónoma de Madrid (2012)

17. Zhang, F.: Improving recommendation lists through neighbor diversification. In: 2009 IEEE International Conference on Intelligent Computing and Intelligent Systems, pp. 222–225. IEEE, New York (2009). https://doi.org/10.1109/ICICISYS.2009.5358201

18. Zhang, M., Hurley, N.: Novel item recommendation by user profile partitioning. In: 2009 IEEE/WIC/ACM International Joint Conference on Web Intelligence and Intelligent Agent Technology, vol. 1, pp. 508–515. IEEE (2009). https://doi.org/10.1109/WI-IAT.2009.85

19. Ziegler, C.N., McNee, S.M., Konstan, J.A., Lausen, G.: Improving recommendation lists through topic diversification. In: Proceedings of the 14th International Conference on World Wide Web - WWW 2005, p. 22. ACM Press, New York, January 2005. https://doi.org/10.1145/1060745.1060754

The OntoOO-Method:
An Ontology-Driven Conceptual Modeling Approach for Evolving the OO-Method

Beatriz Franco Martins$^{(\boxtimes)}$ (iD)

DSIC, Centro de I+D en Métodos de Producción de Software (PROS),
Universitat Politècnica de València, Camino de Vera s/n, 46022 Valencia, Spain
bmartins@pros.upv.es
http://www.pros.upv.es

Abstract. A conceptual model compiler could be the next step in software engineering terms to achieve conceptual programming. In other words, the model is the code instead of the code is the model. This Ph.D. work faces directly this challenge. To make it feasible, we must answer two main research questions: How to integrate models developed by languages supported by ontologies with different ontological commitments? This will be a question solved by characterizing the ontological framework that determines the basic conceptual building units that ontology-driven conceptual models should include. Finally, what is the best approach for the integration process among those models? This will be a question solved by applying the results of the first research question to the OO-Method approach creating an ontologically well-supported method we call OntoOO-Method. The reported Ph.D. work is an advanced state because the ontology resulting from the first research question is almost complete, and now the author is facing the engineering problem of designing the OntoOO-Method approach.

Keywords: Ontology · Ontology-Driven Conceptual Modeling · Ontology-Driven Software Development · Model-Driven Development

1 Introduction

The human capability of representation allows us to communicate and transmit knowledge throughout our lives and for posterity, then since antiquity, the study of this ability has evolved using Ontologies. Indeed, Computer Science incorporates this theme to improve the software systems representation, which the challenge of representing some real-world domain of knowledge accurately and yet remain operational in computational terms.

In this sense, the field of Conceptual Modeling acquired the support of Ontology Engineering, which was born to provide resources and methods to build formal and well-founded models capable of expressing some domain of knowledge as close to reality as possible, called ontologies.

© Springer Nature Switzerland AG 2019
G. Guizzardi et al. (Eds.): ER 2019 Workshops, LNCS 11787, pp. 247–254, 2019.
https://doi.org/10.1007/978-3-030-34146-6_23

According [6], ontologies can be used in several different ways in the development of information systems and basically can be sliced in two main groups: the first one is at the runtime use and the second one is in the development stage (design-time). Thus, as ontologies aim to "drive" software development in many different aspects, this kind of systems are considered Ontology-Driven Information Systems (ODIS) and the development of them is Ontology-Driven Software Development (ODSD).

At the design-time perspective of ODSD, we are interested in two applications: to help knowledge acquisition by using Domain Reference Ontologies [10] and at the design phase to apply Model-Driven Development (MDD) techniques.

There are many proposals to drive the construction of applications using Ontology-Driven Conceptual Modeling (ODCM) [1,17]. Besides, conceptual modeling and ontologies can also be used to support the MDD process [5]. The OO-Method [13,14] incorporates both aspects: ontological foundation and tooling. The Object-Oriented Ontology (O^3) [13] supports the OO-Method, and it has a specific tool, a Conceptual Model Compiler (CMC) called Integranova[1] running it.

Under the MDD field, the notion that "The Conceptual Model is the Code" [4] should strive to promote fast software development, using modeling techniques as support tools. In this context, ontologies can provide a way of increasing quality during application development, as it aims to incorporate the benefits of knowledge acquisition by using domain reference ontologies.

The remainder of this document starts presenting in Sect. 2 the problem faced, then we describe the methodology adopted to investigate this problem in Sect. 3. Section 4 shows the related works of our proposal. Next, Sect. 5 describes our proposal, the actual research stage, and the research work plan. Finally, the conclusions are in Sect. 6.

2   Research Problem

A software system development using a CMC tool and starting from models until the final code by using the best techniques and avoiding traditional codification is a challenge of conceptual modeling in MDD [4].

Bearing in mind that the objective of conceptual modeling is to obtain a description of some conceptualization to produce a conceptual schema, we advocate that is about describing the semantics of software applications at a high level of abstraction. Therefore, our next challenge is to be able to think of software development as *The Conceptual Modeling is Programming*.

Ontologies are concerned to express some domain of knowledge as close to reality as possible [10]. Furthermore, ontologically well-founded languages for ODCM like OntoUML [3] are powerful in expressing domain. Thus, this conceptual modeling approach avoids misunderstandings and other common general languages issues.

---

[1] http://www.integranova.com.

Guarino [6] outsources the "dream" of an ODCM system conceived as an extension of current tools extended with ontological competence, linguistic (terminological) capabilities, ability to reason and criticize the designer's choice with reusability and understandability in mind. This vision is of *The Conceptual Modeling is Programming* (or that *The Model is The Code*) is directly related to both MDD and ODCM subjects. However, in both situations, the models adopted are compromised with different conceptual modeling viewpoints.

While information MDD models are concerned to express some phenomena under the software development viewpoint, ontologies aim to clarify some domain of knowledge about how it is. This distinction happens because different languages have distinct ontological commitments [7]. Therefore, the challenge involves mainly an integration process among models developed by languages supported by different ontologies.

3 Research Methodology and Approach

The Design Science proposed by Wieringa [22] drives our research. This methodology focus on investigating an artifact interacting with a problem context. Besides, it aims to deal with an artifact design to meet some set of requirements according to its stakeholders perspective. In this case, the OntoOO-Method is this artifact and the goal of this Ph.D. research. **The OntoOO-Method is the design and investigation of an ontology-based extension of OO-Method**.

The OntoOO-Method strives to solve a relevant conceptual modeling problem yet without a definitive solution in the context of the MDD. According to the methodology adopted, our research questions must consider who are the stakeholders involved which roles they play and their expectations. Then we may define the research requirements.

In the ambit of this specific research, the stakeholders usually await a new technological resolution or even ignore the problem. As the requirements of a proposed solution must encompass their concerns, we seek within the state-of-art the most relevant works covering our scope. Therefore, the objective goes beyond existing investigations and their approaches. We also intend to settle who the stakeholders are and how they interact with the existent solutions.

As the main topic of this research concerns the Conceptual Modeling subject, then model designers are stakeholders. By the way, they are also the focal points under which each concept to be a model element represented must be consensual. In this case, we must consider they play different roles in the software process, depending on the side they work (client or provider) and how they interact with the models to be produced. Besides, taking into account that this research directly focuses on MDD and Ontology-Driven Modeling Languages then Domain Specialists, Ontology Engineers, and Software Engineers are our main public. Moreover, programmers are negative stakeholders since they are (or perceive) to be hurt by the MDD approach. However, reviews are welcome because this does not mean that these are the only ones whose concerns considered.

From this standpoint, ontologies are the most recent and probably the best way of representing concepts as models under the conceptual modeling perspective. Therefore, the ontological support of this investigation acts both as to its goal as well as its context. In other words, the ontologies appear first as an integral element of the artifact to be produced (OntoOO-Method) and then behind the entire process of designing it, exactly as proposed in [6].

On the design cycle, UFO [9] and O^3 are the ontological support for the OntoUML and OASIS [18] grammars, respectively. Therefore our first questioning aims to identify how their different ontological commitment affects the conceptual models produced by its languages on representing the very same domain of knowledge. For this purpose, it is necessary the support of a *Foundational Ontology*, and we chose UFO because it is a natural choice. We also perform an UFO-based ontological analysis of O^3, since among these ontologies UFO is more general than O^3. This analysis clarifies and provides each language's building blocks semantic and the possible convergence points needed to identify the best approach to follow with the integration of OO-Method models and OntoUML domain reference ontologies.

In the next questioning, we aim to determine what are the design patterns among the involved languages and how each of express particular semantic. For this purpose, we refine the ontological analysis by looking at these patterns in a meta-level. Thus, we raise the architectural set of building blocks for the transformation process as well as the rules to identify in this set which are permissible due to guarantee the claimed semantics.

Finally, working in the validation realm, we must examine the advantages and disadvantages of our approach in comparing with others using empirical studies. Our starting point is comparative with the traditional [20] then we must evolve it by adding the new OntoOO-Method. All in all, we intend to outline how to make a tool to support the OntoOO-Method approach.

4   State of the Art

The search criteria to select relate works focus on proposals that drive the construction of applications using Ontology-Driven Conceptual Modeling (ODCM) and Model-Driven Development (MDD). Indeed, the OO-Method incorporate both aspects. Besides, we also focus on investigations involving the OntoUML approach since the ODSD design-time approach that has been supported by the ODCM in knowledge acquisition has the purpose of drawing nearer real-world phenomena to conceptual modeling.

We evaluate the related works according to its philosophical or pragmatic ontological approach. In this case, we associate the source ontology classification (Reference Ontology or Operational Ontology) with the language adopted, because it is important in this research to estimate the suitability of the grammars. Then we evaluate if the works present sound coverage of the ontological languages involved (Language Coverage). Finally, we focus on the MDD approach used in terms of its platform or tooling to reaching their target languages.

Table 1. Summary of related works

Proposal	Source Ref. Ontology in	Source Oper. Ontology in	Language Coverage	Tool/ Platform	Target
Pergl et al. [15]	OntoUML	—	High	MDD	Implementation Model (UML)
Rybola and Pergl [16]	OntoUML	—	High	MDD	Relational Database (UML)
Homola [11]	OntoUML	—	Medium	Node.js	C#
Valaski et al. [19]	OntoUML	—	High	—	Domain Functional Requirements Heuristic
La-Ongsri and Roddick [12]	OntoER, OntoORM, *OntoUML*[a]	—	Medium	MDD	Relational Database (ER Diagram)
Bartalos and Bielikova [2]	—	OWL	Medium	MDD	JEE (Hibernate)
Weber et al. [21]	—	OWL	Medium	MDD	C++

[a]Ontological Unified Modeling Language (*OntoUML*) that is not UFO-related, Ontological Entity-Relationship (OntoER), and Ontological Object-Role Modeling (OntoORM).

Table 1 summarizes the most relevant studies we've found during the investigation activity cycle of the Design Science Methodology due to answer knowledge questions we proposed.

5   Proposed Solution and Preliminary Results

From the literature study found we note all related works implement the transformation from a conceptual model (domain reference ontology) to the MDD models considering only the structural aspects of the languages involved. However, we advocate that the MDD process also requires ontological support, not only because of the abstraction level transitions but because the language's metamodels involved have different ontological commitments. Therefore, it is fundamental to identify which are the issues related to the semantics of the domain itself and which are features required to a software system design.

At this point, we are not dealing with different models development each one aiming to clarify software aspects. Representations for persistence, behavior, interface, and others are not an issue for software engineering anymore. On the contrary, we advocate the identification of semantic aspects that interfere in how the very same domain conceptualization be models expressed according to different ontological commitments.

The choice to use one particular construct over another is ontological rather than just epistemological [7,8]. Thus, the central idea is to identify among the structural possibilities available for the integration between OntoUML and OO-Method conceptual models produced over its OASIS language, which is the one most ontologically suitable to express the desirable semantics within each perspective instead of treating the transformation of a model into another just as a structural translation between languages.

The OntoOO-Method arise as the main contribution of this research. It has an ontologically structured set of integration patterns among the involved languages (OntoUML and OASIS). Besides, we propose a well-defined framework due to guide this integration process considering the ontological level.

In doing so, we propose the concept of Ontology-Driven Model Integration (ODMI) in which the transformations among this kind of languages must be supported by ontologically well-founded models which describe a conceptualization for the relational aspects among ontologies with different ontological commitments. Figure 1 outlines the ODMI approach proposal to support OntoOO-Method.

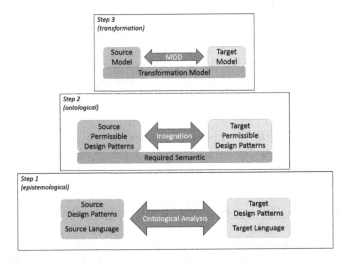

Fig. 1. ODMI supporting the OntoOO-Method.

The integration based on ODMI abides by the classification of KR primitives as proposed in [7,8]. This approach must follow three steps:

1. An epistemological step, in which the involved languages' concept types and their structuring relations establishes the set of transformation patterns to be considered;
2. Then, an ontological step in which decision making occurs by choosing the more appropriate pattern option to be applied to each case to guarantee the correct semantic;
3. And, finally the transformation process itself.

It is also important to highlight that the ontologies use is not a proposition restricted to the ontological step. Conversely, we strongly advocate that an ontological analysis performed at the grammars meta-levels must support the epistemological round.

This work is in the design activity phase of the Design Science methodology when we are producing the documents and artifacts. All stands of our research are available at the author's institutional web page[2]. However, briefly, we present in this session our actual status.

Our current research moment is in the study and development of language design patterns required to reify OntoUML domain reference ontologies into the OO-Method conceptual model, with the support of the produced O^3 ontological analysis. As a work in progress, it is cyclic due to evolve our hypothesis and artifacts.

6   Conclusions

We present our Ph.D. proposal following Wieringa's Design Science methodology. In the initial stages, we have raised the related works with our hypotheses. During this process, we have faced with the study of various issues related to subjects such as MDD, CMC tools, and ODSD. Moreover, we focus our attention on ODCM because it is the primary subject of knowledge acquisition.

In the conceptual modeling perspective, we consider OntoOO-Method fits well with Guarino's proposal [6]. Our intention is also to create ontological support that provides the reification of concepts described with distinct viewpoints, like those adopted by the stakeholders.

As future research steps, we intend to develop the OntoOO-Method bases by evolving them to incorporate domain reference ontologies produced with OntoUML. Our intention is also to create ontological support that provides the reification of concepts described with distinct viewpoints, like those adopted by the stakeholders. Additionally, we intend to suggest a set of features to be as future works made in its CMC tool.

Acknowledgments. This work has been supported by the "Programa Santiago Grisolía" of the "Universitat Poliècnica de València", also has the support of "Generalitat Valenciana" through project IDEO (PROMETEOII/2014/039) and Spanish Ministry of Science and Innovation through project DataME (ref: TIN2016-80811-P).

References

1. Aßmann, U., Zschaler, S., Wagner, G.: Ontologies, meta-models, and the model-driven paradigm. In: Calero, C., Ruiz, F., Piattini, M. (eds.) Ontologies for Software Engineering and Software Technology, pp. 249–273. Springer, Heidelberg (2006). https://doi.org/10.1007/3-540-34518-3_9
2. Bartalos, P., Bielikova, M.: An approach to object-ontology mapping. In: IIT. SRC-Student Research Conference, pp. 9–16 (2007)
3. Benevides, A.B., Guizzardi, G.: A model-based tool for conceptual modeling and domain ontology engineering in OntoUML. In: Filipe, J., Cordeiro, J. (eds.) ICEIS 2009. LNBIP, vol. 24, pp. 528–538. Springer, Heidelberg (2009). https://doi.org/10.1007/978-3-642-01347-8_44

---

[2] http://personales.upv.es/beaframa/research/ontooo-method/ooom.html.

4. Embley, D.W., Liddle, S.W., Pastor, O.: Conceptual-model programming: a manifesto. In: Embley, D., Thalheim, B. (eds.) Handbook of Conceptual Modeling, pp. 3–16. Springer, Heidelberg (2011). https://doi.org/10.1007/978-3-642-15865-0_1
5. Embley, D.W., Thalheim, B.: Handbook of Conceptual Modeling: Theory, Practice, and Research Challenges. Springer, Heidelberg (2012)
6. Guarino, N.: Formal Ontology in Information Systems. In: Proceedings of the 1st International Conference, Trento, Italy, pp. 6–8. IOS Press, June 1998
7. Guarino, N.: The ontological level. In: Philosophy and the Cognitive Sciences (1994)
8. Guarino, N.: The ontological level: revisiting 30 years of knowledge representation. In: Borgida, A.T., Chaudhri, V.K., Giorgini, P., Yu, E.S. (eds.) Conceptual Modeling: Foundations and Applications. LNCS, vol. 5600, pp. 52–67. Springer, Heidelberg (2009). https://doi.org/10.1007/978-3-642-02463-4_4
9. Guizzardi, G.: Ontological Foundations for Structural Conceptual Models. CTIT, Centre for Telematics and Information Technology (2005)
10. Guizzardi, G.: On ontology, ontologies, conceptualizations, modeling languages, and (meta)models. Front. Artif. Intell. Appl. **155**, 18 (2007)
11. Homola, B.D.: Model-driven engineering approach for OntoUML (2016)
12. La-Ongsri, S., Roddick, J.F.: Incorporating ontology-based semantics into conceptual modelling. Inf. Syst. **52**, 1–20 (2015)
13. Pastor, O.: Diseño y Desarrollo de un Entorno de Producción Automática de Software basado en el modelo orientado a Objetos. Ph.D. thesis, Tesis doctoral dirigida por Isidro Ramos, DSIC, Universitat Politècnica de València (1992)
14. Pastor, O., Insfrán, E., Pelechano, V., Romero, J., Merseguer, J.: OO-Method: an OO software production environment combining conventional and formal methods. In: Olivé, A., Pastor, J.A. (eds.) CAiSE 1997. LNCS, vol. 1250, pp. 145–158. Springer, Heidelberg (1997). https://doi.org/10.1007/3-540-63107-0_11
15. Pergl, R., Sales, T.P., Rybola, Z.: Towards OntoUML for software engineering: from domain ontology to implementation model. In: Cuzzocrea, A., Maabout, S. (eds.) MEDI 2013. LNCS, vol. 8216, pp. 249–263. Springer, Heidelberg (2013). https://doi.org/10.1007/978-3-642-41366-7_21
16. Rybola, Z., Pergl, R.: Towards OntoUML for software engineering: transformation of rigid sortal types into relational databases. In: Proceedings of the 2016 Federated Conference on Computer Science and Information Systems, pp. 1581–1591 (2016)
17. Studer, R., Benjamins, V.R., Fensel, D.: Knowledge engineering: principles and methods. Data Knowl. Eng. **25**(1–2), 161–197 (1998)
18. Torres, P.L., Salavert, I.R., Palma, P.S., Pastor, O.: OASIS Versión 3.0 Un enfoque Formal para el Modelado Conceptual Orientado a Objeto. Universidad Politécnica de Valencia (1999). http://users.dsic.upv.es/grupos/oom/oasis.html
19. Valaski, J., Reinehr, S.S., Malucelli, A.: Deriving domain functional requirements from conceptual model represented in OntoUML. In: ICEIS (2017)
20. Verdonck, M., Gailly, F., Pergl, R., Guizzardi, G., Martins, B.F., Pastor, O.: Comparing traditional conceptual modeling with ontology-driven conceptual modeling: An empirical study. Inf. Syst. **81**, 92–103 (2018)
21. Weber, F., Bihlmaier, A., Wörn, H.: Semantic Object-Oriented Programming (SOOP). In: Informatik 2016 (2016)
22. Wieringa, R.J.: Design Science Methodology for Information Systems and Software Engineering. Springer, Heidelberg (2014). https://doi.org/10.1007/978-3-662-43839-8

Stochastic Models to Improve E-News Recommender Systems

Bráulio Miranda Veloso[(✉)] [iD]

Universidade Federal de Ouro Preto, Ouro Preto, MG 35400-000, Brazil
brauliocic091@gmail.com

Abstract. Several recommender systems have been proposed in the literature. Some of them address the problem of recommending news to users of newspaper sites. The context of online news presents some particularities: highly dynamic data volume, users access without registration, quick accesses of a few readings, and content is time-dependent. Online newspapers generate in real-time the recommendation lists with few items. The recommenders have a short time to model access, create the list, and present it to the user. All these characteristics make the problem of news recommendation an exciting challenge that has been studied by the academic community with new proposals. However, scarce works study users reading behavior before proposing new methods. In this work, we are interested in characterizing online newspaper users via stochastic models and using attributes extracted from this characterization in recommender systems. First results demonstrate that models who use only information from the recent past are the best. Next, we will look at whether these models are best, varying data contexts, and how to generate more personalized models. Finally, we intend to add all the knowledge in a recommender system, improving or creating a new one.

Keywords: Stochastic models · Online newspapers · Users behavior · Online readers · Recommender systems

1 Introduction

Recommending items to users on the Web is presented as one of the biggest challenges due to a huge number of content available [5]. Users do not have the time to browse through and see all available items, so a proper recommendation can make the difference between conquering the user or losing him [1].

This work focuses on users behavior of online newspaper to improve news recommender systems [5]. The domain of online newspaper has its peculiarities when compared with other domains of recommender systems [13]. One of the main characteristics is the high dynamism of the items: new items are added continuously to the system, some are updated, and some are removed. Traditional methods of recommender systems such as user-item interaction matrix suffer several implications. As the items are variants, greater control over the matrix

© Springer Nature Switzerland AG 2019
G. Guizzardi et al. (Eds.): ER 2019 Workshops, LNCS 11787, pp. 255–262, 2019.
https://doi.org/10.1007/978-3-030-34146-6_24

is needed [2]. Additionally, users are usually interested in recent articles, such as the latest hour news [4]. This aspect makes the old news start to get uninteresting to users and should not be recommended. Thus, a simple matrix of historical interaction loses its value [12]. Moreover, explicit feedback information, such as ratings is not usual [13]. The common is the user reads the news, searching or choosing from within the ones presented by the layout or by recommendation. After some readings, the user ends the access, without leaving any explicit feedback. Access information, read time, and other implicit feedbacks are the input data commonly considered in online newspaper recommender systems [1,5,11]. Content data (header, body) and meta-data (author, topic, date) are also used for the recommendation task [4,6,7].

There are several proposals for online newspaper systems, some, in particular, focusing on user behavior. The incorporation of user behavior analysis has benefited those proposals by methods that create specific [5,14] or general profiles [8], observe the news context consumed looking for more contextualized information to recommend [4,7,12] and use external data mining to improve user knowledge [10]. Equally, this work has assumed that understanding about the behavior of successive article reads can help in developing better news recommender systems. We are interested in modeling users' accesses to obtain knowledge to improve news recommender systems. We track user readings at the topic level and look at the odds of the next reading being on the same topic or other ones. We study reading habits at the topic level because the most basic level of news suffers many variations, while subjects covered by an online newspaper usually remain stable. Although the amount of news within a particular topic changes over time, the topic interests of users should not change as much.

In [8], the authors studied the individual user reading behavior from an online news portal. They assume a stationary first-order Markov process and estimate the transition probabilities between news topics. No other alternative model was considered, and this casts doubt about the prediction quality one can expect with this single model. Other work shows how to improve the accuracy and diversity of recommender systems using stochastic modeling [7]. From the information of transitions between categories, they create Markov models. They generate two general profiles, one with one-month data and another with all historical data. Then, they try to recommend merging the user's current access with both profiles and compare with the current newspaper recommender system. Therefore, the authors conclude that adjusting the Markov model using data from the previous month can improve diversity while model using all data enhances accuracy. Using only the current user access information with the access of the users generated a minimum of necessary customization without the need of user having to authenticate in the newspaper. Different then that proposal, we are looking for the best models before using them on the system.

The main objective of this project is to investigate how knowledge about the behavior of newspaper users can be inserted back into news recommender systems. As specific objectives of this project, there are: (1) To study and identify which stochastic models should be used to obtain the best results in certain situations; (2) Identify how to add these models to the recommender systems; (3) Evaluate if the insertion of stochastic models improves the recommender systems, making comparisons with other state-of-the-art approaches.

The objectives of this research can be translated into three questions: (1) What is the best model or group of models that best fit the dynamic behavior of online newspaper readers? (2) How can knowledge about the behavior of online newspaper users via stochastic models be inserted back into the systems of online newspapers in order to assist them in the promotion of their newspapers and their user's satisfaction? (3) Do stochastic models improve recommender systems satisfactorily, overcome state-of-the-art methods at levels of precision and accuracy? Also, in what situations?

We are interested in modeling the access of online newspaper users. For this, we define stochastic models as a modeling method. We are looking for the best models, the ones that best fit the users' data. Thus, we proposed five classes with more than 40 different models, and we use two statistical metrics that measure both the degree of fit and the quality of the predictions. We are interested in checking whether stochastic models are proper independent journal descriptors. For this, we have data from two newspapers with unique characteristics: one newspaper has more access than the other, each one has its topics and some similar subjects, each newspaper has its index of a total number of readings per session different from the other, the distribution accesses are different. We use stochastic models because they are models that capture the general essence of users without having to specify the entire reading dynamic, and they are easily estimated. We are looking for not only the best stochastic model but the one that describes the data with the fewest parameters. That is, the model must be easily estimated to be included in the final system.

2   Proposed Classes of Stochastic Models

Let $u \in \mathcal{U} = \{1, 2, \ldots, U\}$ be the index of a user. The sequence of news' topics gives a news-reading session, and it is represented by $S_u = (T_1, \ldots, T_i, \ldots, T_{n_u})$ where n_u is the total number of news read and T_i is the topic of i-th read item. We let $\mathcal{L} = \{1, 2, \ldots, L\}$ represent the set of labels identifying the topics. Adopting a probabilistic model to represent the collection of sessions, we see them as realized trajectories of a discrete-time stochastic process with state space $\mathcal{L}$. Each session generates a random path $\{(1, T_1), (2, T_2), \ldots (n_u, T_{n_u})\}$ in the grid $\mathbb{N} \times \mathcal{L}$. Figure 1a illustrates a session S_u seen as the realized path of a random walk in $\mathbb{N} \times \mathcal{L}$. The user u^* had a reading session $S_{u^*} = (T_1 = 5, T_2 = 5, T_3 = 8, T_4 = 3, T_5 = 3, T_6 = 3)$ generating the shown trajectory.

The joint probability of any sequence of topics in a session is given by multiplying the conditional probabilities of the successive readings conditioned in all previous readings:

$$\mathbb{P}(T_1, T_2, \ldots, T_{n_u}) = \mathbb{P}(T_1) \times \mathbb{P}(T_2|T_1) \times \cdots \times \mathbb{P}(T_{n_u}|T_1, T_2, \ldots, T_{n_u-1}) \quad (1)$$

Given a partial trajectory of a user in a session, we want to estimate the topic of the next news to be read, like in Fig. 1b. In general, to identify the

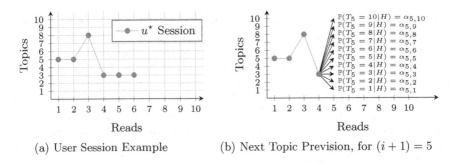

(a) User Session Example   (b) Next Topic Prevision, for $(i+1) = 5$

Fig. 1. News reading session as stochastic process trajectory. (a) shows a user session example. (b) exemplifies next topic previsions ($\alpha_{i+1,l}$) made by a stochastic model, for instant $i + 1 = 5$, where past states $H = (T_1 = 5, T_2 = 5, T_3 = 8, T_4 = 3)$.

probabilities of the next topic: $\mathbb{P}(T_{i+1} = l \mid T_1 = l_1, \ldots, T_i = l_i) = \alpha_{i+1,l}$, where $l_i \in \mathcal{L}$ and $1 < i < n_u$, we need to specify L probabilities for the possible states conditional in all the past states ($l_1, \ldots, l_i$) and this needs to be done for every possible configuration of these previous states. Therefore, the number of probabilities that need to be specified on the $(i+1)$-th step is L^{i+1}. For sessions of length N, it is required $\sum_{i=1}^{N} L^{i+1} = (L^{N+1} - L^2)/(L-1) = O(L^N)$ elements.

All probabilistic models impose constraints on the collection of conditional probabilities that drastically reduce the number of probabilities required to specify the stochastic process distribution fully. These constraints come in the form of assumptions that seek to capture the probabilistic essence of the process. The objective is to formulate a simple, but not trivial, mathematical structure representing the essential and most relevant aspects of the phenomenon and which reduce the required $O(L^N)$ evaluations. We considered a very diverse collection of stochastic models to explain e-news reader behavior. We organize these models into five classes according to how the previous reading history affects the chances of future topics: **Memoryless**, **Short-term Memory**, **Revealed Preference**, **Cumulative Advantage**, and **Geometric Sojourn**. Next, we briefly present only one model of each class we are studying, omitting the maximum likelihood estimation and the independently estimated number of parameters.

2.1   Memoryless Models

The models in these class ignore the previous history when determining the probabilities of the next topic. They represent an idealized and naive standard that is convenient to gauge how far away from these extreme baselines are located the other more sophisticated models as well as the observed data. There are two main models under this class: Uniform Model and Independence Model. For example, the **Independence Model (G1-I)** assumes that the successive topics are independent of each other and depends only the current instant i:

$$\mathbb{P}(T_{i+1} = l \mid T_1 = l_1, \ldots, T_i = l_i) = \mathbb{P}(T_{i+1} = l) \tag{2}$$

2.2   Short-Term Memory Models

In these class, all model assumes that the next topic probabilities are influenced only by the most recently read news, a limited past. There are three types of models in this class, not counting their variations: Stay Model, Markov Model, and Higher-Order Markov Model. One is the **Time-Variant Markov model (G2-Mk)**, who assumes that the next topic depends only on the current topic:

$$\mathbb{P}(T_{i+1} = l | T_1 = l_1, T_2 = l_2, \ldots, T_i = l_i) = \mathbb{P}(T_{i+1} = l | T_i = l_i) \tag{3}$$

2.3   Revealed Preference Models

In this class, we use a specific function focused on a targeted topic $T_{i+i} = l$ to model the probability of topic l being the next reading in the session. This function varies with the model, and it collects information from the entire past, not only from the most recent readings as in the previous class. There are four types of models in this class, despite their variations: Visit Record Model, Topic Duration Model, Last Visit Duration Model, and Readings After Departure Model.

The **Visit Record Model (G3-VR)** uses the sum of the number of target-topic readings in the past. Let $S_i^l = s$ be the number of times a user read news from the l topic in a session of size i: $S_i^l = \sum_{j=1}^{i} I[T_j = l]$, where I is the indicator function. For $s \in [0, \ldots, i]$, the Visit Record Model assumes that:

$$\mathbb{P}(T_{i+1} = l | T_1 = l_1, \ldots, T_i = l_i) \propto \mathbb{P}(T_{i+1} = l | S_i^l = s) \tag{4}$$

2.4   Cumulative Advantage Models

In this class, the successive topic choices alter future probabilities in a way that some topics acquire advantage concerning the others. Reading topic l leads to an increase in its probability. There are two types of models in this class, despite their variations: Additive Cumulative Advantage Model and Multiplicative Cumulative Advantage Model. The **Additive Cumulative Advantage Model (G4-CA)** assumes that a bonus β_l is added cumulatively and in an additive way to a base probability π_l:

$$\mathbb{P}(T_{i+1} = l | T_1 = l_1, \ldots, T_i = l_i) \propto \pi_l + \beta_l S_i^l \tag{5}$$

2.5   Geometric Sojourn Models

The last class of models assumes that the permanence in a topic follows a geometric distribution G. Given that there will be a change of topic, a transition function governs how the new topic is selected. There is only one type of model in this class, the Geometric Sojourn Model, varying in the way of estimating the theta parameter and the re-normalization of the probability of topic change. Per example, let d_i is equal the number of topic-duration and let θ_l is the topic-specific geometric distribution parameter, the **Geometric Sojourn Model with Simple Re-normalization (G5-GS)** assumes that:

$$\mathbb{P}(T_{i+1} = l | T_1 = l_1, \ldots, T_i = l_i) = \begin{cases} \mathbb{P}(G(\theta_l) \geq d_i + 1) & \text{if } l = l_i \\ \mathbb{P}(G(\theta_l) = d_i) \times \mathbb{P}(l | l_1, \ldots, l_i) & \text{if } l \neq l_i \end{cases} \tag{6}$$

2.6   Baseline Model

We define an additional model based on the current recommender system per newspaper, **Recommender Based Model (BL-R)**. Let R represent the set of news recommended at the i-reading and $m_{i+1}(l|l_i)$ be the number of news in R which belongs to topic l after reading news from topic l_i. The baseline model assumes that, if the recommender system is effective, then we should have the probability that the next news topic is from topic l is proportional to $m_{i+1}(l|l_i)$. That is, we assume that:

$$\mathbb{P}(T_{i+1} = l|T_1 = l_1, \ldots, T_i = l_i) \propto m_{i+1}(l|l_i) \tag{7}$$

2.7   First Results

Using data from two online newspapers, we estimate the models and test their characteristics. The data comprises two months of millions of user accesses from two different online newspapers, each with its distinct subjects. Two tests were performed in each database, using five-fold cross-validation criteria. First, we used the **Akaike Information Criterion (AIC)** [3] given by: $AIC(M) = 2 \ln L(M) - 2df(M)$, where $\ln L(M)$ is the log-likelihood for a model M, and $df(M)$ is the number of independent parameters estimated in the model. We intend to verify how the models fit the data, the higher the AIC value, the better the model result. Second, we used an error metric that demonstrates from the actual values what the model choices and the user's choices were. We used the **Brier Score (BS)** [9] given by: $BS(i, M) = \frac{1}{N_i} \sum_{S \in \mathcal{S}} \sum_{l \in \mathcal{L}} (M(\alpha_{i,l}) - S(i, l))^2$, where $M(\alpha_{i,l})$ is the probability given by model M to topic l in instant i, and $S(i, l)$ is the binary information that the i-th news of the session S is or is not from topic l. The lower the BS value, the better the model.

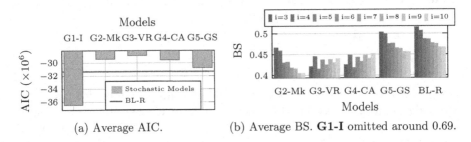

(a) Average AIC.   (b) Average BS. **G1-I** omitted around 0.69.

Fig. 2. First results. (a) shows the stochastic models average AIC. (b) shows the stochastic models average BS per values of instants 3 to 10.

We present in Fig. 2 only the results of data from one newspaper, and only from the five models explain before. The results from other data are similar. The results from other stochastic models are equivalent to the selected class model, despite some variations. In general, we have that practically all models fit the user's reading dynamics better than the baseline model (**BL-R**). No model was worse than the naive models of Memoryless class. The Higher-Order Markov Models or **G3-VR** and other models of the Preference Revealed class are better than the Markov Model (**G2-Mk**). All models in Cumulative Advantage Class, like **G4-CA**, were better than the baseline model (**BL-R**) and were slightly below the **G2-Mk** but not overcome it. The **G5-GS** and other models in the Geometric Sojourn Class were better than the **BL-R**, but they were worse than models of the Cumulative Advantage class.

3   Discussion

We are investigating which models best represent the general reading behavior of users. When comparing several stochastic models, we can see which ones fit the data better and which ones err less. From now, models that work with low past are the best. Despite that, we do not focus on only one model because we know that models can be context-dependent. This is one of the future tasks, to identify which models are best by varying the context: assiduous/infrequent readers, long/short sessions, profiles generated by different time intervals (for example, week by week a new estimated model), fast/long readings sessions, and restrictive/eclectic tastes users (usual number of distinct topics read). Another future task is to study the personalization of stochastic models. Be it generating user-specific models, or using Bayesian techniques to consider how far a user is from the general model and thus make personalization by weights. The last step will be to add the best models in recommender systems. We hope to demonstrate the value of stochastic models in capturing users' reading habits and how these patterns can be useful features to recommender systems.

We have data from two real newspaper with a large amount of access. Each newspaper had information about their recommender system and their click-through rate (CTR) [5]. On the final, we can measures how better are our results compared to the newspaper's ones, by the CTR metric. Before that, we will use a test/training scheme that observes the temporal order of the data. In this way, the tests will bring results that are more faithful to the reality, because, in the online newspapers' sites, the news emerge over time, changing the number of articles available and viewed by topic. Then, we must train the models simulating an online test, where only the sessions made by users and articles published before that moment are present in the historical data used to adjust the models. To evaluate if the insertion of stochastic models improves the recommender systems, we will compare this with other state-of-the-art recommender systems approaches, like [5,7,10,12,14].

This work is expected to be completed until March 2021. We have plan to publish the results in conferences like ACM Conference on Recommender Systems (https://recsys.acm.org/), and International World Wide Web Conference (https://www2019.thewebconf.org/), or Journals like ACM Transactions on Knowledge Discovery from Data (https://tkdd.acm.org/).

References

1. Ahmed, A., Teo, C.H., Vishwanathan, S., Smola, A.: Fair and balanced: learning to present news stories. In: Proceedings of the Fifth ACM International Conference on Web Search and Data Mining, Seattle, Washington, USA, pp. 333–342 (2012)
2. Bogers, T., van den Bosch, A.: Comparing and evaluating information retrieval algorithms for news recommendation. In: Proceedings of the 2007 ACM Conference on Recommender Systems, Minneapolis, MN, USA, pp. 141–144 (2007)
3. Burnham, K.P., Anderson, D.R.: Model Selection and Multimodel Inference: A Practical Information-theoretic Approach. Springer, New York (2003). https://doi.org/10.1007/b97636
4. Campos, P.G., Díez, F., Cantador, I.: Time-aware recommender systems: a comprehensive survey and analysis of existing evaluation protocols. User Model. User Adapt. Interact. **24**(1–2), 67–119 (2014)
5. Das, A.S., Datar, M., Garg, A., Rajaram, S.: Google news personalization: scalable online collaborative filtering. In: Proceedings of the 16th International Conference on World Wide Web, Banff, Alberta, Canada, pp. 271–280 (2007)
6. De Francisci Morales, G., Gionis, A., Lucchese, C.: From chatter to headlines: harnessing the real-time web for personalized news recommendation. In: Proceedings of the 5th ACM International Conference on Web Search and Data Mining, Seattle, Washington, USA, pp. 153–162 (2012)
7. Epure, E.V., Kille, B., Ingvaldsen, J.E., Deneckere, R., Salinesi, C., Albayrak, S.: Recommending personalized news in short user sessions. In: Proceedings of the 11th ACM Conference on Recommender Systems, Como, Italy, pp. 121–129 (2017)
8. Esiyok, C., Kille, B., Jain, B.J., Hopfgartner, F., Albayrak, S.: Users' reading habits in online news portals. In: Proceedings of the 5th Information Interaction in Context Symposium, Regensburg, Germany, pp. 263–266 (2014)
9. Hernández-Orallo, J., Flach, P., Ferri, C.: Brier curves: a new cost-based visualisation of classifier performance. In: Proceedings of the 28th International Conference on Machine Learning (ICML 2011), Bellevue, Washington, USA, pp. 585–592 (2011)
10. Hsieh, C.K., Yang, L., Wei, H., Naaman, M., Estrin, D.: Immersive recommendation: news and event recommendations using personal digital traces. In: Proceedings of the 25th International Conference on World Wide Web, Republic and Canton of Geneva, Switzerland, pp. 51–62 (2016)
11. Hu, Y., Koren, Y., Volinsky, C.: Collaborative filtering for implicit feedback datasets. In: 8th IEEE International Conference on Data Mining, Pisa, Italy, pp. 263–272 (2008)
12. Li, L., Chu, W., Langford, J., Schapire, R.E.: A contextual-bandit approach to personalized news article recommendation. In: Proceedings of the 19th International Conference on World Wide Web, Raleigh, North Carolina, USA, pp. 661–670 (2010)
13. Tavakolifard, M., et al.: Workshop and challenge on news recommender systems. In: Proceedings of the 7th ACM Conference on Recommender Systems, pp. 481–482 (2013)
14. Zhao, Z., Cheng, Z., Hong, L., Chi, E.H.: Improving user topic interest profiles by behavior factorization. In: Proceedings of the 24th International Conference on World Wide Web, Florence, Italy, pp. 1406–1416 (2015)

Author Index

Printed in the United States
By Bookmasters